EXPLORING
THE ARTS

This publication was funded in part by a grant from the National Endowment for the Arts, an independent agency of the federal government. Additional funding was provided by The George Gund Foundation of Cleveland, Ohio. Action for Children's Television is grateful for the support of these two institutions and for their help in making *Exploring the Arts* possible.

EXPLORING THE ARTS

Films and Video Programs for Young Viewers

by
PAULA ROHRLICK
Action for Children's Television

Foreword by
David Rockefeller, Jr.
Chairman, The Arts, Education and Americans, Inc.

R. R. BOWKER COMPANY
New York and London, 1982

Published by R. R. Bowker Company
1180 Avenue of the Americas, New York, NY 10036
Copyright © 1982 by Xerox Corporation
Printed and bound in the United States of America

Library of Congress Cataloging in Publication Data

Rohrlick, Paula.
   Exploring the arts.

   Includes indexes.
   1. Arts—Juvenile films—Catalogs.
2. Arts—Study and teaching—Juvenile
films—Catalogs. I. Action for Children's
Television.   II. Title.
NX633.R64   1982   016.7'002454   82-9588
ISBN 0-8352-1515-6

Jacket photo credits: *The Tap Dance Kid,* Learning Corporation of America; *Degas in the Metropolitan,* Pyramid Film & Video; *The Incredible Book Escape,* Bosustow Entertainment for CBS Library.

To my husband, Fred

Contents

Appendixes

Foreword

With this book, Action for Children's Television (ACT) has demonstrated that film and video can be among the most effective means of presenting and teaching the arts.

What of the arts in contemporary American culture? Have technology and science perhaps taken us beyond a need for artistic expression? I doubt it. If the arts are not a "necessary" component of civilization, why has every culture developed unique art forms? In many cultures, the arts are woven into every fabric of life, just as fibers are interlaced into carrying baskets. For others, the arts have been primarily entertainment, intellectual stimulation, or the tools of politics and war.

Today, due to financial cutbacks, there are classrooms and schools, even entire districts, without live instruction in the arts. The question is: do we wait for better times or do we take steps to fill the gap?

We must fight to restore arts programs in the classroom, but meanwhile I believe we must also look for alternative modes of educating a generation who cannot wait for the society to renew itself. In fact, it may be film and video that will rescue the arts for our culture. If we receive most of our information and entertainment from film and television, then perhaps we should yield to the inevitable and concen-trate on improving the quality of what is available on TV, particularly for children.

The inherent characteristics of film and video reinforce their roles as both arts instructors and arts purveyors. With the great improvements in video and audio technology, there is no art form that cannot be adequately represented by screen and soundbox. Of course, the television image is different from the real thing, but not nearly so different as the sound quality of 78 rpm records and the flickering images of the first "talkies." Modern camera techniques have brought film and video recording of dance, opera, symphony, and theater to high arts in themselves.

And what art-filled journeys we can make through film and video, whether the subject is painting, sculpture, architecture, or a panoply of crafted objects!

Film and video—with their capacity to draw near, to inspect, as well as to draw back, to give context—are ideal tools for educating children (or anyone) about the arts.

More power to the medium and to ACT for surveying the materials available and for presenting them here in such an accessible fashion!

David Rockefeller, Jr.
Chairman, The Arts, Education and
Americans, Inc.

Preface

> There was a child went forth every day,
> And the first object he look'd upon, that
> object he became,
> And that object became part of him for the
> day or a certain part of the day,
> Or for many years or stretching cycles of years.
>
> *Walt Whitman*

The arts have an essential role to play in children's development. Exposure to music, painting, literature, and other branches of creative expression is a necessity, not a luxury, in children's lives. The arts can expand young people's horizons; introduce them to new ways of thinking, feeling, and looking at the world; stimulate them to express themselves; and bring them great pleasure. Most important, being exposed to creativity can inspire children to create.

Television and film are ideal media for presenting the arts to children. Not only can they be considered art forms in and of themselves, but they have the capacity to analyze and teach the art process. Close-ups can demonstrate exactly how a potter centers clay on the wheel; the camera can catch a dancer in midpirouette and examine his or her movements step-by-step. Children are sometimes exposed to the arts through classroom experiences, but they deserve the opportunity to encounter the arts on an individual basis as well as in school, for entertainment as well as for education. Children need to see, hear, and experience the arts in order to be enriched by them.

To this end, Action for Children's Television (ACT), with the help of grants provided by the National Endowment for

the Arts and The George Gund Foundation, has compiled this book of film and video programs on the visual, performing, and literary arts for children. ACT has been concerned with programming in the arts for a long time. Founded in 1968, ACT is a national nonprofit child advocacy organization that works to improve children's experiences with television. Its two primary goals are to increase diversity in children's programming and to eliminate commercial abuses in children's television. As part of the first of these goals, we have worked to bring public attention to special subject areas, such as the arts, which are all too often neglected by children's television. ACT has held a national symposium and a number of regional workshops on the subject of children's television and the arts. In 1979 ACT compiled *Promise and Performance: ACT's Guide to Television Programming for Children, Volume II: The Arts,* a series of essays on art education and the media by artists, teachers, TV producers, and other experts, and in 1982 ACT published *Arts for Young Audiences: An ACT Handbook,* containing suggestions for bringing the arts to children through television.

ACT's years of experience have shown us that although many excellent arts programs for children have been produced, they have not been widely publicized or distributed, especially on television. The existence of cultural cable television channels such as ARTS, Bravo, CBS Cable, and The Entertainment Channel indicates that the demand for arts programming for adults is being met, but so far children's needs have been largely overlooked. ACT hopes that as a result of this book more young people will have a chance to see more art on TV and in schools, libraries, and museums, and that this will give them an opportunity to explore their own potential as creative people.

Exploring the Arts: Films and Video Programs for Young Viewers provides a selected, annotated collection of productions for young people, ages 2 to 15, on the visual, performing, and literary arts. In selecting the 568 films and video programs included in this book, we considered thousands of titles and screened hundreds of productions, combed distributors' catalogues and lists of award winners. We solicited the opinions and advice of children, teenagers, parents, educators, librarians, artists, and media reviewers and specialists. We looked for films and programs that

Depict or discuss one or more of the arts in a meaningful way.

Are comprehensible, engaging, and attractive to young people.

Are creative, imaginative, stimulating, and enjoyable.

Are suitable for children or adolescents in both content and style.

Are of high technical quality.

Are not stereotyped in relation to race, sex, or age, or unnecessarily violent.

Films and video productions of all lengths, from many different countries, are represented. The majority of the productions date since the early 1970s, although classic older films are included as well.

This collection is not intended to be a list of "ACT-approved" programs. Instead, it offers suggestions for broadcasters, cable programmers, educators, artists, art administrators, librarians, and others who can find ways to use these productions, grouped in presentations or individually. Many of the films and programs appeal to adults as well as to children. All kinds of productions were considered in making this selection, not just those specifically aimed at children, because ACT believes that most good films and video programs can communicate something to all ages. However, films and programs should always be prescreened before being shown to children, to determine suitability for a particular audience.

Part I organizes the films and programs under the different branches of the arts—visual, performing, and literary—in alphabetical order by title. In Part II, annotated resource lists of awards and festivals, organizations, periodicals, and books and articles provide additional information. Also included are a subject and a title index; a listing of filmmakers, producers, and directors; and a directory of distributors with addresses and telephone numbers to help readers find out about rental or purchase fees and the availability of broadcasting and cablecasting rights.

For details about the descriptive cataloguing information provided for each entry, see Key to Entry Format.

This book could not have been written without the help of the ACT staff. I would also like to thank Euclid J. Peltier, Coordinator of Audio Visual Services of the Boston Public Library; Candace Boyden, Programming Director, Massachusetts Educational Television; Maureen Gaffney, Executive Director, Media Center for Children; Carolyn Markuson, Director of School Libraries, Brookline Public Schools; Michael Nicholson, Director of Off the Wall Cinema; Al Hurwitz, Sharon Lichtman, and the staff of the film libraries of Boston University, Harvard University, and the Newton and Brookline school systems for their valuable advice and assistance.

Key to Entry Format

[1]IN PRAISE OF HANDS

[2]28 min. [3]16mm, ¾" U-Matic, ½" Beta,
   ½" VHS
[4]color [5]live action [6]nonverbal
[7]Distributor: National Film Board of Canada
[8]Producers: Tom Daly and Colin Low
[9]Director: Donald Winkler
[10]Canada [11]1974 [12]ages 9 up
[13]Award: First International Craft Film Festival

[14]A fascinating visual tribute to crafts-people at work in their native lands. Filmed in the Canadian Arctic, Finland, India, Nigeria, Japan, Mexico, and Poland, it shows in loving detail the special skills of artisans working at stone sculpture, pottery, ceramics, weaving, dyeing, puppet making, and embroidery. Although the production is sensitive and beautifully filmed, its length and lack of commentary (only the sound of crafts-in-progress is used) make it more appropriate for older children.

1. Title of film or program.
2. Length of production in minutes.
3. Film and videocassette formats in which the production is available.
4. Indication that the production is in color, black and white, or both.
5. Indication of live action or animation. Live action is the filming of an actual sequence of events; animation is the frame-by-frame manipulation of images (drawings, objects, or people).
6. A nonverbal notation means that the production may have music or sound effects, but lacks comprehensible dialogue or narration. No designation here indicates the film does have extensive dialogue or narration.
7. Distributor of production. Addresses and telephone numbers are listed in Appendix 2. Distributors can be contacted for information on cost and availability of films or programs.
8,9. Names of producers and directors are provided when available. Where appropriate, the names of film-makers or production companies are included.
10. Country in which the film or program was produced.

11. Year of production.
12. Suggested age level; may be listed as span of years (6–8) or age followed by "up" (9 up). "Up" indicates that the production should interest viewers from the indicated age through adults. Productions should be screened to determine suitability for a particular audience.
13. List of any awards won in film and television festivals. A selected list of awards and festivals relating to children and the arts is found in Part II.
14. An evaluative description of the content and style of the entry. Also included in the annotation, where applicable, is the availability of foreign-language or captioned versions.

Glossary of Animation Terms

Animation: Drawings, objects, or people are filmed one shot or frame at a time, then moved slightly and filmed again, so that an illusion of movement is created when the film is shown.

Cameraless Animation: Drawings are made or etched directly on a clear piece of film. (See *Hen Hop; Ink, Paint, Scratch*)

Cel Animation: Characters and objects in the foreground are drawn on a sheet of clear celluloid; the background is drawn on other sheets of celluloid. The different sheets are then layered. (See *The Hare and the Tortoise; How We Made "The Devil and Daniel Mouse"*)

Clay Animation: Figures made of clay are filmed one position at a time so that they appear to be moving when the film is projected. (See *Claymation; Whazzat?*)

Cut-Out Animation: Characters and backgrounds cut out from paper, fabric, or other materials form the visuals. (See *The Isle of Joy; The Fisherman and His Wife*)

Iconographic Animation: Movement of the camera over still illustrations imparts a sense of motion. (See *Apt. 3; Norman the Doorman*)

Object Animation: Small three-dimensional objects are photographed one position at a time to create a feeling of movement. (See *The Bead Game*)

Pixillation: People are filmed one frame at a time; in between shots they change positions so that they can appear to be leaping tall buildings in a single bound or achieving other unusual special effects. (See *The Wizard of Speed and Time*)

Puppet Animation: Puppets or dolls appear to move when they are arranged in slightly different positions in different shots. (See *Puppets of Jiri Trnka; The Shoemaker and the Elves*)

Sand Animation: Figures formed in sand are photographed frame by frame. (See *The Owl Who Married a Goose*)

Silhouette Animation: Flat puppets with hinged joints are filmed to show their profiles. (See *Aucassin and Nicolette*)

Photo Credits

A Is for Architecture: A National Film Board of Canada film distributed in the United States by International Film Bureau Inc.

Closed Mondays: Courtesy of Pyramid Film & Video.

Houses Have History: Produced by Churchill Films.

This Is Your Museum Speaking: Photo courtesy of the National Film Board of Canada.

The Bronze Zoo: Distributed by Texture Films, Inc.

Degas in the Metropolitan: Courtesy of Pyramid Film & Video.

Harold and the Purple Crayon: From the Weston Woods production based on the book illustrated by Crockett Johnson.

The Incredible San Francisco Artists' Soap Box Derby: Phoenix/BFA Films & Video, Inc.

Nevelson in Process: Photo courtesy of Films Inc.

Two Centuries of Black American Art: Courtesy Pyramid Film & Video

In Praise of Hands: Photo courtesy of the National Film Board of Canada.

The First Moving Picture Show: Phoenix/BFA Films & Video, Inc.

Hen Hop: A National Film Board of Canada film distributed in the United States by International Film Bureau Inc.

Never Give Up: Imogen Cunningham: Phoenix/BFA Films & Video, Inc.

The Wizard of Speed and Time: Courtesy of Pyramid Film & Video.

Duel-Duo: Photo courtesy of the National Film Board of Canada.

Let It Bee: Vivaldi's "Concerto in C-dur": Photo courtesy of Films Inc.

Monsieur Pointu: Courtesy of Pyramid Film & Video.

Mountain Music: Courtesy of Pyramid Film & Video.

New York City Too Far from Tampa Blues: Time-Life Video.

Sunshine's on the Way: Photo courtesy of Learning Corporation of America.

Ballet Adagio: Courtesy of Pyramid Film & Video.

Dance on a May Day: Photo courtesy of Learning Corporation of America.

Pas de Deux: Photo courtesy of Learning Corporation of America.

A Special Gift: Time-Life Video.

The Tap Dance Kid: Photo courtesy of Learning Corporation of America.

Paul Robeson: Tribute to an Artist. Photo courtesy of Films Inc.

The American Short Story Series: The Greatest Man in the World: Courtesy of Perspective Films & Video.

The Case of the Elevator Duck: Photo courtesy of Learning Corporation of America.

The Incredible Book Escape: Produced by Bosustow Entertainment for CBS Library.

Lafcadio, the Lion Who Shot Back: Photo courtesy of Learning Corporation of America.

The Little Prince: Billy Budd Films, distributor.

Rookie of the Year: Time-Life Video.

Where the Wild Things Are: From the Weston Woods production based on the book illustrated by Maurice Sendak.

Summer of My German Soldier: Photo courtesy of Learning Corporation of America.

Arrow to the Sun: Distributed by Texture Films, Inc.

The Big Bang and Other Creation Myths: Courtesy of Pyramid Film & Video.

Hansel and Gretel: An Appalachian Version: Photo courtesy of Tom Davenport Films.

Little Red Riding Hood: A Balinese-Oregon Adaptation: Distributed by Texture Films, Inc.

A Story—A Story: From the Weston Woods production based on the book illustrated by Gail E. Haley.

Strega Nonna: From the Weston Woods production based on the book illustrated by Tomie de Paola.

Zlateh the Goat: From the Weston Woods production based on the book written by Isaac Bashevis Singer.

Part I
Films and
Video Programs

1
Visual Arts

Arts Overview, Museums, Architecture————————————

A IS FOR ARCHITECTURE (Revised)

14 min.   16mm, ¾" U-Matic, ½" Beta,
   ½" VHS   color   animation
Distributor: International Film Bureau
Producers: Colin Low and Tom Daly
Directors: Gerald Budner and Robert Verrall
Canada   1973   ages 9 up

A IS FOR ARCHITECTURE

This thought-provoking, clearly explained, animated history of architecture shows that what people build expresses what they value. Beginning with the pyramids and moving up to the skyscrapers of today, the film illustrates how buildings reflect the philosophical outlook of the time. The classical music used as

background to the narration also matches the spirit of each civilization depicted. Available in Spanish as *Arquitectura, el Espejo de la Historia.*

ART IS

28 min.   16mm   color   live action
Distributor: Modern Talking Picture Service
Producers: Associated Council of the Arts and
   Sears, Roebuck
USA   1972   ages 9 up
Awards: CINE Golden Eagle; Bronze Award, Interna-
   tional Film and TV Festival of New York; Golden
   Camera Award, U.S. Industrial Film Festival

A diverting and well-photographed look at paintings, music, sculpture, ballet, and mime. Highlights include Leonard Bernstein rehearsing an orchestra and Edward Villella and Patricia McBride dancing. Children particularly like the mime section with Tony Montanaro. Although this production was sponsored by the Sears-Roebuck Foundation, it is not a plug for the company. The film is available on free loan; borrower pays return postage only.

CLOSED MONDAYS

8 min.   16mm, ¾" U-Matic, ½" Beta, ½" VHS
   color   animation   nonverbal
Distributor: Pyramid
Filmmakers: Will Vinton and Bob Gardiner
USA   1974   ages 9 up
Awards: Academy Award; International Film Critics
   Award, Annecy (France) International Animated
   Film Festival; Maxi Award, *Media & Methods*

CLOSED MONDAYS

A man wanders into a museum and is first shocked, then moved, as paintings and objects come to life. Done in a remarkable combination of animation and three-dimensional clay figures, this film may confuse younger children, but it fascinates older ones.

CREATIVE KIDS SERIES

5 programs   16mm, ¾" U-Matic, ½" Beta,
   ½" VHS   color   live action
Distributor: Films Inc.
Producer: WGBH-TV for "Zoom"
USA   1974–76   ages 6–11

This series is part of the Emmy Award–winning Public Broadcasting Service (PBS) series "Zoom." A participatory magazine show for preteens, "Zoom" offers a potpourri of features for children, many suggested by children. The episodes are lively and stimulating, and the production values are excellent. These sequences feature vignettes of children who are involved in the arts.

More Than a Snapshot. 10 min.
   Neighborhood Portraits. Natches displays his photographic portraits of friends and neighbors, and discusses whom he likes to photograph and his techniques.
   Shooting on Location. Tess helps her stepfather photograph sea otters in the Monterey Harbor, and shows how she works with the animals.

Everybody Likes Jazz. 10 min.
   Dixieland. Dwight, a drummer for his church in New Orleans, says he likes his neighborhood because the older people help the younger ones with their music.
   Ragtime. Chris lives in St. Louis and enjoys playing the piano, particularly the music of Scott Joplin.

The World Is a Stage. 14 min.
   Clown. Scott belongs to a clown club, and he and the other children in the

club learn to apply clown makeup and dress in clown costumes.

New York Dance. Yvette is a member of a children's dance theater. In addition to dancing with the group, she teaches younger children, and the film climaxes with a performance of a Jamaican dance.

Experiments in Design. 9 min.
Illustrated Book. Katherine demonstrates how she printed her own book.
Tree House. John is building a tree house in the New Hampshire woods.

On Stage and Screen. 10 min.
"*Such a Ham.*" Andy, a self-confessed ham, plays the part of the lion in *The Wizard of Oz* with the Boston Children's Theater.
"*That's a Take.*" Tom makes his own videotapes, and shows how he directs a performance, tapes it, and then screens the tape.

HOUSES HAVE HISTORY

15 min.   16mm, ¾" U-Matic, ½" Beta, ½" VHS
  color   live action
Distributor: Churchill Films
Director: Paul Fillinger
USA   1980   ages 9 up

A beguiling look at old houses and house renovation. The film follows a group of children as they draw a Victorian house, tour a restored neighborhood, talk to longtime residents, and repair and renovate stairways and windows. Architectural details and structural styles are examined, and the value of preservation and restoration is stressed in this lively, well-paced presentation, enhanced by catchy music.

IMAGES AND THINGS

30 programs, 20 min. each   16mm, ¾" U-Matic,
  ½" Beta, ½" VHS   color   live action
Distributor: Agency for Instructional Television
Producers: Kentucky Authority for ETV, Lexington;
  KETC-TV, St. Louis; and Educational Film
  Center, North Springfield, Va.

HOUSES HAVE HISTORY

USA   1971   ages 9–11
Award: CINE Golden Eagle

This creative, visually exciting series is designed to sharpen children's awareness of art in the world around them and to increase their understanding of its relationship to their own lives. The programs do not closely follow any standard school curriculum, but they can be used in art or creative writing courses, and individual programs can be appreciated for their entertainment value. Prepared by art educators, the series focuses on the arts as they speak about life through a variety of themes, in order to encourage art appreciation, art criticism, and artistic performance. A 138-page teacher's guide is available, as well as three 30-minute teacher programs and a learning resources kit with slides of art images appearing in the series.

Module Blue

Sea Images. People's varied responses to the sea are shown through numerous art images.

Street Furniture. The function and appearance of streets and the design and location of street furniture are examined as spaces for living and as sources of imagery for artists.

People Working. Six artists working in different media describe and demonstrate their work and discuss the personal rewards of creating.

Everyone Makes Things. Similarities and differences in artistic and industrial forming processes are shown.

The Human Image. Artists' treatment of the human image expresses different personal and social concepts and attitudes.

Module Green

Spaces to Live In. A look at manmade environments and the problems of designing living space.

All Kinds of Houses. Various architectural solutions to housing needs are examined.

Buildings for Work and Play. A survey of architectural styles in office buildings, air terminals, schools, and cultural centers.

Plazas, Malls and Squares. Manmade outdoor environments are studied in paintings and in reality around the world.

Here to There. Transportation and the design of transport modes are this program's theme.

Module Red

Houses for Worship. Religious architecture and its relationship to religious ceremonies are examined.

Pageants, Parades, and Festivals. Special occasions involve imaginative planning and hard work, and the contributions to these celebrations by artists around the world are shown.

Remembering Happy Times. A look at how art preserves pleasant experiences of the past.

Groups of People. The interaction of people in groups can be a source of imagery for artists.

Stars and Heroes. The variety of ways in which art has been used to honor prominent people, both fictional and real, is shown.

Module Brown

How About a Spoon. The reasons that objects are designed as they are is the subject of this program.

Signs of the Times. A study of signs and symbols as they have developed in various times and cultures.

Things to Use. Manufactured objects used in daily life illustrate the variety of forms that function dictates.

Make Yourself Comfortable. An examination of solutions to the problems of furniture design.

Play's the Thing. Toys and playthings reveal the customs, skill, and imagination of their makers.

Module Yellow

Faces of Nature. An illustration of the fact that many art forms have their origins in natural forms.

Making the Unseen Visible. Various kinds of photography and cinematography used in scientific research can also be a source of imagery for artists.

Birds, Bees, and Bugs. Animal forms are often sources of ideas for artists and designers.

Man: Friend and Enemy of Nature. What people have done both to care for and to harm the earth, as depicted by artists.

Land Images. Natural images inspire different interpretations by different artists.

Module Orange

Wrappings and Trappings. A look at how costumes and clothing are made and used by different people around the world.

Changing Your Looks. Body decoration and adornment are used in various ways and for various reasons to change the looks of people in different times, societies, and cultures.

Getting the Message. An examination of the arts as a form of communication and a way of conveying ideas and feelings.

Dreams and Fantasy. A study of the ways that fantasies and dreams have been presented in art.

Devils, Monsters and Dragons. Frightening art images are seen as ways to control fear and to ward off harm.

MUSEUM: BEHIND THE SCENES AT THE ART INSTITUTE OF CHICAGO

28 min.   16mm   color   live action
Distributor: The American Federation of Arts
Producer: Chuck Olin Associates for the Art Institute of Chicago
Director: John Mason
USA 1979   ages 12 up
Award: Red Ribbon, American Film Festival

This engrossing and informative film reveals the backstage workings of a great museum. It stands out because it clearly depicts the "hows" and "whys" of museum activities. Curators are shown at work on exhibits, and they discuss how they acquire artworks and how they hang them to achieve particular effects. Conservators demonstrate the techniques they use to maintain and restore paintings. An interesting sequence shows how photographic techniques help them discover a new figure in a painting. This film offers an unusual angle on art that helps viewers understand how museums function.

NORMAN THE DOORMAN

15 min.   16mm, ¼" U-Matic, ½" Beta, ½" VHS
   color   animation
Distributor: Weston Woods
Producer: Morton Schindel
Director: Cynthia Freitag
USA 1971   ages 6–8

Norman, a feisty mouse who lives in a museum, enters an art contest. His wire-sculpture entry wins, and Norman is granted his greatest desire—a tour of the museum's upstairs galleries. Don Freeman's fanciful illustrations, animated iconographically, complement the gently humorous tone of his writing.

NOTES ON THE POPULAR ARTS

20 min.   16mm, ¼" U-Matic, ½" Beta, ½" VHS
   color   live action and animation
Distributor: Pyramid
Producer/director: Saul Bass
USA 1978   ages 12 up
Awards: Gold Cindy, Information Film Producers of America; Silver Venus, Best Short Film, Miami Film Festival; CINE Golden Eagle; First Prize, Hemisfilm International Film Festival

Entertaining and insightful sketches explore the effects of film, television, popular music, and popular novels on society.

Various film techniques and special effects are used to show how the popular arts expand experience and fulfill fantasies in a production that is both lyrical and funny.

RIGHT ON/BE FREE

15 min.   16mm, ¾" U-Matic, ½" Beta, ½" VHS
   color   live action
Distributor: FilmFair Communications
Filmmaker: Sargon Tamimi
USA   1971   ages 9 up
Award: San Francisco International Film Festival

Although the title may sound dated, this film is a fresh and vital celebration of some aspects of the black cultural experience, and it succeeds admirably. Music, poetry, painting, and dance are the arts briefly examined. The dance segment, which features the extraordinary Judith Jamison elegantly gliding around in a concrete setting, is especially good. The camera work throughout has a rhythm to it, and the effective use of close-ups and pans makes even static presentations dramatic and involving.

THIS IS YOUR MUSEUM SPEAKING

13 min.   16mm, ¾" U-Matic, ½" Beta, ½" VHS
   color   animation
Distributors: Coe, National Film Board of Canada
Producers: Robert Verall and Derek Lamb
Director: Lynn Smith
Canada   1979   ages 9 up
Awards: Ottawa International Animated Film Festival; Bronze Plaque, Columbus Film Festival Chris Awards; Annecy (France) International Animated Film Festival; San Francisco International Film Festival

History comes alive in an intriguing and humorous fashion for a night watchman and his dog, Fang, when they encounter characters emerging from the walls and halls of the museum. Guided by the resident muse, they witness an eighteenth-century duel, converse with a Rembrandt painting, and question an Egyptian pha-

THIS IS YOUR MUSEUM SPEAKING

raoh. The unusual and beautiful animation was done with pastel chalks worked directly under the camera on special "sanded" art paper.

WHY MAN CREATES

25 min. 16mm, ¾" U-Matic, ½" Beta, ½" VHS
   color   live action and animation
Distributor: Pyramid
Producer/director: Saul Bass
USA   1968   ages 9 up
Awards: Academy Award; Blue Ribbon, American
   Film Festival; Grand Prize, Berlin Film Festival;
   Gold Hugo, Chicago Film Festival; Gold Medal,
   Moscow Film Festival; Maxi Award of the De-
   cade, Media & Methods; Golden Gate Award,
   San Francisco International Film Festival

A superlative, stimulating experience in both form and content, this is an exploration of the nature of the creative process. The film is organized into eight sections, including a funny animated history of ideas, a look at the young creator's struggle, a parable about a rubber ball that bounces to a different drummer, and an examination of why people need to create. It is witty, imaginative, and provocative, and the photography is stunning.

YOU CALL THAT ART?!

29 min.   ¾" U-Matic, ½" Beta, ½" VHS
   color   live action
Distributor: PBS Video
Producer: WTTW-TV, Chicago
USA   1978   ages 12 up

This survey of different approaches to contemporary art offers exciting images and a relaxed pace. Actor Meshach Taylor has a pleasant, chatty style as the host, and the production is enhanced by good photography and agreeable music. Well-chosen examples of work by Claes Oldenburg and Andy Warhol, among others, are examined, as well as such unusual pieces of environmental art as Christo's Running Fence, an 18-foot-high nylon fence stretched across nearly 25 miles of northern California.

Painting, Drawing, and Sculpture

THE ARTIST WAS A WOMAN

54 min.   16mm, ¾" U-Matic   color and b&w
   live action
Distributor: ABC Wide World of Learning
Producers: Mary Bell and Suzanne Bauman
Director: Suzanne Bauman
USA   1980   ages 12 up
Awards: Red Ribbon, American Film Festival;
   Midwest Film Conference; CINE Golden Eagle

A beautifully crafted, enlightening look at women artists. Actress Jane Alexander narrates as the camera examines paintings by female artists over the last four centuries. Anecdotes and quotations by the artists and their contemporaries are woven into the narration, and scholars, including Germaine Greer, comment on the problems encountered by women painters. This film effectively lays to rest the question "Why are there no great women artists?" by presenting the work of a number of great women artists while prompting a feeling for the difficulties they encountered because they are female.

BLACK DAWN

20 min.   16mm, ¾" U-Matic   color   animation
Distributor: Icarus Films
Producers/directors: Robin Lloyd and Doreen Kraft
USA   1980   ages 9 up
Awards: Lille Film Festival, France; Annecy
   (France) International Animated Film Festival

THE BRONZE ZOO

The history and folklore of Haiti are retold through animated paintings of 13 Haitian artists, rhythmic music, and resonant (although heavily accented) narration. The brilliant, glowing colors of the primitive paintings make up for the sometimes static quality of the animation. This is an authentic, colorful, entertaining expression of a rich culture. French and Creole versions available.

A BOY CREATES

10 min.   16mm, ¾" U-Matic, ½" Beta, ½" VHS
  color live action nonverbal
Distributor: Encyclopaedia Britannica
Filmmaker: Tom Harris
USA 1971 ages 6–11

A young black boy transforms discarded objects into sculpture in this slow-paced but engaging film. He turns bottles, plastic pieces, driftwood, and metal odds and ends that he finds on a beach into creative figures and constructions. Child viewers may be inspired to attempt their own statues with recycled material.

THE BRONZE ZOO

16 min.   16mm, ¾" U-Matic, ½" Beta, ½" VHS
  color   live action
Distributor: Texture
Filmmaker: Sonya Friedman
USA 1973 ages 6 up
Awards: Francis Scott Key Award, Baltimore International Film Festival; ALA Notable Film for Children

Shay Rieger's unusual bronze animal sculptures are part fantasy, part reality. This well-paced film follows a sculpture of a yak from its conception in the artist's mind to its modeling in her studio, casting at the foundry, and final placement at a city library. Rieger narrates and gives some insights into the creative process, and the ancient art of bronze casting is clearly demonstrated.

THE CLAY CIRCUS

12 min. 16 mm, ¾" U-Matic, ½" Beta, ½" VHS
  color live action nonverbal
Distributors: Texture, Coe
Filmmaker: Herman J. Engel
USA 1973 ages 6 up

A celebration of sculpture in the appealing context of the circus. The freewheeling colors, movement, and excitement of actual circus acts are related to sculptures inspired by the circus. Shay Rieger is shown sketching the action in the rings and then transforming her sketches into clay sculptures in her studio. This is an interesting study of a sculptor at work on an ever-popular subject.

DEGAS IN THE METROPOLITAN

10 min.   16mm, ¾″ U-Matic, ½″ Beta, ½″ VHS
  color   live action
Distributor: Pyramid
Filmmakers: Charles Eames and Ray Eames
USA   1979   ages 12 up
Award: Learning A/V Award, *Learning* Magazine

Piano music by Chopin and Satie sets the relaxed pace for this informative and keenly observed introduction to the works of Edgar Degas. In 1977, New York City's

DEGAS IN THE METROPOLITAN

Metropolitan Museum of Art organized its comprehensive collection of Degas's work into a special exhibition, and this film is a study of that exhibit. The curator of the exhibition, Charles Moffett, provides the insightful voiceover narration.

ESKIMO ARTIST—KENOJUAK

20 min.   16mm, ¾″ U-Matic, ½″ Beta, ½″ VHS
  color   live action
Distributor: National Film Board of Canada
Producer: Tom Daly
Director: John Feeney
Canada   1964   ages 9 up
Awards: British Film Academy; New York Film
  Festival

An engrossing look at an artist of an unfamiliar culture. Kenojuak lives on Baffin Island and during the harsh winter she makes striking drawings, which are carved in stone by artisans and printed on paper. Her inspirations come from legends and the stark landscape, and her work reflects the Eskimo belief in ecological unity. Kenojuak's thoughts on her culture and her art constitute the film's commentary. The beautiful photography shows her with her family in their igloo as well as at work on her art.

FOUR ARTISTS PAINT ONE TREE

16 min.   16mm   color   animation
Distributor: Walt Disney
USA   1964   ages 9 up

This film emphasizes different ways of seeing things and the importance of individual style. It begins with Walt Disney talking about painting and showing animation artists at work on *Sleeping Beauty*. Then four artists from Disney's studio go out and paint the same subject, an oak tree, to illustrate different approaches and interpretations. Each artist talks about how he sees the tree and plans to paint it, and watching them at work on their canvases demonstrates the process of transforming a vision into reality. Available in Spanish.

FROM THE MIXED UP FILES OF MRS. BASIL E. FRANKWEILER

105 min.   16mm, 35mm, ¾" U-Matic, ½" Beta,
½" VHS   color   live action
Distributor: Films Inc.
Director: Fielder Cook
USA   1978   ages 6 up

Claudia and her brother Jamie run away from home to live in the Metropolitan Museum of Art, where they come upon a breathtaking statue. While trying to find out who made it, they arrive at the grand estate of the eccentric Mrs. Frankweiler (played by Ingrid Bergman), where the mystery is solved. This affecting and suspenseful drama is based on the Newbery Medal-winning book by E. L. Konigsburg.

FULL CIRCLE: THE WORK OF DORIS CHASE

9½ min.   16 mm, ¾" U-Matic, ½" Beta, ½" VHS
color   live action
Distributor: Perspective Films
Producer: Elizabeth Wood
Director: Doris Chase
USA   1974   ages 9 up

Doris Chase, an innovative sculptor, painter, filmmaker, and videomaker, shows and explains her work in this interesting documentary. Her spare, clean forms are frequently designed to be used, not just admired, and one of the film's highlights is watching dancers incorporate her movable sculptures into the choreography. Chase's sculptured forms for children were made specifically for crawling under, over, and through, and she has also created huge kinetic sculptures.

GALLERY

6 min.   16mm, ¾" U-Matic, ½" Beta, ½" VHS
color   live action   nonverbal
Distributor: Pyramid
Filmmaker: Ken Rudolph
USA   1971   all ages

An exciting whirlwind tour of the highlights of Western art from its beginnings to the present. Using split screens, tilts, pans, and other cinematic effects, the filmmaker has taken over 2,000 paintings, drawings, and etchings and synchronized the pacing of the stills with classical music. The art flies by at a great speed, but the effect is stimulating, and the image juxtaposition is often witty. Children of any age enjoy it, but older children who are able to recognize some of the famous works get a special kick from it.

GEORGIA O'KEEFFE

60 min.   16mm, ¾" U-Matic   color   live action
Distributor: Films Inc.
Producer/director: Perry Miller Adato
USA   1977   ages 12 up
Awards: Red Ribbon, American Film Festival; Award for Directorial Achievement, Directors Guild of America (the first time to a woman); Clarion Annual Award, Women in Communication; Christopher Award; Peabody Award; CINE Golden Eagle; Bronze Hugo, Chicago International Film Festival

A first-class portrait of an excitingly original artist and woman. This film was first broadcast on PBS in honor of O'Keeffe's ninetieth birthday in 1977. Georgia O'Keeffe's striking style in her life and in her art is clearly evident in interviews with her in the present as well as through the paintings, letters, home movies, and photographs that illuminate her past. The photographs are by her famous photographer husband, Alfred Stieglitz, and they are truly extraordinary. This film is part of the WNET series "The Originals: Women in Art."

GRAVITY IS MY ENEMY

26 min.   16mm, ¾" U-Matic, ½" Beta, ½" VHS
color   live action
Distributor: Churchill Films
Filmmakers: John Joseph and Jan Stussy
USA   1977   ages 12 up
Awards: Academy Award; San Francisco International Film Festival; CINE Golden Eagle; American Film Festival

A moving and genuinely inspirational portrait of an articulate young artist. Mark Hicks was paralyzed from the neck down by a fall from a tree at the age of 12. With his parents' help, he adjusted to life as a quadriplegic. Hicks attended college, over the objections of some professors, and developed into an exceptional modern painter, using pencils and brushes held in his mouth. Hicks talks about his life and his art, and we see him with his family and at his canvases. The film concludes with the opening of his one-man show at a California art gallery. This excellent documentary, which has been shown on PBS, emphasizes the artist's ability, not his disability; the focus is on his work. Sadly, Mark Hicks died shortly after this film was made.

HAROLD AND THE PURPLE CRAYON

8 min.   16mm, ¾" U-Matic, ½" Beta, ½" VHS
   color   animation
Distributor: Weston Woods
Producer: Morton Schindel
Director: David Piel
USA   1969   ages 2–5

HAROLD AND THE PURPLE CRAYON

A little boy named Harold has a wondrous purple crayon that brings to life whatever he draws. In this film, based on the book by Crockett Johnson, Harold draws an apple tree (and a dragon to guard it), a road to walk down, a mountain to climb, and a boat to ride in. The animation consists of line drawings (as the credits have it, "lighting and scenery by Harold"), which suit the simple story line. Preschoolers love resourceful Harold and his imaginative adventures, and they may be inspired to draw along with him. Available in Danish. See also *Harold's Fairy Tale* and *A Picture for Harold's Room*, in this section.

HAROLD'S FAIRY TALE

8 min.   16mm, ¾" U-Matic, ½" Beta, ½" VHS
   color   animation
Distributor: Weston Woods
Producer: Morton Schindel
Director: Gene Deitch
USA   1974   ages 2–5
Awards: Grand Prize, Harrisburg Film Festival;
   Silver Hugo, Chicago International Film Festival

Little Harold draws an enchanted garden with his magic purple crayon and steps inside it. He saves the garden from a giant witch and makes it bloom again, drawing his way in and out of a variety of strange and wonderful experiences along the way. In this happy blend of fantasy and reality, based on the book by Crockett Johnson, everything always turns out fine. Available in Danish, Dutch, and Swedish. See also *Harold and the Purple Crayon* and *A Picture for Harold's Room*, in this section.

HENRY MOORE: MASTER SCULPTOR

15½ min.   16mm, ¾" U-Matic, ½" Beta, ½" VHS
   color   live action
Distributor: Centron
Producer: Centron Corporation
Great Britain   1976   ages 9 up
Awards: CINE Golden Eagle; Silver Screen Award;
   U.S. Industrial Film Festival; Bronze Plaque, Columbus Film Festival Chris Awards; Red Ribbon, American Film Festival

This sensitive, contemplative film focuses on the artist as much as on his art. Henry Moore is shown at work in his studio, demonstrating and clearly explaining the process of carving, casting, and finishing his large bronze pieces. He also talks about his philosophy of art, life, and sculpture, and beautiful views of Moore's monumental outdoor sculptures illustrate the words. The film conveys a warm feeling toward Moore and his art, and a sense of what sculpture is all about.

IMAGES OF THE WILD

22 min.   16mm   color   live action
Distributor: Benchmark Films
Producers: Beryl Fox, Don Hopkins
Director: Norman Lightfoot
Canada   1981   ages 9 up

Canadian artist Robert Bateman specializes in paintings of wild animals in their natural environment. This captivating, beautifully filmed production follows him into the Canadian wilderness and on

safari in East Africa as he studies his subjects. Bateman collects rocks, branches, and even elephant dung in order to later reconstruct an animal's environment, and he takes photographs and makes preliminary sketches and clay models before beginning to paint. His aim is to make his oil paintings as true to life as possible, and he succeeds admirably. Young viewers enjoy seeing both the animals and Bateman's paintings of them, and the narration does a good job of explaining his techniques.

THE INCREDIBLE SAN FRANCISCO ARTISTS' SOAP BOX DERBY

24 min.   16mm, ¼" U-Matic, ½" Beta, ½" VHS   color   live action
Distributor: Phoenix
Producer/director: Amanda C. Pope
USA   1977   ages 9 up
Award: ALA Selected Film for Young Adults

THE INCREDIBLE SAN FRANCISCO ARTISTS' SOAP BOX DERBY

The imagination and energy of over 100 Bay Area artists are celebrated in this film about an artist-built "car" exhibition/ derby. Cars in the form of bananas, tennis shoes, bathtubs, and other unlikely designs—even a car made out of bread—are displayed and then raced downhill. The artists themselves narrate this entertaining, clever, and well-paced production.

ISABELLA AND THE MAGIC BRUSH

14 min.   16mm, ¾" U-Matic, ½" Beta, ½" VHS
    color   animation
Distributors: Coe, FilmFair Communications
Producer/director: Barbara Dourmashkin
USA   1977   ages 2–11
Awards: Ruby Slipper, Seventh International Children's Film Festival; Bronze Plaque, Columbus Film Festival Chris Awards; Best Film for Children, Canadian Association for Young Children, Child Film Festival

A delightful fantasy based on a Chinese tale about a little girl who wants to be an artist. Poverty, a tyrant king, the court painter, and her parents all stand in her way until Isabella wishes for and receives a brush—a magic brush that gives life to whatever she paints. Renaissance music, clever and colorful animation, and a terrific sense of humor combine to make an enchanting film that children really enjoy.

LEONARDO'S DIARY

9 min.   16mm, ¾" U-Matic, ½" Beta, ½" VHS
    color   live action and animation   nonverbal
Distributor: Perspective
Producer: Kratky Film, Prague
Czechoslovakia   1977   ages 9 up

Animated drawings from Leonardo da Vinci's diary and notebooks are intercut in intriguing ways with sepia-colored live-action footage. The juxtaposition of images (for example, footage of athletic competitions with animation of a battle scene) is clever and stimulating.

THE LIVING STONE

31 min.   16mm, ¾" U-Matic, ½" Beta, ½" VHS
    color   live action
Distributor: National Film Board of Canada
Producer: Tom Daly
Director: John Feeney
Canada   1958   ages 12 up
Award: Robert J. Flaherty, London

Eskimo sculptors believe their task is to release the image they see imprisoned in the rough stone. Behind their inspiration is faith in the supernatural. This film centers around an old legend about the carving of the image of a sea spirit to bring food to a hungry camp. It is a moving and absorbing tale that conveys a sense of the Eskimo way of life as well as a feeling for the art of Eskimo carving.

MAUD LEWIS: A WORLD WITHOUT SHADOWS

10 min.   16mm, ¾" U-Matic, ½" Beta, ½" VHS
    color   live action
Distributors: Coe, Phoenix
Producer: Kathleen Shannon
Director: Diane Beaudry-Cowling
Canada   1978   ages 12 up

An affectionate and nostalgic look at the bright, detailed primitive paintings of the late Maud Lewis. The film moves from paintings to real-life scenes of rural Nova Scotia in a slow, harmonious series of dissolves. This National Film Board of Canada production is enhanced by piano music.

MIRRORS: REFLECTIONS OF A CULTURE

18 min.   16mm, ¾" U-Matic, ½" Beta, ½" VHS
    color   live action
Distributor: Churchill Films
Filmmaker: Millie Paul
USA   1980   ages 12 up

This excellent documentary examines the proud spirit and products of three Chicano muralists. The artists and their community helpers are shown decorating barrios, schools, and churches in the Denver area with bold, colorful, highly symbolic images. Stirring guitar music and fine cinematography enhance this portrayal of artists who glory in their heritage.

NEVELSON IN PROCESS

30 min.   16mm, ¾″ U-Matic, ½″ Beta, ½″ VHS
   color   live action
Distributor: Films Inc.
Producer: Perry Miller Adato
Directors: Susan Fanshel and Jill Godmilow
USA   1977   ages 12 up
Award: Red Ribbon, American Film Festival

NEVELSON IN PROCESS

Louise Nevelson is a forthright, dynamic person and an outstanding sculptor. Both aspects of the woman come across clearly in this fine film. She talks about her life and her long fight to gain recognition for her art, and she comments on her work. The real treat, however, is watching her at work in the foundry and at her studio as she creates two new sculptures, one of metal and one of wood. This film is part of WNET's "The Originals: Women in Art" series, broadcast on PBS.

NORMAN ROCKWELL'S WORLD... AN AMERICAN DREAM

25 min.   16mm   color   live action
Distributor: Films Inc.
Producer: Concepts Unlimited
Director: Robert Deubel
USA   1973   ages 9 up
Awards: Academy Award; CINE Golden Eagle;
   Silver Phoenix, Atlanta Film Festival; Bronze
   Plaque, Columbus Film Festival Chris Awards

A warm look at a beloved artist. The beautiful, simple, nostalgic world of Norman Rockwell is depicted through reenactment, stills, paintings, old film footage, and scenes of Rockwell at 78 in his hometown of Stockbridge, Massachusetts. The film shows how Rockwell's work reflects American culture, history, beliefs, and customs. It also offers a portrait of a vital man who truly cared about the people he painted. An exceptionally well-produced art film.

A PICTURE FOR HAROLD'S ROOM

6 min.   16mm, ¾″ U-Matic, ½″ Beta, ½″ VHS
   color   animation
Distributor: Weston Woods
Producer: Morton Schindel
Director: Gene Deitch
USA   1971   ages 2–5

Harold decides he needs a picture on his wall, so he draws one with his magic purple crayon, which brings whatever he draws to life. When Harold steps inside the picture, he finds he is a giant, towering over a town. Based on Crockett Johnson's book, this film is a treat for young viewers. Available also in Danish and Turkish. See also *Harold and the Purple Crayon* and *Harold's Fairy Tale* (this section).

PORTRAIT OF GRANDPA DOC

28 min.   16mm, ¾″ U-Matic, ½″ Beta, ½″ VHS
   color   live action
Distributor: Phoenix
Producer: Diane Baker
Director: Randal Kleiser
USA   1977   ages 9 up

Awards: Red Ribbon, American Film Festival; Best of Festival, Birmingham International Educational Film Festival; Georgia Film Festival on Aging; First Prize, Jacksonville Film Festival; San Francisco International Film Festival

Greg, a young artist preparing for his first one-man show, struggles to complete a portrait of his grandfather (beautifully played by Melvyn Douglas). As Greg paints, he reflects on his childhood and the time he and his grandfather spent together. Grandpa Doc was the first to encourage Greg to express himself through art, and the film depicts the very special bond between the two. The cinematography is excellent, and the plot is very moving. This production was presented as an "ABC Short Story Special."

SANDSONG

20 min.   16mm, ¾" U-Matic, ½" Beta, ½" VHS
   color   live action
Distributors: Coe, Wombat
Producer/director: Stuart A. Goldman
USA   1980   ages 9 up

An engaging film about a unique art form. Gerry Lynas is shown creating sand sculpture on a Fire Island, New York, beach as the tide pulls out. Using his hands, a Frisbee, a trowel, a shovel, and seashells, he creates huge animal and human heads and forms that resemble architectural ruins, as curious onlookers gather. Beach sounds and instrumental music provide a background for the comments of Lynas and observers. Still photographs show some of Lynas's previous work as the tide comes in and washes away his current sand sculpture.

TWO CENTURIES OF BLACK AMERICAN ART

26 min.   16mm, ¾" U-Matic, ½" Beta, ½" VHS
   color   live action
Distributor: Pyramid
Producer: Pyramid Films
Director: Carleton Moss
USA   1976   ages 12 up

This survey of black American art covers the work of artisans, painters, and sculptors of the nineteenth and twentieth centu-

TWO CENTURIES OF BLACK AMERICAN ART

ries. It focuses on 14 individuals, from the early portrait painter Joshua Johnson to such modern artists as John Rhodden, and it shows how black art has been seen differently in different eras. The camera shows artists at work and presents finished works of art. Most of the artists are not widely known, but the narration provides some background and the brief look at their work is tantalizing. The overall effect is to impress the viewer with the range and quality of black American art.

Crafts

ANONYMOUS WAS A WOMAN

28 min.   16mm, ¾" U-Matic   color   live action
Distributor: Films Inc.
Producer: Perry Miller Adato
Director: Mirra Bank
USA   1978   ages 12 up

A thoughtful look at the origins of American folk art traditions, this film pays tribute to the scores of unknown women of the eighteenth century who stitched and painted attractive items to decorate their homes and to express themselves. Engravings, costumed recreations, and expressively read excerpts from letters, diaries, and journals supplement the display of handsome objects that testify to the creative spirit of early American women. This film, part of WNET's "The Originals: Women in Art" series, has been shown on PBS.

APPLE DOLLS

19 min.   16mm, ¾" U-Matic, ½" Beta, ½" VHS
   color   live action
Distributor: Wombat
Producer: Bernard B. Sauermann
USA   1978   ages 12 up
Award: Birmingham International Educational Film
   Festival

Urvé Buffey demonstrates the North American pioneer craft of carving expressive faces from apples, drying them, and dressing them up to create unique dolls. Buffey has a leisurely, gentle manner and clearly demonstrates her easy-to-follow instructions. This is a slow-paced but enjoyable introduction to an intriguing craft.

AT YOUR FINGERTIPS

6 programs, 10 min. each   16mm, ¾" U-Matic,
   ½" Beta, ½" VHS   color   live action
Distributors: PCI, Coe Films
Producer: ACI Films
USA   1969   ages 6–11

This engaging crafts series encourages creativity and makes use of inexpensive and easily obtainable materials. It shows children how they can make their own playthings instead of buying them, and features children demonstrating how to make the objects. Also available in French.

At Your Fingertips—Boxes. Boxes, cartons, and containers seen at a supermarket are transformed at home into cars, animals, villages, playhouses, and tunnels. *Award:* Silver Medal, Venice Film Festival.

At Your Fingertips—Cylinders. Using materials found in the home, such as rollers from paper towels and bathroom tissue, children build totem poles, rockets, and other toys. With cutout additions, they construct animals and sculptures.

At Your Fingertips—Floats. After exploring why some things float and others sink, children make their floating playthings, including boats and a floating man.

At Your Fingertips—Grasses. Different kinds of grasses can be used in different ways. A design is made by placing paper over grass stalks and rubbing with a crayon, and long stalks can be woven into belts, costumes, and headdresses.

At Your Fingertips—Play Clay. This film shows how to mix flour, salt, and water to make a claylike dough, which can be dyed or painted. Children create animals, human figures, and elements for a necklace, and then finish the objects with a lacquer spray.

At Your Fingertips—Sugar and Spice. Confectioner's sugar can be combined with water to make a paste, which is then dried in molds. Children demonstrate how to create party favors, Easter eggs, a snowman, and decorations for a Christmas tree.

HORSE FLICKERS

10 min. 16mm, ¾" U-Matic, ½" Beta, ½" VHS
    color live action nonverbal
Distributor: Texture
Producers: Jim Gruebel and Rhonda Raulston
Director: Bill Stitt
USA 1977 ages 6 up

Fast-moving fun. Filmmaker-artist Stitt set up a camera directly above a bare barn floor and took stop-action pictures of a series of horse images. The horse creations are made of every material imaginable, from feathers to newspapers, sleeping bags, and broomsticks. The pixillation technique makes them appear to be moving, running, jumping, and vanishing in a flash. Music by John Reubourn and Jack Nitzsche accompanies the amusing, inventive action.

IN PRAISE OF HANDS

28 min. 16mm, ¾" U-Matic, ½" Beta, ½" VHS
    color live action nonverbal
Distributor: National Film Board of Canada
Producers: Tom Daly and Colin Low
Director: Donald Winkler
Canada 1974 ages 9 up
Award: First International Craft Film Festival

A fascinating visual tribute to craftspeople at work in their native lands. Filmed in the Canadian Arctic, Finland, India, Nigeria, Japan, Mexico, and Poland, it shows in loving detail the special skills of artisans

IN PRAISE OF HANDS

working at stone sculpture, pottery, ceramics, weaving, dyeing, puppet making, and embroidery. Although the production is sensitive and beautifully filmed, its length and lack of commentary (only the sound of crafts-in-progress is used) make it more appropriate for older children.

MARIA OF THE PUEBLOS

15 min.   16mm, ¾" U-Matic, ½" Beta, ½" VHS
   color   live action
Distributor: Centron
Producer: Cleman Film Enterprises
Director: Maurice Prather
USA   1971   ages 9 up
Award: Chris Statuette, Columbus Film Festival
   Chris Awards

Maria Martinez was a famous and successful American Indian potter. As a young woman, she accidentally discovered the long-forgotten secret process for creating iridescent black pottery. She shared her techniques with family and friends in her Pueblo Indian village of San Ildefonso, New Mexico, and helped lift the village out of poverty. Despite poor sound, the film gives a good sense of the life of the Pueblos and shows the step-by-step process of making their beautiful pottery.

MY HANDS ARE THE TOOLS OF MY SOUL

54 min.   16mm, ¾" U-Matic, ½" Beta, ½" VHS
   color   live action
Distributor: Texture
Producer: Swanni Films, Inc.
Director: Arthur Barron
USA   1977   ages 12 up
Awards: Best Documentary, Hemisfilm International Film Festival; CINE Golden Eagle

This well-photographed, low-key documentary emphasizes the close relationship between native American arts and nature. Native Americans consider art a part of life, so this film is as much about Indian culture as about their art, poetry, and handicrafts. Still photographs illustrate art of the past, while present-day art is

explained as we watch it being created. An Iroquois mask maker carves out a medicine man's mask from a living tree, and a medicine dance demonstrates how the mask is used to drive away evil. Pottery making, blanket and basket weaving, and sand painting are shown, and their relationship to activities of daily life is described. Poetry and statements by native Americans provide the narration, with background Indian music. This is an authentic and absorbing look at the role of art in the lives of native Americans.

PUPPET MAGIC

12 min.   16mm, ¾" U-Matic, ½" Beta, ½" VHS
   color   live action
Distributor: International Film Bureau
Producer: Internews Productions
Directors: Christian Depovere and Patrick Wilcox
Belgium   1977   ages 6–11

The short history of puppets that begins this film points out that in ancient times many people thought puppets were magic. This clearly presented, absorbing production demystifies puppets by showing how they are made and by introducing the "magicians," the puppeteers. The puppeteers demonstrate various kinds of puppets and staging and show how marionettes are constructed. They then make the marionettes come to life in performances. Available in French as *La Vie Tient à Plus d'un Fil.*

PYSANKA: THE UKRAINIAN EASTER EGG

14 min.   16mm, ¾" U-Matic, 1" & 2" Masters
   color   live action
Distributor: ICAP
Filmmaker: Slavko Nowytski
USSR   1975   ages 9 up
Awards: CINE Golden Eagle; ALA Selected Film for Young Adults

An eye-pleasing study of the art of egg painting. The narration relates the history of the craft, from its origins in a pagan sun cult in the Ukraine to its adoption in the celebration of the modern Christian Easter. The camera shows an artist at work painting an egg, and dozens of her finished creations are displayed. The rich detail of the eggs is brought out by the skillful use of closeups. Musical background is provided by a choral chant and a lyrical string instrument.

QUILTS IN WOMEN'S LIVES

28 min.   16mm   color   live action
Distributor: New Day Films
Producer/director: Pat Ferrero
USA   1980   ages 12 up
Awards: Emily Award and Blue Ribbon, American
   Film Festival; First Place, Fine Arts, San Fran-
   cisco International Film Festival; Gold Cindy,
   Best Documentary, Information Film Producers
   of America; New York International Film Festival

Traditional quiltmakers share their art and their lives in this warm, beautiful film. Seven women, including a California Mennonite, a black Mississippian, a Bulgarian immigrant, and others of similarly varied backgrounds and interests, discuss their quilting and their strong feelings about it. They talk about the inspirations for their work and the joy of the creative process. Lovely cinematography shows the women at work and the quilts they have made.

STAINED GLASS—PAINTING WITH LIGHT

20 min.   16mm, ¾" U-Matic, ½" Beta, ½" VHS
   color   live action
Distributor: Barr
Filmmaker: Hans Halberstadt
USA   1974   ages 12 up
Awards: Birmingham International Educational
   Film Festival; National Educational Film Festival

Artists and craftspeople are shown designing and constructing stained glass windows and lampshades in this attractive, straightforward film. The emphasis is on the process of creating stained glass,

rather than on the history of the craft. The camera work is well done, offering many closeups of the craftspeople, who explain their techniques as they work.

UNDER THE COVERS: AMERICAN QUILTS

11 min.   16mm, ¾" U-Matic, ½" Beta, ½" VHS
   color   live action
Distributor: Pyramid
Filmmaker: Millie Paul
USA   1976   ages 9 up
Awards: Learning A/V Award, Learning Magazine;
   CINE Golden Eagle

A well-photographed, visually exciting look at traditional American quilts, with lively background banjo music. The narration covers the history of quilting, and the film emphasizes the importance of quilting in the lives of early American women. Brief interviews with modern quiltmakers point out the recent revival of interest in the craft.

WORLD CULTURES AND YOUTH

26 programs, 25 min. each   16mm, ¾" U-Matic,
   ½" Beta I and II, ½" VHS   color   live action
Distributor: Coronet
Producers/directors: Paul Saltzman and Deepa
   Saltzman
1980–1982   ages 9 up

This excellent series celebrates the creative potential of youth. Young people ages 10–17 are shown at work on a wide variety of crafts in their native lands. These films are more than just handicraft travelogues, however. The individuality of each young craftsperson is stressed, and the audience gets a sense of what the work means to them and of their doubts as well as their pride. The connection between each craft and the culture in which it is practiced is also an important part of these sensitive productions. The photography throughout is first class.

Yoshiko the Papermaker (Japan). Yoshiko Fujimoto, 13, is learning to make paper by hand, a time-consuming art that has been practiced in her Japanese village for hundreds of years. *Awards:* Red Ribbon, American Film Festival; Golden Babe, Chicagoland Educational Film Festival; Best Arts Film and Best Editing, Yorktown, Canada, International Film Festival; Top 20 Award, Cleveland Instructional Film Festival

Ming-Oi the Magician (Hong Kong). Sixteen-year-old Ming-Oi Kwan lives in Hong Kong. She is studying the ancient art of Chinese magic and hopes to become a professional magician.

Lee's Parasol (Thailand). Lee Nakhampa, 15, lives in a Thai village and works with her mother making and painting beautiful, delicate parasols.

Gopal's Golden Pendant (India). In Jaipur, India, ten-year-old Gopal Dyar is carrying on a family tradition as he learns gold and silver enameling.

Hasan the Carpetweaver (India). Under the direction of his grandfather, 12-year-old Hasan Gulam Dhar of the Kashmir province of India struggles to become a master carpet weaver.

Jafar's Blue Tiles (Iran). An ancient tomb in Jafar Esarbaksh's Iranian village is being restored. With his father's help, 14-year-old Jafar learns to make clay tiles and apply the special turquoise blue glaze.

Serama's Mask (Bali). Serama Samadi E-Gusti Mura, 16, carves a ceremonial mask and performs a demanding dance in order to become principal dancer in the troupe of his Balinese village. *Award:* Honor Film Award, Pacific Film Festival

Slima the Dhowmaker (Tanzania). Slima Juma, 14, is an apprentice dhowmaker, helping to build the wooden sailing boats called dhows in his Tanzanian village.

Francesco the Potter (Greece). On the Greek island of Sifnos, Francesco Lomines, 14, works at becoming a master potter. Under his uncle's supervision, he makes a pair of candlesticks for a local church festival, which he attends.

Steffan the Violinmaker (West Germany). Steffan Keller, 16, of West Germany, is carrying on a family tradition by learning to make violins.

Valerie's Stained Glass Window (France). Sixteen-year-old Valerie Foucault lives in Chartres, France, which is famous for its cathedral. Inspired by the windows of the cathedral, Valerie designs and assembles her first stained glass window. *Award:* Honorable Mention, Columbus Film Festival Chris Awards

Amy the Photographer (USA). Amy Hobby, 13, is interested in hard-edge photography. She takes, develops, and exhibits her photographs, and this film shows her preparing for an important art festival.

Julia the Gourdcarver (Peru). In a village in the Andes Mountains of Peru, Julia Flores Sanabria, 11, carves the story of her life on a gourd and sells it at the market. *Award:* Golden Babe, Chicagoland Educational Film Festival

Lena the Glassblower (Sweden). Seventeen-year-old Lena Sundberg decides to follow a career in glassblowing after working in a famous Swedish glassworks company.

Igor and the Dancing Stallions (Yugoslavia). Igor Lang, 16, rides and trains the famous dancing white stallions of Lipizza, Yugoslavia.

Gilberto's Mayan Dream (Guatemala). Fourteen-year-old Gilberto Leopoldo learns traditional Guatemalan weaving techniques from his father.

Richard's Totem Pole (Canada). Richard Harris, a 16-year-old Gitskan Indian living in British Columbia, helps his father carve a totem pole and discovers his heritage in the process.

Laroussie the Saddlemaker (Morocco). Twelve-year-old Laroussie Moushing lives in Fez, Morocco. He works as a brass and copper apprentice with his father, but his true love is horses and he makes a saddle in his uncle's saddle shop.

Yang-Xun the Peasant Painter (China). Yang-Xun, 15, attends summer art classes. He hopes one day to be accomplished in a new style of peasant painting.

Tanya the Puppeteer (USSR). Twelve-year-old Tanya Nicolev of Moscow is chosen by the famous Sergi Obratsov Puppet Theatre to participate in a season-long workshop.

Kathy's Pacing Horse (Australia). Australian rancher Kathy Sargent, 17, works at training an injured horse named Alchemy to race.

Anessi's Barkcloth Art (Tonga). Twelve-year-old Anessi of the South Pacific kingdom of Tonga makes a barkcloth to give to her cousin as a wedding gift.

Joshua's Soapstone Carving (Canada). Joshua Quamluk, 14, an Innuit (Eskimo) who lives on the coast of Hudson Bay, takes up his family's tradition of carving soapstone.

Yohannes the Silversmith (Ethiopia). Twelve-year-old Yohannes Mengesha lives in northwest Ethiopia and wants to be a doctor, but his parents want him to learn a trade first. They apprentice him to a master silversmith, and Yohannes casts a beautiful Coptic cross.

Shao-Ping the Acrobat (China). Sixteen-year-old Shao-Ping, a member of Shanghai Acrobatic Team No. 3, rehearses some new routines.

Kurtis, Hollywood Stuntman (USA). Kurtis Epper Sanders, 12, is part of a large family that does stunt work in Hollywood. He and his mother perform some spectacular stunts to demonstrate how they are done. *Award:* Silver Plaque, Chicago International Film Festival

Film, Animation, and Photography

ANIMATION PIE

25 min.   16mm   color   live action and animation
Distributor: Film Wright
Filmmaker: Robert Bloomberg
USA   1974   ages 6 up
Award: American Film Festival

A creative and enjoyable introduction to animation techniques. The young students of an animation workshop held in Concord, California, are shown making flipbooks, drawing on film, experimenting with pixillation, and doing clay animation. Their finished products are clever and funny, but not so polished that they would discourage other children from trying animation. On the contrary, this is the kind of film that makes young viewers want to go out immediately and try some of the techniques themselves.

THE BEAD GAME

6 min.   16mm, ¾" U-Matic, ½" Beta, ½" VHS
  color   animation   nonverbal
Distributors: Coe, Pyramid
Producer: National Film Board of Canada
Director: Ishu Patel
Canada   1978   ages 6 up
Awards: Blue Ribbon, American Film Festival; Best Short Film, British Academy of Film Art

In this fascinating example of object animation, thousands of glass beads are arranged and rearranged to form the outlines of creatures. Beginning with amoeba-like shapes and progressing through evolution to humans, the forms battle for survival and struggle for power until humans finally unleash forces that cannot be controlled. The throbbing beat of the Indian tamboura matches the mood of the metamorphosing images, which flash in brilliant colors. Older children will get the underlying message about our destructive potential more readily than younger children, but everyone can appreciate the artistry of the animation.

CAMERA MAGIC: THE ART OF SPECIAL EFFECTS

15 min.   16mm, ¾" U-Matic, ½" Beta, ½" VHS
   color   live action
Distributor: Pyramid
Filmmakers: Paul Burnford and Jerry Samuelson
USA   1973   ages 9 up

"In this film we are out to trick you . . . be prepared for some surprises," the narration warns at the start. Teenage boys demonstrate, often humorously, how amateur filmmakers can produce such special effects as fast and slow motion, pixillation, and multiple images. Visually stimulating, with good musical accompaniment, this film will entertain and inspire young filmmakers.

A CHAIRY TALE

10 min.   16mm, ¾" U-Matic, ½" Beta, ½" VHS
   b&w   animation   nonverbal
Distributor: International Film Bureau
Producer: National Film Board of Canada
Director: Norman McLaren
Canada   1957   all ages
Awards: London Film Festival; Venice Film Festival

This modern parable is a classic film, and glorious fun to watch. A man attempts to subdue an unruly chair that moves about so that he cannot sit on it. He stalks it, wrestles it, ignores it, and dances with it, in a struggle first for mastery and then for understanding. Sitar music by Ravi Shankar enhances Norman McLaren's delightful pixillation technique.

CLAYMATION

17 min.   16mm   color   live action and
   animation
Distributor: Billy Budd Films
Filmmakers: Will Vinton and Susan Shadburn
USA   1978   ages 9 up
Awards: Best in Show, Motion Picture Seminar of the Northwest; Gold Cindy, Information Film Producers of America; Bronze Award, San Francisco International Film Festival; Special Awards Jury Prize, Marin County National Film Competition; CINE Golden Eagle; Second Prize, Animation, Columbus Film Festival Chris Awards; Silver Plaque, Chicago International Film Festival; Silver Venus Medallion, Miami International Film Festival; First Prize, High Plains Film Festival; Special Jury Award, Hemisfilm International Film Festival; Learning A/V Award, *Learning* Magazine; Film as Art Award, National Educational Film Festival

A fascinating and entertaining documentary on the art of clay animation. The animators at the Will Vinton studio show what they do and how they do it. The processes are clearly explained and humorously depicted. Much of the film is illustrated in clay animation, and clips from other Will Vinton productions (*Closed Mondays, Mountain Music, Rip Van Winkle, Martin the Cobbler*) are shown.

DOCUMENTARY

135 min.   16mm, ¾" U-Matic, ½" Beta, ½" VHS
   color and b&w   live action
Distributor: Texture
Producers: Herman J. Engel and Sonya Friedman
USA   1978   ages 12 up

A unique anthology of sequences from the world's most renowned documentary films, including *Nanook of the North, Triumph of the Will,* and *Harlan County, U.S.A.,* makes this a valuable resource for film study as well as an entertaining and informative production. The selections span five decades and many countries, and each sequence is preceded by a brief introduction that places it in historical context. Elizabeth Swados composed and conducted the background music, and Galway Kinnell narrates.

FILM: THE ART OF THE IMPOSSIBLE

27 min.   16mm, ¾" U-Matic, ½" Beta, ½" VHS
   color   live action
Distributor: Learning Corporation of America
Producer: Robert Saudek
Director: Michael Ritchie
USA   1972   ages 9 up

Exciting, well-chosen action clips from *Birth of a Nation, Potemkin, Footlight Parade, King Kong, Lawrence of Arabia, The African Queen,* and director Michael Ritchie's own *Downhill Racer* are used to illustrate how seeing can be believing in the world of film. Ritchie narrates and demonstrates some of the devices film-makers use to make scenes look realistic and to heighten drama. The film offers an interesting glance behind the lens that helps make clear how movies are made and how directors and film editors work, highlighted by thrilling film sequences.

THE FIRST MOVING PICTURE SHOW

7 min.   16mm, ¾" U-Matic, ½" Beta, ½" VHS
   color   animation
Distributor: Phoenix
Filmmaker: Nancy Faye Karkowsky
USA   1973   ages 2–8

A clay horse munching on flowers becomes a model for a clay man, who draws a series of pictures of the animal in different positions. The man discovers that when the drawings are viewed in sequence, the horse appears to be moving, and he invites all his friends to see his "first moving picture show." Historically, the motion picture actually was discovered accidentally in the course of an artistic study of horses in motion, and this ingenious introduction to motion picture theory makes the process clear to even the youngest children.

FRAME BY FRAME

13 min.   16mm,   ¾" U-Matic, ½" Beta, ½" VHS
   color   live action and animation
Distributor: Pyramid
Filmmakers: Paul Burnford and Jerry Samuelson
USA   1972   ages 9 up
Award: CINE Golden Eagle

An effective if overly fast survey of single-frame animation techniques: filming still pictures, flicker filming, cutout animation, cel animation, object and people animation, direct images on film, and time-

THE FIRST MOVING PICTURE SHOW

sequence filming. The still-picture and flicker-filming techniques whiz by so quickly that they can be hard on the eyes, but in general the examples of animation shown are excellent and enjoyable. This is a creative film that encourages creativity.

HEN HOP

4 min.   16mm, ¾" U-Matic, ½" Beta, ½" VHS
   color   animation   nonverbal
Distributors: Coe, International Film Bureau
Filmmaker: Norman McLaren
Canada   1942   all ages
Awards: Brussels Film Festival; Gijon (Spain) International Cinema Contest for Children and Teen-agers

This sprightly dance of chicken and egg is a good example of McLaren's technique of cameraless animation. The images are drawn directly on the film, and they cavort to the rhythms of French Canadian barn dance music.

HEN HOP

HISTORY OF ANIMATION

21 min.   16mm   color and b&w   live action and animation
Distributor: Walt Disney
USA   1975   ages 12 up

Although this production naturally features the animation done at the Disney studio, it also provides an interesting and clearly explained history of the art. Walt Disney, acting as host, begins with examples of cave paintings, in which double pairs of legs on animals suggest movement, and ends up with the inventors who created the techniques that made animation possible. Disney's narration is pedantic, but the examples shown are engaging. They include demonstrations of toys whose revolving images led to the development of animation and historic footage from such productions as *Steamboat Willie,* an early Mickey Mouse cartoon.

HOW WE MADE "THE DEVIL AND DANIEL MOUSE"

22 min.   16mm, ¾" U-Matic, ½" Beta, ½" VHS
   color   live action and animation
Distributor: Beacon Films
Producers: Patrick Loubert and Michael Hirsh
Director: Clive A. Smith
USA   1978   ages 12 up

An intriguing documentary that clearly demonstates how this animated film was made. Each stage in the production process is described and illustrated, from storyboard to sound track, drawings and animation, and film clips from *The Devil and Daniel Mouse* (see Chapter 2, Music section) show the impressive result. Although this film would be useful in filmmaking classes, it works well as entertainment, especially when shown after *The Devil and Daniel Mouse.*

IDA MAKES A MOVIE AND LEARNS TO TELL THE TRUTH

22 min.   16mm, ¾" U-Matic, ½" Beta, ½" VHS
   color   live action
Distributor: Learning Corporation of America
Producer: Linda Schuyler
Director: Kit Hood
Canada   1980   ages 6–11

One dull summer day young Ida learns of a children's filmmaking festival and decides to enter. She chooses neighborhood littering as her theme and talks her friend Cookie and her brother Fred into acting in her movie, while she dons a beret and directs the action. Ida is delighted when her masterpiece is picked as a finalist in the competition, but is dismayed to learn that the judges think it is an antiwar piece. How spunky Ida resolves this dilemma is the climax of this well-photographed, realistic, and amusing tale, based on the book by Kay Chorao.

INK, PAINT, SCRATCH

11 min.   16mm, ¾" U-Matic, ½" Beta, ½" VHS
   color   animation
Distributors: Coe, Little Red Filmhouse
Filmmaker: Robert Swarthe
USA   1979   ages 6 up

Swarthe, who was director of animation on *Close Encounters of the Third Kind,* provides three examples of cameraless animation. Each example is a complete film and is preceded by a verbal and visual description of the techniques needed to achieve the effects with easily found materials, such as toothbrushes. The narration is relatively easy for children to understand. The first two examples are abstract films; bright colors, lively music, and humorous sound effects keep children's attention. The third film has a central character and is more engaging.

KICK ME

8 min.   16mm, ¾" U-Matic, ½" Beta, ½" VHS
   color   animation   nonverbal
Distributors: Coe, Little Red Filmhouse
Filmmaker: Robert Swarthe
USA   1975   all ages
Awards: CINE Golden Eagle; San Francisco Outstanding Theatrical Short; Bronze Plaque, Columbus Film Festival Chris Awards; Silver Cup, Best Film on Art, Salerno (Italy); Prize of the City of Gijon, Gijon (Spain) International Cinema Contest for Children and Teenagers

A witty cartoon drawn directly on frames of 35mm motion picture film, *Kick Me* tells an action-packed story whose main characters are a tiny pair of legs, a

baseball, and a gang of spiders. An adversary in the plot is the film itself. At one point the frame line jumps into the frame, and later the film appears to catch fire and burn. A wide range of funny and clever effects is achieved with simple figures, brightly colored backgrounds, sound effects, and music in this offbeat piece of cameraless animation.

LIFE GOES TO THE MOVIES

5 programs   16mm, ¾" U-Matic, ½" Beta II,
   ½" VHS   color and b&w   live action
Distributor: Time-Life Video
Producers: Time-Life Films and 20th-Century Fox TV
USA   1977   ages 12 up

This lively, entertaining history of the movies from the 1930s to the 1970s was originally presented as an "NBC Big Event." Hosts Henry Fonda, Shirley MacLaine, and Liza Minnelli, movie stars of three different generations, examine American films in the context of what was happening in the country at the time the films were produced. News photos illustrate the narration. The highlights are, of course, the clips from feature films of the various eras, and they are featured in abundance in each episode. The episodes can be shown individually or together.

The Golden Age of Hollywood. 34 min.
The War Years. 35 min.
The Post-War Years. 20 min.
The Fifties. 27 min.
The Movies Today. 37 min. *Award:* Chris Statuette, Columbus Film Festival

THE LIGHT FANTASTICK

58 min.   16mm, ¾" U-Matic, ½" Beta, ½" VHS
   color   live action and animation
Distributor: National Film Board of Canada
Producer: Wolf Koenig
Directors: Rupert Glover and Michel Patenaude
Canada   1974   ages 12 up
Awards: Blue Ribbon, American Film Festival; Special Jury Prize, San Francisco International Film Festival

A highly enjoyable and informative survey of animation at the National Film Board of Canada (NFB). Narrated in part by some of the artists and directors themselves, the film alternates marvelous clips from a wide variety of films with a history of animation at the NFB. The sound track is not up to the standard of the visuals, but this is still an excellent film both for entertainment and for educational purposes.

THE MAKING OF STAR WARS

52 min.   16mm, ¾" U-Matic, ½" Beta, ½" VHS
   color   live action
Distributor: Films Inc.
Producer: Gary Kurtz
Director: Robert Guenette
USA   1979   ages 6 up

Narrated by robots R2-D2 and C3-PO and by William Conrad, this is an amusing and fascinating behind-the-scenes look at the techniques used to obtain the amazing special effects in the Academy Award–winning film *Star Wars*. Clips demonstrate the movie-making process, the locations and sets where the picture was filmed are shown, and interviews with major actors and director George Lucas are included. See also *SPFX: The Making of The Empire Strikes Back,* later in this section.

MASTERPIECE

14 min.   16mm   color   live action and animation
Distributor: Yellow Ball Workshop
Producer: Department of Public Education, Fine Arts Museum of Boston
Director: Yvonne Anderson
USA   1980   ages 9 up

Nine teenage filmmakers animate their favorite paintings at Boston's Museum of Fine Arts. This is a good film to inspire children to think imaginatively when looking at famous works of art. Animation techniques include xerography, cutouts, multilevel cels, and three-dimensional paper sculpture, and the techniques are explained. Yellow Ball Workshop specializes in teaching children how to make animated films, and it distributes animated films made by children.

MINDSCAPE

8 min.   16mm, ¾" U-Matic, ½" Beta, ½" VHS
   b&w   animation   nonverbal
Distributor: Pyramid
Producer: National Film Board of Canada
Director: Jacques Drouin
Canada   1976   ages 12 up
Awards: Special Jury Prize, Ottawa International Animation Film Festival; Special Diploma, Oberhausen Film Festival; Bronze Hugo, Chicago International Film Festival; Grand Prize, Baltimore Film Festival; Best Film of Festival, Kenyon College Film Festival; Bronze Medallion, Hemisfilm International Film Festival; Silver Venus, Best Film of Festival, Virgin Islands International Film Festival

A painter steps into the landscape he is painting and travels the regions of the imagination. The images of this film were created by manipulating 240,000 pins on a perforated screen, a technique invented by Alexandre Alexeieff and Claire Parker. The result is a somber, surreal, dreamlike experience, fascinating both visually and intellectually.

MOVIE STUNTMEN

28 min.   16mm, ¾" U-Matic, ½" Beta, ½" VHS
   color   live action
Distributor: Learning Corporation of America
Producer: Brian Trenchard Smith
Australia   1975   ages 9 up
Award: Columbus Film Festival Chris Award

A tense and exciting behind-the-scenes look at the dangerous world of movie stuntmen. Five Australians are shown planning and performing a number of death-defying stunts, including surviving dynamite blasts, falling off horses and out of flaming cars, and jumping from high cliffs. The men explain what they are doing and how they feel about it, and they also reveal the hazards that confront them despite all their precautions; indeed, we

NEVER GIVE UP: IMOGEN CUNNINGHAM

see some accidents occur. Children are riveted by all the thrills, chills, and spills.

NEVER GIVE UP: IMOGEN CUNNING-HAM

28 min.   16mm, ¾" U-Matic, ½" Beta, ½" VHS
    color   live action
Distributor: Phoenix
Producer/director: Ann Hershey
USA   1975   ages 12 up
Awards: USA Film Festival; Mid-West Film Confer-
    ence; Blue Ribbon, American Film Festival

A winning portrait of the late photographer, then 92. Cunningham talks about her life and her art honestly and with a sense of humor. Interviews in which she chats amusingly about herself and the people she has known alternate with montages of her stunning photographs to give a sense of both the artist and her work.

PUPPETS OF JIRI TRNKA

26 min.   16mm, ¾" U-Matic, ½" Beta, ½" VHS
    color   live action and animation
Distributor: Phoenix
Producers/directors: Bruno Sefranka and Jiri Trnka
Czechoslovakia   1973   ages 6 up

Jiri Trnka is world famous for his bewitching puppet-animated films, such as *Song of the Prairie*. This film shows him at work in his studio creating his detailed, expressive puppets and painstakingly filming them one tiny movement at a time to create the illusion of motion on the screen. Excerpts from some of his works are shown. Children are equally fascinated by Trnka's puppet making and by his filmmaking technique.

THE RED BALLOON

34 min.   16mm   color   live action   nonverbal
Distributors: Macmillan, Twyman
Producer/director: Albert Lamorisse
France   1956   all ages
Awards: Academy Award; Cannes International
    Film Festival; Edinburgh Film Festival; Prix Louis
    Delluc; "Best Film of the Decade," American
    Film Festival

This wonderful fantasy about a young boy and a balloon is a film classic and an outstanding example of a visual essay. Beautiful photography by Edmond Sechan shows how the boy finds and befriends the balloon, which takes on a life of its own and follows him everywhere. As they walk through the streets of Montmartre, a gang of street urchins spies the balloon and sets out to destroy it. They succeed at last, but in a joyful ending all the other balloons in Paris swoop down on the boy and carry him up into the sky.

SPFX: THE MAKING OF THE EMPIRE STRIKES BACK

52 min.   16mm, ¾″ U-Matic, ½″ Beta, ½″ VHS
  color   live action
Distributor: Films Inc.
Producers: Guenette and Schnickel
Director: Robert Guenette
USA   1980   ages 6 up

This engrossing documentary explains and demonstrates how the special effects used in the film *The Empire Strikes Back* were achieved. It also provides historical background on special effects and presents clips from *King Kong, Close Encounters of the Third Kind,* and *2001: A Space Odyssey.* Some of the techniques shown are stop action, models, miniatures, and illustrations, and the film also covers sound effects and musical scores. This is a sure hit with *Star Wars* fans. See also *The Making of Star Wars,* earlier in this section.

TRACK STARS: THE UNSEEN HEROES OF MOVIE SOUND

8 min.   16mm, ¾″ U-Matic, ½″ Beta, ½″ VHS
  color   live action   nonverbal
Distributor: Learning Corporation of America
Producer/director: Terry Burke
Canada   1979   ages 6 up
Awards: Academy of Canadian Cinema; Canadian Film & Television; Chicago International Film Festival; Moscow Film Festival; National Educational Film Festival

A fast-paced introduction to sound effects. A burglar attempts to steal company se-

crets and is pursued by the night watchman. There is no dialogue, but the sound effects tell the story. By using the split-screen technique, the film demonstrates how two enterprising studio technicians create the sounds. Children love this outstanding film and want to see it again. It can also be used in filmmaking classes to illustrate the making of a sound track.

THE WIZARD OF SPEED AND TIME

3 min.   16mm, ¾″ U-Matic, ½″ Beta, ½″ VHS
  color   animation   nonverbal
Distributor: Pyramid
Filmmaker: Mike Jittlov
USA   1980   all ages
Awards: Grand Prize, Aspen Film Festival; Diploma, Oberhausen Film Festival

This astonishing example of pixillation was originally created to illustrate special effects for an episode of "The Wonderful World of Disney." There are 22,000 separate shots in the film's three minutes, and the action is breathtakingly fast. The film is delightfully silly. A Green Wizard (portrayed by the filmmaker) blasts out of a mountain cave, zips down a highway, and roars around the world—until he slips on a banana peel and crashes into a movie studio. Then he resurrects the smashed equipment and leads a dance of tripods,

THE WIZARD OF SPEED AND TIME

cameras, lights, and film cans. This is marvelous entertainment for both children and adults, and it could also be useful in filmmaking classes.

YELLOW SUBMARINE

85 min.   16mm   color   animation
Distributor: Twyman
Producer: King Features-Subafilms
Director: George Dunning
Great Britain   1968   all ages
Awards: New York Film Critics' Circle; National
   Society of Film Critics

The amazing animation of this film made it an instant classic. All sorts of animation styles are represented, and the psychedelic, pop-art result is wild and wonderful. The film features cartoon caricatures of the Beatles, with musical numbers from their "Sgt. Pepper's Lonely Hearts Club Band" album. The plot concerns the Beatles' efforts to save Pepperland from the Blue Meanies, nasty creatures who run around draining color from their victims and bopping them on the head with green apples. A delightful experience.

2
Performing Arts

Music

ANTONIA: PORTRAIT OF A WOMAN

58 min.   16mm, ¾" U-Matic, ½" Beta, ½" VHS
  color   live action
Distributor: Phoenix
Producer: Rocky Mountain Productions, Inc.
Directors: Judy Collins and Jill Godmilow
USA   1974   ages 12 up
Award: Blue Ribbon and Emily Award, American
  Film Festival

A warm and affecting portrayal of 73-year-old Antonia Brico, an acclaimed piano teacher and symphonic conductor. This beautifully constructed documentary by Brico's former student Judy Collins captures her teacher's love of life and love of music. It depicts her determination in the face of discrimination, as she seeks to lead a major symphony orchestra in a field dominated by men. This is a sensitive study of a fascinating woman.

APT. 3

8 min.   16mm, ¾" U-Matic, ½" Beta, ½" VHS
  color   animation
Distributor: Weston Woods
Filmmaker: Alexander Cochran
USA   1977   ages 2–8
Award: Gold Venus Medallion, Virgin Islands In-
  ternational Film Festival

Sam and his brother Ben hear wistful harmonica music in their apartment building one day and set out to find where it is coming from. They discover a blind man who plays for them, and they make friends

with him. Subtle tones of gray, green, and purple match the mood of this poignant story, adapted from Ezra Jack Keats's book and done in iconographic animation. The appealing music is by Sugar Blue. Also available in Spanish.

BLACK MUSIC IN AMERICA: FROM THEN TILL NOW

28 min.   16mm, ¾" U-Matic, ½" Beta, ½" VHS
  color   live action
Distributor: Learning Corporation of America
Producer: Black Music Association
USA   1971   ages 9 up

The history of black people's contribution to American music is traced in rare footage of Louis Armstrong, Mahalia Jackson, Duke Ellington, B. B. King, Count Basie, Bessie Smith, and Sly and the Family Stone, among others. Woodcuts, stills, and film clips that show the history of blacks in America and relate it to the music of the times are interspersed with outstanding performances.

BLACK MUSIC IN AMERICA: THE SEVENTIES

32 min.   16mm, ¾" U-Matic, ½" Beta, ½" VHS
  color   live action
Distributor: Learning Corporation of America
Producer: Black Music Association
USA   1979   ages 9 up

Exciting clips of some 75 performers show the growth and influence of black music and musicians in the 1970s. This film takes up where *Black Music in America: From Then Till Now* (see preceding entry) leaves off. It covers musical highlights of the 1970s from the Motown sound of Diana Ross to the disco beat of Donna Summer. Isaac Hayes and Dionne Warwick narrate.

THE BOLERO

26 min.   16mm, ¾" U-Matic, ½" Beta, ½" VHS
  color   live action
Distributor: Pyramid
Filmmakers: Allan Miller and William Fertik
USA   1972   ages 9 up
Awards: Academy Award; Gold Medal, Atlanta
  Film Festival; Gold Cup, Buenos Aires Film Festival; Award of Merit, Melbourne Film Festival

Zubin Mehta conducts the Los Angeles Philharmonic in an exciting performance of Ravel's *Bolero,* filmed so as to coordinate the visuals with the music. The cinematography and sound are superb. This outstanding film humanizes the orchestra by showing individual musicians talking about the problems and satisfactions they encounter in their careers.

THE BOY WHO HEARD MUSIC

13 min.   16mm, ¾" U-Matic, ½" Beta, ½" VHS
  color   live action   nonverbal
Distributors: Coe, Texture
Filmmaker: Franck le Flaguais
Canada   1976   ages 6–8

An enchanting fantasy about a little boy who roams through the colorful old streets of Quebec in a red toy car. He meets a kindly but mysterious old man who gives him a magical gift: the ability to make astounding, resounding organ music emerge from ordinary objects. What's more, he can share the music with his friends. The stirring score is by Dietrich Buxtehude, the seventeenth-century German master composer.

CLOSE HARMONY

30 min.   16mm, ¾" U-Matic, ½" Beta, ½" VHS
  color   live action
Distributor: Learning Corporation of America
Filmmaker: Nigel Noble
USA   1980   ages 9 up
Awards: CINE Golden Eagle; Academy Award,
  Best Documentary

This warm, sensitive documentary records an unusual intergenerational experiment. Music teacher Arlene Symons brought together fourth and fifth graders of Friends School in Brooklyn and members of the Council Center for Senior Citizens to rehearse and perform a joint concert. The resulting chorus ranged in age from 9 to 90. The concept of breaking down the barriers between these two age groups is inspired and inspiring; they make joyful music together.

DEL MERO CORAZÓN: LOVE SONGS OF THE SOUTHWEST

28 min.   16mm, ¾" U-Matic, ½" Beta, ½" VHS
  color   live action
Distributor: Brazos Films
Producer: Chris Strachwitz
Director: Les Blank
USA   1979   ages 9 up
Awards: Gold Medal, Houston International Film
  Festival; CINE Golden Eagle; First Place, Poetry
  Film Festival, San Francisco; Oberhausen Film
  Festival; Edinburgh Film Festival; Bronze Cindy,
  Information Film Producers of America; London
  Film Festival; Bilbao (Spain) Film Festival

"Del mero corazón" means "straight from the heart." In this vivid and engrossing documentary, filmmaker Les Blank tours the norteña (Mexican-American) musical tradition. He goes beyond just presenting songs and performers by showing the culture in which this rhythmic music developed. The camera travels the barrios of the Southwest, from barbeques to cantinas, a church and a cemetery, and conveys a sense of the music's context. Lyrics sung in Spanish are translated into English subtitles on the screen.

THE DEVIL AND DANIEL MOUSE

24 min.   16mm, ¾" U-Matic, ½" Beta, ½" VHS
   color   animation
Distributor: Beacon Films
Producers: Patrick Loubert and Michael Hirsh
Director: Clive A. Smith
Canada   1978   ages 6 up
Awards: Best Production for Children, Childfilm
   Festival; Henry Fonda-River City Film Award,
   River City Film Conference

Elaborate and imaginative cel animation makes this musical fable based on Stephen Vincent Benét's short story "The Devil and Daniel Webster" a standout. A folk-singing mouse sells her soul to the devil in order to become a rock star. Pleasurably scary, with lots of comic touches and catchy tunes by John Sebastian, this production captivates children. See also *How We Made "The Devil and Daniel Mouse"* (Chapter 1), a film about the making of this film.

DIRO AND HIS TALKING MUSICAL BOW

13 min.   16mm, ¾" U-Matic   color   live action
Distributor: African Family Films
Producer/director: Jim Rosellini
West Africa   1979   ages 6 up
Award: American Film Festival

An intriguing look at a musician and the unusual instrument that is his specialty. The film follows Diro Dah of the Lobi tribe of West Africa as he makes, tunes, and plays a kankarama, or musical bow. Then he plays a musical game with the village children, using his talking bow to lead them to a hidden object.

DUEL-DUO

2 min.   16mm, ¾" U-Matic, ½" Beta, ½" VHS
   color   animation   nonverbal
Distributors: Coe, National Film Board of Canada

Producer: Gaston Sarault
Director: Jean-Michel Labrosse
Canada   1975   all ages

A clarinet and a trumpet meet, compete, compromise, and finally harmonize. A fast and funny film done in very simple animation that has the two characters cavorting against a background of vibrant changing colors.

DUEL-DUO

THE FOOLISH FROG

8 min.   16mm, ¾" U-Matic, ½" Beta, ½" VHS
   color   animation
Distributor: Weston Woods
Producer: William Bernal
Director: Gene Deitch
Czechoslovakia   1971   ages 2–8
Awards: Red Ribbon, American Film Festival; Chris
   Certificate, Columbus Film Festival Chris Awards

A farmer makes up a song about a bullfrog and gets the whole countryside singing. Pete Seeger sings and plays the catchy tune. Cheerful, simple animation and lively banjo picking make for a joyful film that children like to clap along with.

FROM JUMPSTREET

13 programs, 30 min. each   ¾" U-Matic, ½" Beta,
   ½" VHS   color   live action
Distributor: Great Plains National
Producer: WETA-TV, Washington, DC
USA   1979–1980   ages 12 up

The history of black music, from its African origins to its influence on modern American music, is explored in this exciting series. Oscar Brown, Jr., singer and songwriter, is the host for the programs. Each episode features performances and commentary by well-known contemporary entertainers. Photographs and film clips of famous black musicians of the past are shown as well. This series, shown on PBS, the Public Broadcasting Service, has been recommended by the National Education Association and the Music Educators National Conference and endorsed by the National Dance Association. The programs are closed-captioned for the hearing impaired.

Jazz Vocalists. Al Jarreau and Carmen McRae are featured.

Gospels and Spirituals. With the Reverend James Cleveland and the D.C. Mass Choir of the Gospel Workshop of America, as well as the Mighty Clouds of Joy.

Blues—Country to City. Willis Dixon and his Chicago Blues All-Stars and Sonny Terry and Brownie McGhee perform.

The West African Heritage. Featuring Alhaji Bai Konte, Dembo Konte, Hugh Masekela, and the Wo'se Dance Theater.

Early Jazz. With Alvin Alcorn and his Tuxedo Band, and Roy Eldridge.

Dance to the Music. Honi Coles and the Rod Rodgers Dance Troupe perform.

Jazz People. Dizzy Gillespie, Jackie McLean, and James Moody are featured.

The Black Influence in Theatre and Film. Pearl Bailey and L. O. Sloane's Black and White Refined Jubilee Minstrels appear.

Jazz Gets Blue. Roy Eldridge and Jackie McLean are featured.

Soul. Stevie Wonder performs.

The Recording Industry. With George Benson and Quincy Jones.

Rhythm and Blues. Featuring The Dells and Bo Diddley.

The Source of Soul. Chuck Brown and the Soul Searchers and Michael Babtunde Olatunji perform.

GIVE MY POOR HEART EASE: MISSISSIPPI DELTA BLUESMEN

22 min.   16mm   color   live action
Distributor: Center for Southern Folklore
Filmmaker: William Ferris
USA   1975   ages 12 up
Awards: CINE Golden Eagle; American Film Festival; Ann Arbor Film Festival

Featuring performances and comments by the legendary B. B. King, this authentic and engrossing documentary examines the sound and background of the blues experience. Musicians talk about the origins of the blues, which were often inspired by trouble with love, poverty, and the law. Sometimes it is difficult to understand the musicians' explanations, but their performances, recorded in concerts and in jam sessions, communicate clearly and memorably.

THE GUITAR: FROM STONE AGE THROUGH SOLID ROCK

14 min.   16mm, ¼" U-Matic, ½" Beta, ½" VHS   color   live action and animation
Distributors: Xerox, Coe
Producer: Stephen Bosustow Productions, Inc.
USA   1970   ages 6 up
Awards: Columbus Film Festival Chris Award; CINE Golden Eagle

A delightful film that traces the history of the guitar with humor, striking visuals, and a rollicking sound track. Although the history is presented very quickly, it does convey a good sense of the guitar's development and the variety of music played on it. The sound quality is excellent, particularly in the live classical selection by world-famous guitarist Laurindo Almeida that concludes the film.

HOMAGE TO FRANÇOIS COUPERIN

2 min. 16mm color animation nonverbal
Distributors: International Film Foundation, Coe
Filmmaker: Philip Stapp
USA 1965 all ages

A beguiling visual interpretation of an enchanting piece of music. Delicately drawn butterflies and dragonflies flit about to the music of *Les Papillons* by the eighteenth-century French composer François Couperin. The movements of the images are coordinated with the piano melody, so that when there is a variation on the musical theme, the butterfly ballet is depicted in a different, more abstract, and stylized manner.

HUSH LITTLE BABY

5 min. 16mm, ¾″ U-Matic, ½″ Beta, ½″ VHS
   color animation
Distributor: Weston Woods
Producer: Morton Schindel
Director: Alexander Cochran
USA 1976 ages 2–5

A little boy in colonial America is lulled to sleep with promises of gifts. Iconographic animation of Aliki's beautifully painted illustrations on wood in warm, soft colors match the quiet mood of the lullaby. The song is sung twice; the words are shown on the screen the second time around. This is a lovely experience for younger children.

I KNOW AN OLD LADY WHO SWALLOWED A FLY

6 min. 16mm, ¾″ U-Matic, ½″ Beta, ½″ VHS
   color animation
Distributor: International Film Bureau
Producer: Colin Low
Director: Derek Lamb
Canada 1966 ages 2–8

Burl Ives sings and plays this old favorite with zest. The lady in question swallows an improbable succession of animals, to the endless amusement of younger children. The droll, colorful images match the nonsense lyrics perfectly.

THE ISLE OF JOY

7 min. 16mm, ¾″ U-Matic, ½″ Beta, ½″ VHS
   color animation nonverbal
Distributor: Perspective Films
Filmmaker: Marshall Izen
USA 1972 all ages
Award: CINE Golden Eagle

Pieces of brightly colored paper, cut and shaped in the style of Matisse, come alive to Debussy's *Isle of Joy*. Abstract leaves, boats, people, flowers, birds, and fish cavort in a fanciful ballet that creates a truly joyful mood, a treat for both the eye and the ear.

AN ITALIAN IN ALGIERS

10 min. 16mm, 35mm color animation
   nonverbal
Distributor: Distribution Sixteen
Filmmakers: Emanuele Luzzati and Giulio Gianini
Italy 1970 ages 6 up
Award: USA International Animation Film Festival

Rossini's glorious music accompanies the adventures of two newlyweds in this splendidly animated film. The couple's boat is swept away in a storm and they are washed up on a hostile shore. The wife is imprisoned in a sultan's harem but manages to escape, and she and her husband lead their would-be captors on a wild chase back to the sea. Since the film is not narrated, the plot may confuse some children, but the story is really just a vehicle for the music and the rich, unusual cutout animation. The film can be enjoyed on these levels alone. See also *Pulcinella,* later in this section.

THE JOY OF BACH

58 min. 16mm color live action
Distributor: Lutheran Film Associates Library
Producer: Lothar Wolff
Director: Paul Lammers
USA, East Germany 1979 ages 9 up
Awards: Prize of the Public, Eighth Besançon
   (France) International Musical and Choreo-
   graphic Film Festival; CINE Golden Eagle

The life and career of Johann Sebastian Bach are traced in an outstanding production that celebrates his music and its influence over the last two centuries. First shown on PBS in a 90-minute version, this fast-moving extravaganza was filmed in five countries. It features a variety of performances of Bach's works, both traditional and nontraditional: Yehudi Menuhin, Rosalyn Tureck, the East German Berlin Chamber Orchestra, the Brooklyn Boys Choir, and the Swingle Singers are just some of the performers. British actor Brian Blessed serves as host and also acts out vignettes of Bach's life. The inventive production of the film, which intersperses past and present, musical performances and dramatic reenactments, makes this a lively and unique experience.

KUUMBA: SIMON'S NEW SOUND

8 min. 16mm color animation
Distributors: Beacon, Coe
Producer: Carol Munday Lawrence
Directors: Jane Aaron and Bob Bloomberg
USA 1978 ages 6–11
Awards: Best of Festival, Black Filmmakers Hall of
    Fame; Red Ribbon, American Film Festival;
    CINE Golden Eagle; ALA Notable Film for Children; Third Award, Marin County National Film
    Competition

This realistic, warm, and cheerful folktale from Trinidad explains the origin of the steel drum. On the eve of Carnival, young Simon searches for a musical instrument to play. He experiments with the noises made by household objects, but it is the rain plunking on an old oil drum that gives Simon the idea for the "special sound" he has been seeking. The cutout figures were done by children and the animation by adults, producing colorful and appealing visuals. Music by the Louis Arnold Steel Drummers.

THE LAST MEOW: SIBELIUS'S "VALSE TRISTE"

7 min. 16mm color animation nonverbal
Distributor: Films Inc.

Producer/director: Bruno Bozzetto
Italy 1979 ages 9 up

Bruno Bozzetto is one of Italy's most famous and admired filmmakers. He is best known for his highly creative animation, and this film is a good example of his work. It is a segment from Bozzetto's feature film *Allegro Non Troppo*, which is a parody of Disney's *Fantasia*. This episode is more poignant than satirical, however. An emaciated cat with huge, sad eyes prowls the ruins of a house, remembering the warmth and happiness of the past. Sibelius's *Valse Triste*, performed by the Berlin Philharmonic Orchestra, accompanies the cat's reminiscences. The striking animation, which vividly contrasts times past and times present, provides an excellent visual interpretation of the sad, sentimental music. See also *Let It Bee: Vivaldi's "Concerto in C-dur,"* later in this section.

THE LEGEND OF JOHN HENRY

11 min. 16mm, ¼" U-Matic, ½" Beta, ½" VHS
    color animation
Distributor: Pyramid
Producer: Stephen Bosustow Productions
Director: Sam Weiss
USA 1974 ages 9 up
Awards: Special Jury Award and Gold Medal, Atlanta International Film Festival; Learning A/V
    Award, *Learning* Magazine; First Prize—Ethnic
    History, Birmingham International Educational
    Film Festival; Trophy of the Asturias, Gijon
    (Spain) International Cinema Contest for Children
    and Teenagers; ALA Notable Film for Children

Roberta Flack sings this folk ballad about a proud steel-driver for the railroad who tries to race a steam drill through a tunnel and dies in the attempt. The jazz-blues style of the singing and the abstract quality of the strongly colored animation make this tribute to the dignity of the human spirit attractive primarily to older children.

LET IT BEE: VIVALDI'S "CONCERTO IN C-DUR"

4 min. 16mm color animation nonverbal
Distributor: Films Inc.
Producer/director: Bruno Bozzetto
Italy 1979 ages 6 up

This drolly titled tale is a segment from Bozzetto's feature film *Allegro Non Troppo*, a set of cartoons inspired by classical works of music (see also *The Last Meow: Sibelius' "Valse Triste,"* earlier in this section). *Let It Bee* is a beautifully animated, amusing visual interpretation of Vivaldi's "Concerto in C-dur," performed by the Berlin Philharmonic Orchestra. It features a honeybee busily preparing a picnic in a lovely glade. A human couple, also picnicking, disrupts her meal until, in exasperation, the bee sends them on their way with a well-placed sting. The brightly colored backgrounds are gorgeous, and children enjoy the bee's revenge.

LET IT BEE: VIVALDI'S "CONCERTO IN C-DUR"

LISTEN!

10 min. 16mm, ¾" U-Matic, ½" Beta, ½" VHS
  color live action
Distributors: Coe, FilmFair Communications
Filmmakers: Brian Neary and J. V. DiMuro II
USA 1972 ages 6 up

A marvelous imagination stimulator. A small, ornate box appears as an offscreen voice invites another person inside to "see" the music. The host plays different musical works and encourages his guest to describe how the music makes him feel. The visuals—of wind, hot sun, water, skiing, a storm, and other images—match the guest's descriptions. A creative and enjoyable experience. Also available in Spanish.

LOVE OF LIFE

91 min. 16mm color live action
Distributor: New Yorker Films
Producer: Bernard Chevry
Directors: François Reichenbach and S. G. Patris
France 1968 ages 12 up
Award: Academy Award, Best Documentary

This joyous documentary celebrates pianist Arthur Rubinstein, one of the world's great musicians. The filmmakers followed Rubinstein in his travels around the world, culminating in a concert in Jerusalem. The special qualities of both the man and the musician come across clearly in home movies and scenes of Rubinstein reminiscing about his past and telling jokes, as well as through watching his concert performances.

THE MAGIC PIPES

15 min. 16mm, ¾" U-Matic, ½" Beta, ½" VHS
  color live action
Distributor: Sterling
Producer: Dokumenta Productions
Austria 1979 ages 2–11

An enchanting experience. Lush cinematography by Kurt Jetmar captures the old-world flavor of Kufstein, an Austrian town high in the Tyrolean Alps. Kufstein's giant organ regularly rings out and reassures the townspeople busy at their work and crafts that all is well, until one day the organ player falls asleep at his instrument. He dreams of pressing a strange new key that speeds up and slows down people's actions in time with the music. The special effects amuse child viewers and may be of interest to filmmaking classes as well.

MAHALIA JACKSON

34 min.   16mm, ¾" U-Matic, ½" Beta, ½" VHS
  color   live action
Distributor: Phoenix
Producer/director: Jules Victor Schwerin
USA   1974   ages 12 up

A moving portrait of the late singer, known as "the queen of the gospels," who popularized the religious music of American blacks. Studs Terkel narrates this CBS News production, which emphasizes the joys and triumphs of Jackson's life. Stills show the slavelike living conditions of her family when she was growing up in New Orleans, and the film includes footage of her funeral in Chicago in 1972. The best parts are her performances. Jackson is shown belting out 11 songs in her inimitable voice, including "Go Tell It on the Mountain," "When the Saints Go Marching In," and "He's Got the Whole World in His Hands."

MELODY

8 min.   16mm, ¾" U-Matic, ½" Beta, ½" VHS
  color   animation
Distributor: PCI
Producer: Sandler Films
USA   1972   ages 2–8

An engaging fantasy about a young bird named Melody who sings instead of chirps. She leaves home to find someone who understands her and at last meets a trumpet, who introduces her to the other members of the orchestra. The film is also available in Spanish and in a version in which English and Spanish phrases are used alternately, called *Melody: Bilingual* (15 min., 1974). Spanish narration is by Ricardo Montalban.

MR. GOSHU, THE CELLIST

19 min.   16mm, ¾" U-Matic, ½" Beta, ½" VHS
  color   animation
Distributors: Coe, International Film Bureau
Producer: Gakken Film
Japan   1969   ages 2–8

Puppets are used to tell the story of a young cellist who struggles to play as well as the conductor of the orchestra demands. As he practices, he is visited by various animals who give him the encouragement he needs to work harder. At concert time, he is rewarded by a standing ovation. The theme may be saccharine, but the detailed little puppets are appealing.

MONSIEUR POINTU

12 min.   16mm, ¾" U-Matic, ½" Beta, ½" VHS
  color   live action   nonverbal
Distributor: Pyramid
Producer: René Jodoin
Directors: Bernard Longpré and André Leduc
Canada   1975   all ages
Awards: Special Prize, Geneva Festival of the Short
  Film; 30,000 Peseta Prize, Bilbao Festival, Spain

A fiddler finds that his fiddle, bow, hat, shoes—even his limbs—persist in behaving as if they had a life of their own. They fly out of his grasp and around the room, shrink, expand, and change shape to the lively rhythms of Monsieur Pointu's fiddle tunes, thanks to the technique of pixillation. The film is a combination of music, magic, and mime—and it's pure fun.

MONSIEUR POINTU

MOUNTAIN MUSIC

MOUNTAIN MUSIC

9 min.   16mm, ¾″ U-Matic, ½″ Beta, ½″ VHS
   color   animation   nonverbal
Distributor: Pyramid
Filmmaker: Will Vinton
USA   1975   all ages
Awards: First Prize, National Educational Film Fes-
   tival; CINE Golden Eagle; First Prize, Animation,
   Hemisfilm International Film Festival

A trio plays music in the wilderness, beginning with folk tunes and moving into hard rock. They gradually increase the volume and add electronic hardware until nature rebels. Wonderful clay animation depicts the progression. Younger children will enjoy the clever sights and sounds; older children will appreciate the allegory.

MUSIC AND ME

28 programs, 15 min. each   ¾″ U-Matic, ½″ Beta,
   ½″ VHS   color   live action
Distributor: Agency for Instructional Television
Producer: WDCN-TV, Nashville
USA   1979   ages 8–9

These entertaining, straightforward instructional programs attempt to develop children's understanding and appreciation of musical instruments, concepts, and traditions by building on their exposure to contemporary music. Each program encourages student participation and emphasizes how music is related to other art forms and to other aspects of life. Music of all kinds, from classical to Dixieland, Gershwin, jazz, and music of native Americans, as well as country music and rock 'n' roll, is performed by a variety of musicians. Nan Gurley, a professional singer and teacher, is writer-producer and acts as host. A 48-page teacher's guide is available.

Music and Me
Use Your Voice to Sing
Music of Inspiration
Note Value
I Got the Beat
The Percussion Family

Intervals
Melodies
Makin' Sweet Harmony
The Keyboard Family
The Ballad
The Brass Family
The String Family
Meter Reader
Music of Afro-America
The Woodwind Family
Tempo and Dynamics
The Folk Song
Music of South America
Music of the First Americans
Music of the U.S.A. I
Music of the U.S.A. II
Music of the U.S.A. III
The Best of Me

Four holiday specials are available:

Songs of Halloween. Award: Best Instructional Television Program and Innovative Production, SECA
Songs of Thanksgiving
Music of Christmas and Hanukkah I
Music of Christmas and Hanukkah II

NEW YORK CITY TOO FAR FROM TAMPA BLUES

47 min.   16mm, ¾″ U-Matic, ½″ Beta, ½″ VHS
    color   live action
Distributor: Time-Life Video
Producer: Daniel Wilson
Director: Ron Finley
USA   1979   ages 9 up
Awards: CINE Golden Eagle; Blue Ribbon, American Film Festival

Tom, a Puerto Rican newcomer to Brooklyn, faces many challenges: new friends, intimidating gangs, family tension, and a shortage of cash. He forms a successful rock 'n' roll duo with his streetwise shoeshine partner Aurelio, only to find the pleasure of earning so much money undermined by the defensiveness of his father, a proud truckdriver out on strike. The performances are excellent and so is the music. From the novel by T. Ernesto Bethancourt; presented as an "NBC Special Treat."

NEW YORK CITY TOO FAR FROM TAMPA BLUES

ONE GENERATION IS NOT ENOUGH

23 min.   16mm, ¾″ U-Matic, ½″ Beta, ½″ VHS
    color   live action
Distributor: De Nonno Pix
Producer/director: Tony De Nonno
USA   1979   ages 12 up
Award: Blue Ribbon, American Film Festival

Nineteen-year-old Nicholas Frirsz is a fourth-generation violin maker. He and his father, Max, work together creating exquisite musical instruments in their small Manhattan shop. This subtle, sensitive film follows Nicky as he works on a viola under his father's supervision, but the film is as much about the relationship between father and son as it is about the art of making instruments. Max, who was born in Hungary, feels that Nicky should be content with his profession and his way of life. Nicky, born in the United States, has his doubts, but nevertheless admires his father's skills and works hard at his art.

PAGANINI STRIKES AGAIN

45 min.   16mm, ¾″ U-Matic, ½″ Beta, ½″ VHS
    color   live action

Distributor: Janus
Producer: Cyril Randell
Director: Gerry O'Hara
Great Britain   1977   ages 6–11

This film is part of the collection of the Children's Film Foundation (CFF) of Great Britain. CFF specializes in films specifically designed for children's enjoyment. Its research shows that children like to see child actors and animals, and that they appreciate humor and straightforward, exciting stories with lots of action. CFF films usually include as many of these elements as possible, and consequently they are highly successful with young audiences. This particular CFF film is about young musicians who become amateur detectives when they get involved in a mystery that only they can solve. This involving adventure is based on a story by Benjamin Lee.

PATRICK

7 min.   16mm, ¾" U-Matic, ½" Beta, ½" VHS
   color   animation   nonverbal
Distributor: Weston Woods
Producer: Morton Schindel
Director: Gene Deitch
Czechoslovakia   1975   ages 2–8
Awards: Gold Medal, Atlanta International Film
   Festival; Bronze Plaque, Columbus Film Festival
   Chris Awards

A lanky young man buys a fiddle from a junkman in the marketplace. The joyous music he plays (variations on a theme by Dvořák) makes everyone and everything in the countryside bloom with color and happiness. This lovely, lyrical film has the same effect on young children, who enjoy its appealing animation and infectious tune. From the book by Quentin Blake.

PAVAROTTI AT JUILLIARD, PROGRAM 1

30 min.   16mm, ¾" U-Matic, ½" Beta, ½" VHS
   color   live action
Distributor: Phoenix
Producer/director: Nathan Kroll
USA   1979   ages 12 up

Awards: Blue Ribbon, American Film Festival;
   CINE Golden Eagle

Luciano Pavarotti, the famous Italian operatic tenor, is seen working with opera students at the Juilliard School of Music in New York. His love for music and his easy, relaxed manner with the young singers and the audience make this an involving and enjoyable experience even for non-opera lovers. This film, one of a series of six on Pavarotti produced for PBS, shows him helping three students, answering questions from the audience about his own training, and gloriously singing a piece from Buononcini's *Griselda*.

PEOPLE DON'T DANCE TO JAZZ

30 min.   16mm, ¾" U-Matic, 1" & 2" Masters
   color   live action
Distributor: ICAP
Producer/director: Michael N. Pressman
USA   1979   ages 12 up

An unsentimental film about a critical day in the life of a teenage musician. Eric is struggling with a decision about his musical ambitions. His friends in a rock band want him to perform with them, but he finds that he is more attracted to jazz. At the same time, he has to face his parents' divorce. The music is appealing, and young adolescents identify with Eric's dilemmas.

PETER AND THE WOLF

28 min.   16mm, ¾" U-Matic, ½" Beta, ½" VHS
   color   live action
Distributor: Pyramid
Producer/director: Dan Bessie
USA   1981   ages 2–8

This captivating version of Sergei Prokofiev's musical story is set in turn-of-the-century America. Ray Bolger, the charming on-camera storyteller, introduces the characters and their musical themes as the Santa Cruz Chamber Orchestra performs in a sunlit forest glade. In a refreshingly nonviolent variation on the traditional tale, young Peter traps the wolf with the help of a little bird and triumphantly marches the caged wolf off to the zoo, accompanied by three bumbling comic hunters. Excellent editing makes the animals' actions believable and exciting to watch. This film is a rare treat for younger children.

PULCINELLA

10 min.   16mm, 35mm   color   animation
  nonverbal
Distributor: Distribution Sixteen
Filmmakers: Emanuele Luzzati and Giulio Gianini
Italy   1973   ages 6 up
Awards: Italian Film Critics Award; Grand Prize,
  Moscow Film Festival

Pulcinella, a lazy scoundrel, would rather sleep than work. When his exasperated wife drives him from the house, he sneaks up to the roof to continue his nap, and there he dreams a wild adventure involving ballet, music, monsters, a circus, and a chase. Pulcinella's droll escapades make children laugh. The lush, colorful cutout animation by Luzzati and Gianini is paced to Rossini's music.

ROMEO AND JULIET IN KANSAS CITY

28 min.   16mm, ¾" U-Matic, ½" Beta, ½" VHS
  color   live action
Distributor: Pyramid
Producer/director: Allan Miller
USA   1975   ages 12 up

Superb photography shows the Kansas City Philharmonic playing Tchaikovsky's *Romeo and Juliet* Overture for an audience of young adults. Conductor Jorge Mester introduces the performance by explaining how the music relates to the play. The filmmaking is in rhythm with the music, and the camera alternates between the audience and the orchestra to convey the involvement of both the teenagers and the musicians.

SCOTT JOPLIN: KING OF RAGTIME COMPOSERS

15 min.   16mm, ¾" U-Matic, ½" Beta, ½" VHS
  color   live action
Distributor: Pyramid
Filmmaker: Amelia Anderson
USA   1977   ages 9 up

An engrossing biography of the famous black composer whose syncopated ragtime rhythm was all the rage at the turn of the century. Joplin's life is illustrated in lively vignettes: his boyhood study of classical music, his development of a new form of popular music, his discovery in a dance hall by a music publisher, and his great initial success. When he turned to composing more serious pieces, however, the public rejected him. He died an early and impoverished death. The film traces the origins and development of ragtime music using early film footage and also shows a modern production of Joplin's neglected folk opera *Treemonisha*.

STREET MUSIQUE

9 min.   16mm, ¾" U-Matic, ½" Beta, ½" VHS
  color   live action and animation   nonverbal
Distributor: Learning Corporation of America
Producer: National Film Board of Canada
Director: Ryan Larkin
Canada   1973   ages 9 up
Awards: Chicago International Film Festival; Co-
  lumbus Film Festival Chris Awards; Oakland
  Film Festival

A fantasy inspired by street musicians and their music. Pixillated shots of street musicians inspire line drawings that grow, flow, and change into brilliant color designs and abstractions. The images are clever, beautiful, and ever changing, moving in rhythm with the music. Filmmaking classes may be interested in this fine film as an example of animation and visual rhythm.

SUNSHINE'S ON THE WAY

SUNSHINE'S ON THE WAY

47 min. (full version), 37 min. (edited version)
16mm, ¾" U-Matic, ½" Beta, ½" VHS
color   live action
Distributor: Learning Corporation of America
Producer: Doro Bachrach
Director: Robert Mandel
USA   1980   ages 12 up
Awards: Two Emmys

Fifteen-year-old Bobba June Strang works at a nursing home after school. She aspires to be a jazz trombonist and she encourages some of the elderly residents to form their own jazz group. When her idol, the great jazz trombonist T. P. Jackson (played by Scatman Crothers), is forced to move into the home after a stroke, the group's ambitions grow by leaps and bounds. When they are invited to appear on "The Tonight Show," Bobba June organizes the trip to Hollywood over her mother's objections and ends up playing the trombone on camera. The plot may be farfetched, but Bobba June's relationship with her mother is realistic and the music is catchy. This entertaining production was presented as an "NBC Special Treat."

TOOT, WHISTLE, PLUNK AND BOOM

10 min.   16mm   color   animation
Distributor: Walt Disney
USA   1953   ages 6–11
Award: Academy Award, Best Short Subject

An amusing look at the origin and development of musical instruments. Professor Owl tells his class about the four different types of instruments—brass, woodwinds, strings, and percussion—which he labels toot, whistle, plunk, and boom according to how they produce sound. It is fast-paced fun, as well as being educational.

Available in French, Italian, Portuguese, and Spanish.

THE VIOLIN

24 min.   16mm, ¾" U-Matic, ½" Beta, ½" VHS
    color   live action
Distributor: Learning Corporation of America
Filmmaker: George Pastic
Canada   1973   ages 9 up
Awards: Oakland Film Festival; Columbus Film
    Festival Chris Awards; International Children's
    Film Festival

A young boy who wants to learn the violin meets an old man who teaches him. They become friends and when the old man moves on, he leaves his own violin for the boy. The old man provides the voice-over narration, which is hardly necessary since this is such a good visual narrative. The cinematography is outstanding, and the film offers a positive portrayal of the elderly. It is sentimental, but also very affecting.

WHAT TIME IS THE NEXT SWAN?

8 min.   16mm, ¾" U-Matic, ½" Beta, ½" VHS
    color   live action

Distributor: Phoenix
Producer/director: Wayne Wadhams
USA   1975   ages 12 up

A behind-the-scenes look at the serious and funny aspects of mounting an opera. Conductor Sarah Caldwell is shown working with her Opera Company of Boston and talking with staff and performers. This tribute to one of opera's leading figures is brief but vivid, and entertaining even for viewers who are not opera fans.

A WORLD IS BORN

20 min.   16mm   color   animation   nonverbal
Distributor: Walt Disney
USA   1940   ages 6 up

Disney's famous feature film *Fantasia* is not available for rental or sale, but this excerpt is typical of the film's extraordinary animation illustrating classical pieces of music. Stravinsky's *The Rite of Spring*, played by Leopold Stokowski and the Philadelphia Orchestra, is used in this sequence as inspiration for a dramatic depiction of evolution and warring dinosaurs.

Dance

BALLET ADAGIO

10 min.   16mm, ¾" U-Matic, ½" Beta, ½" VHS
    color   live action   nonverbal
Distributor: Pyramid
Producer/director: Norman McLaren
Canada   1972   ages 12 up
Awards: Silver Medal, Atlanta Film Festival;
    Bronze Plaque, Columbus Film Festival Chris
    Awards

This production features a Canadian duo, David and Anna Marie Holmes, dancing Messerer's ballet *Spring Water* to music by Albinoni. The dancers are filmed in slow motion against a blue-black background on a bare stage, which makes them appear to be weightless, floating in space. Special lighting illuminates the dancers from all sides, so that a three-dimensional, sculptural effect is created. Both the dancing and the filmmaking techniques are breathtakingly beautiful.

CHERRY TREE CAROL

10 min.   16mm, ¾" U-Matic, ½" Beta, ½" VHS
    color   live action
Distributor: PCI
Producer: Educational Broadcasting Corporation
USA   1975   ages 9 up
Award: CINE Golden Eagle

BALLET ADAGIO

Choreographer Agnes de Mille's Appalachian Dance Troupe performs this beautiful adaptation of a traditional Christmas carol. The carol is sung by a black folk singer with a lovely voice, and the dancers wear pioneer-style clothing. The song is based on a folk tale that tells of Jesus commanding a cherry tree to bend so that his mother can gather the fruit, and the folk ballet the dancers perform is appropriately reverent and graceful.

THE CHILDREN OF THEATER STREET

90 min.   16mm, ¾" U-Matic   color   live action
Distributor: Corinth
Producer: Earle Mack

Directors: Earle Mack and Robert Dornhelm
USSR   1977   ages 9 up
Nijinsky went there; so did Pavlova, Balanchine, Nureyev, Makarova, and Baryshnikov. The famous Vaganova Choreographic Institute, located on Theater Street in Leningrad, is one of the great ballet schools of the world. This beautifully filmed documentary, narrated by Princess Grace of Monaco, shows episodes in a typical year of the school. It focuses on the rigorous training that 11-year-old Angelina and 12-year-old Alec, two new students, must undergo. Children identify with the struggles of the young dancers, and the dance sequences are lovely.

DANCE ON A MAY DAY

11 min.   16mm, ¾" U-Matic, ½" Beta, ½" VHS
   color   live action
Distributor: Learning Corporation of America
Producers: Michael Herz, Lloyd Kaufman, and
   George Manasse
Director: John Avildsen
USA   1978   ages 9 up
Awards: Dance Film and Video Festival; Columbus
   Film Festival Chris Awards

This exuberant display of modern dance
by a troupe of young boys is a joy to
watch. Ballet star Jacques d'Amboise
founded the National Dance Institute to
introduce boys to dance, and this film
records one of their presentations. Director John Avildsen (who directed *Rocky*)
follows the boys from early interviews
through the demanding training to their
exciting, energetic performance.

FULL OF LIFE A-DANCIN'

29 min.   16mm, ¾" U-Matic, ½" Beta, ½" VHS
   color   live action
Distributor: Phoenix
Filmmakers: Robert Fiore and Richard Nevell
USA   1978   ages 12 up

Deep within the Great Smoky Mountains
of North Carolina, a traditional American
folk dance known as "clogging" is still
proudly practiced by the mountain
people. The champion clog team is the
Southern Appalachian Cloggers, and this
rousing film follows them through rehearsals and performances, and in their daily
lives. Some background on this energetic
dance form would have added to the
film's interest, but nevertheless it is an
enjoyable look at a unique activity and the
people who so obviously take pleasure in
doing it.

IN A REHEARSAL ROOM

11 min.   16mm, ¾" U-Matic, ½" Beta, ½" VHS
   color   live action   nonverbal
Distributors: Films Inc., Coe
Producer/director: David Hahn
USA   1976   ages 12 up
Award: Silver Hugo, Chicago Dance Film Festival

Two dancers (Cynthia Gregory and Ivan
Nagy of the American Ballet Theatre)

DANCE ON A MAY DAY

limbering up at the bar flirt with their eyes and then move into a beautiful, romantic pas de deux. The camera moves with the graceful dancers and creates an ethereal mood. The choreography is by William Carter and the music is Pachelbel's lovely *Canon in D*.

NIKKOLINA

28 min.   16mm, ¾" U-Matic, ½" Beta, ½" VHS
color   live action
Distributor: Learning Corporation of America
Producers/directors: Glen Salzman and Rebecca Yates
USA   1978   ages 6 up
Awards: Canadian Child Film Festival; Columbus Film Festival Chris Awards; Jacksonville Film Festival; National Educational Film Festival; ALA Notable Film for Children

A young Greek-American girl comes to appreciate her Greek heritage in this perceptive, well-acted film. Forced to give up a skating competition for a family wedding, Nikkolina ends up enjoying herself immensely. When she is given an unexpected second chance at the competition, she combines her newly learned Greek dancing with her figure skating in a winning performance.

NO MAPS ON MY TAPS

58 min.   16mm, ¾" U-Matic, ½" Beta, ½" VHS
color and b&w   live action
Distributor: Direct Cinema
Producer/director: George T. Nierenberg
USA   1978   ages 12 up
Awards: Blue Ribbon, American Film Festival; Best Film, Dance Film and Video Festival; Bronze Hugo, Chicago International Dance Film Festival; selected as U.S. Prix Italia Entry

This warm, involving documentary is a delight to watch. It presents tap dancing as a joyous expression of black American culture. Three top tap dancers, Bunny Briggs, Chuck Green, and Howard (Sandman) Sims, are shown performing and reminiscing about their art. Clips from older films give a sense of the history of

PAS DE DEUX

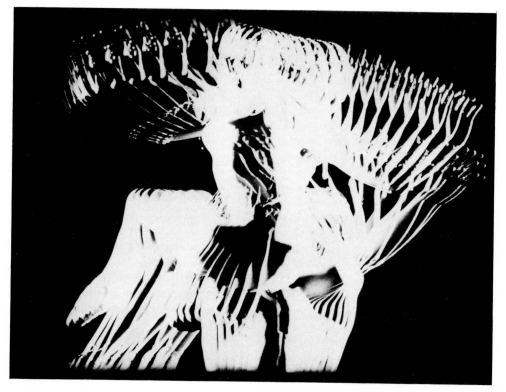

tap dance and show some legendary tap dancers in action.

PAS DE DEUX

14 min.   16mm, ¾" U-Matic, ½" Beta, ½" VHS
   b&w   live action   nonverbal
Distributor: Learning Corporation of America
Filmmaker: Norman McLaren
Canada   1969   ages 9 up
Awards: American Film Festival; Columbus Film
   Festival Chris Awards; Philadelphia Film Festival

McLaren's exquisite and innovative film classic is too abstract for younger children, but older ones find it mesmerizing. Through optical printing and stroboscopic effects, a classical dance performed by Margaret Mercier and Vincent Warren of Les Grands Ballets Canadiens becomes a succession of multiple images folding and unfolding with astounding grace and beauty.

PETER RABBIT AND TALES OF BEATRIX POTTER

98 min.   16mm, ¾" U-Matic, ½" Beta, ½" VHS
   color   live action   nonverbal
Distributor: Films Inc.
Director: Reginald Mills
Great Britain   1971   ages 6 up

Ballet for children has rarely been better. Members of Britain's Royal Ballet, wearing animal costumes and masks, perform episodes from five of Beatrix Potter's stories. The imaginative dances were partly filmed outdoors in Potter's own Lake District. Musical background is supplied by the Covent Garden Opera House orchestra.

THE RED SHOES

134 min.   16mm, ¾" U-Matic, ½" Beta, ½" VHS
   color   live action
Distributor: Learning Corporation of America
Producers/directors: Michael Powell and Emeric
   Pressburger
Great Britain   1948   ages 9 up
Awards: Academy Awards, Best Art Direction,
   Sets, and Musical Score

This dazzling display of dance captures the imagination of older children. The plot, based on a story by Hans Christian Andersen, concerns a ballerina whose role as prima ballerina in the ballet, *The Red Shoes*, begins to take over her life. The ballet itself concerns a young girl whose ballet slippers possess magical powers and dance her to death.

SIU MEI WONG: WHO SHALL I BE?

17 min.   16mm, ¾" U-Matic, ½" Beta, ½" VHS
   color   live action
Distributor: Learning Corporation of America
Producer: Michael Ahnemann
USA   1970   ages 9–11

A realistic and affecting story about Siu Mei, an 11-year-old girl who wants more than anything to be a ballerina. Her father, however, thinks Chinese lessons are more important than ballet lessons. This simple, low-key story follows Siu Mei through a day in her life that culminates in a confrontation with her father. Set in Los Angeles's Chinatown, the dialogue is mostly in Chinese, with English subtitles.

A SPECIAL GIFT

47 min.   16mm, ¾" U-Matic, ½" Beta, ½" VHS
   color   live action
Distributor: Time-Life Video
Producer: Martin Tahse
USA   1979   ages 9 up
Awards: Peabody Award; Ohio State Award; Blue
   Ribbon, American Film Festival

A sensitive drama about a junior high school boy who faces the first big dilemma of his life when he must choose between playing in his basketball team's season opener or beginning ballet rehearsal for his first professional role—a lead in *The Nutcracker* with the Los Angeles Ballet Company. Peter's struggle with the prejudices of his father and friends is presented realistically and sympathetically in this "ABC Afterschool Special," based on the book by Marcia L. Simon.

A SPECIAL GIFT

THE TAP DANCE KID

49 min. (full version), 33 min. (edited version)
    16mm, ¾" U-Matic, ½" Beta, ½" VHS
    color   live action
Distributor: Learning Corporation of America
Producer: Evelyn Barron
Director: Barbara Grant
USA   1979   ages 9 up
Awards: Emmy Award; Columbus Film Festival
    Chris Awards; Hawaii Film Festival; Los Angeles
    International Children's Film Festival; MIFED
    Film Festival; USA Film Festival; ALA Notable
    Film for Children

Eight-year-old Willie Sheridan dreams of tap dancing on Broadway, despite his parents' objections. His equally ambitious 12-year-old sister Emma, who wants to be a lawyer and heads a neighborhood "Children's Rights Crusade," takes on Willie as a test case. While the sophisticated humor of this "NBC Special Treat" often seems more appropriate for adults than for children, children like the film and sympathize with Willie. Louise Fitzhugh's novel *Nobody's Family Is Going to Change* provided the inspiration for this production.

TAPDANCIN'

75 min.   16mm   color   live action
Distributor: Blackwood
Producer/director: Christian Blackwood
USA   1980   ages 12 up

A loving tribute to veteran tap dancers and to the popularity of the art in the 1940s, this is also a look at the younger tap dancers who are responsible for a resurgence of interest in this rhythmic American dance form. Famous tap dancers strut their stuff in archival and contemporary clips, and various practitioners discuss tap dance yesterday and today. It is fun to watch, but the film's length makes it best for older children.

THE TAP DANCE KID

TEACH ME TO DANCE

29 min.   16mm, ¾" U-Matic, ½" Beta, ½" VHS
    color   live action
Distributor: Films Inc.
Producer: Vladimir Valenta
Director: Anne Wheeler
Canada   1978   ages 6 up

Lesia, a young Ukrainian immigrant living in rural Alberta, Canada, in 1919, plans to perform a Ukrainian dance with her English-Canadian friend Sarah at their school's Christmas pageant. Although anti-Ukrainian hostility and the prejudices of their fathers spoil their plans, the girls find a way to dance together on Christmas Day anyway. Photographed in glowing tones in authentic settings, this touching story succeeds despite some stiff acting.

TEALIA

10 min.   16mm, ¾" U-Matic, ½" Beta, ½" VHS
 color   live action   nonverbal
Distributor: Phoenix
Producer: Ellen Jane Kutten
Director: George Paul Csicsery
USA   1978   ages 9 up
Awards: CINE Golden Eagle; Moscow International Film Festival; Certificate of Merit, New York Dance Film Festival; San Francisco International Film Festival

To the music of Gustav Holst's *The Planets*, Betsy Erickson and Vane Vest of the San Francisco Ballet Company dance a beautiful modern ballet based on the movements of the tealia, a sea anemone. The creative and unusual choreography is by John McFall. The dancers wear decorated pink leotards and move in synchronization against a black background; the overall effect of the movements, costumes, and music is stunning.

TWYLA THARP: MAKING TV DANCE

58 min.   16mm, ¾" U-Matic, ½" Beta, ½" VHS
 color and b&w   live action
Distributor: Phoenix
Producer: The Twyla Tharp Dance Foundation
Director: Don Mischer
USA   1980   ages 12 up

Twyla Tharp is an innovative choreographer, and this interesting piece of video is a good introduction to her style of dance. In it she explores the relationship between the technology of television and the art of dance. Four performances by members of her dance troupe illustrate the principles of speed, repetition, focus, and retrograde. Tharp herself is shown rehearsing a piece called *Once More Frank* with Mikhail Baryshnikov, and she and members of her company dance an exciting new work called *Country Dances*. The behind-the-scenes parts of this presentation are unfortunately not up to the high quality of the dancing.

Theater and Mime

THE ART OF SILENCE: PANTOMIMES WITH MARCEL MARCEAU

13 films   16mm, ¾" U-Matic, ½" Beta II, ½" VHS
 color   live action
Distributor: Encyclopaedia Britannica Educational Corporation
Producer/director: John Barnes
USA   1975   ages 9 up

The master of mime, Marcel Marceau, talks about his art and performs many of his most famous routines in this series. His French accent is sometimes hard to understand, but his movements and gestures in performance are wonderfully expressive. Other than Marceau's introductions and the occasional, highly effective use of music, the programs are silent.

Pantomime: The Language of the Heart. 10 min. Marceau explains how body movement and gestures communicate attitudes and emotions. Brief clips from the pantomimes presented in the other programs in this series vividly illustrate his words.

Bip Hunts Butterflies. 10 min. Marceau's famous tragicomic character, Bip, captures a fragile butterfly.

The Sideshow. 9 min. In this pantomime, Marceau depicts circus performers demonstrating their skills. *Award:* Certificate of Honor, Dance Film and Video Festival of New York City

Bip at a Society Party. 14 min. Bip creates a world of fun at an imaginary party.

The Painter. 8 min. Mime can make the invisible seem real, as Marceau shows in this fantasy.

Bip as a Skater. 8 min. Bip struggles, on illusionary ice, to become a great skater. *Award:* Certificate of Merit, Dance Film and Video Festival of New York City

The Cage. 9 min. This classic mime sequence is an allegory about freedom and confinement.

The Hands. 7 min. The hands represent the battle between good and evil in this symbolic pantomime. *Award:* Bronze Plaque, Columbus Film Festival Chris Awards

The Dream. 9 min. Marceau interprets the idea of dreaming through dancelike movements. *Award:* Certificate of Merit, Dance Film and Video Festival of New York City

Bip as a Soldier. 17 min. Bip plays at being a soldier until he discovers the tragic side of war. *Award:* Certificate of Honor, Dance Film and Video Festival of New York City

The Maskmaker. 9 min. Marceau impersonates the different faces of humanity. *Award:* Certificate of Honor, Dance Film and Video Festival of New York City

Youth, Maturity, Old Age, Death. 8 min. The seven ages of humankind, from birth to death, are the subject of this pantomime. *Award:* Certificate of Merit, Dance Film and Video Festival of New York City

The Creation of the World. 11 min. Marceau enacts the biblical version of creation.

BEWARE, BEWARE MY BEAUTY FAIR

29 min.   16mm, ¾" U-Matic, ½" Beta, ½" VHS
   color   live action
Distributor: Phoenix
Producer: Tom Daly
Directors: Peter Svatek and Jean LaFleur
Canada   1973   ages 9 up

Young members of the Children's Theater of Montreal perform this intriguing play-within-a-play. During the rehearsals for a school play based on "The Beauty and the Beast," a mysterious drama unfolds backstage as someone or something menaces Beauty. This suspenseful fantasy ends happily, after a chase that parallels the action onstage.

CITY LIGHTS

87 min.   16mm, 35mm, ¾" U-Matic, ½" Beta, ½" VHS   b&w   nonverbal
Distributor: Films Inc.
Director: Charles Chaplin
USA   1931   ages 6 up

Charlie Chaplin, as the Tramp, falls in love with a blind girl and steals money to have her sight restored. This sentimental pantomime is classic Chaplin, with many unforgettably funny sequences.

THE CONCERT

12 min.   16mm, ¾" U-Matic, ½" Beta, ½" VHS
   color   live action   nonverbal
Distributor: Pyramid
Filmmakers: Claude Chagrin and Julian Chagrin
Great Britain   1974   all ages
Awards: Golden Bear, Best Short Film, Berlin International Film Festival; Learning A/V Award, *Learning* Magazine

A funny fantasy in mime about a concert pianist who uses a London street crossing (located behind the Royal Albert Hall) as a keyboard, which he plays with his feet. Julian Chagrin bounds from note to note while attempting to cope with the obstacles posed by oncoming cars, police, other musicians, and a dog. This is delightful entertainment, simple enough for even the youngest to get the point, clever enough for everyone to enjoy.

THE GOLD RUSH

81 min.   16mm, 35mm, ¾" U-Matic, ½" Beta,
   ½" VHS   b&w   nonverbal
Distributors: Films Inc., Macmillan
Producer/director: Charles Chaplin
USA   1925   ages 6 up

Chaplin stars as the Lone Prospector who travels to the Klondike to find gold and make his fortune. Some of the funniest scenes take place when he is trapped in an Alaskan cabin with the bearlike Big Jim McKay and reduced to dining on boiled shoe. Children love the pathetic little character and his wild adventures in the northern snows, and they appreciate his expressive pantomime.

KEITH

10 min.   16mm   color   live action   nonverbal
Distributors: Billy Budd, Coe
Producer/director: Frank Moynihan
USA   1973   all ages

A captivating display of mime for children and adults alike. Keith Berger, a young mime artist, performs his impression of a mechanical man. The film opens on Keith sitting outdoors by a sculpture and shows his face in progressive stages of makeup. To the accompaniment of suspenseful piano music, he moves like a robot from the sculpture down to the ground as curious passersby gather to watch. Invisible walls then spring up and threaten to crush him, but he manages to break free.

LORRAINE HANSBERRY: THE BLACK EXPERIENCE IN THE CREATION OF DRAMA

35 min.   16mm   color   live action
Distributor: Films for the Humanities
Filmmaker: Ralph Tangney
USA   1975   ages 12 up

An appreciative biography of the gifted playwright whose premature death from cancer at age 34 ended a successful career. Using film clips and photos of her childhood in Chicago as well as compelling sequences from her plays, *A Raisin in the Sun, The Sign in Sidney Brustein's Window,* and *Les Blancs,* the film conveys Hansberry's dedication to equal rights for all and to her art, in her own words and voice.

MAX

20 min.   16mm, ¾" U-Matic, ½" Beta, ½" VHS
   color   live action
Distributors: Carousel, Coe
Producers/directors: Joseph Gilford and Jennifer
   Lax
USA   1974   ages 12 up

Lynn, an ambitious understudy rehearsing after hours in a Broadway theater, encounters Max, a helpful night watchman and ex-vaudevillian. He reminisces about seeing Judy Garland in performance, and Lynn is so impressed by Max's own performance that they end up working on a scene together. Comedian Jack Gilford plays the role of Max with sensitivity and humor. This enjoyable piece of fiction will be especially appreciated by aspiring young actors and actresses.

MIME VIGNETTES/MUMMENSCHANZ

30 min.   16mm, ¾" U-Matic, ½" Beta, ½" VHS
   color   live action
Distributor: Argus
Producer: Arthur Shafman
Director: Jim Talbot
USA   1978   ages 6 up

For those who have never seen Mummenschanz on stage, this film of some of their creative and witty performances is a good substitute. In 14 sequences, the mime troupe uses simple costumes and unusual masks to portray all sorts of creatures, concepts, and emotions.

MODERN TIMES

85 min.   16mm, 35mm, ¾″ U-Matic, ½″ Beta,
  ½″ VHS   b&w   nonverbal
Distributor: Films Inc.
Director: Charles Chaplin
USA   1936   ages 6 up

Charlie Chaplin tries his hand at a variety of jobs in this classic comedy that mocks the industrial age. He battles machinery and the system in his inimitable style of mime, and his eloquent gestures and expressions as he confronts a world obviously out to get him leave children rolling in the aisles with laughter.

THE MORNING SPIDER

22 min.   16mm, ¾″ U-Matic, ½″ Beta, ½″ VHS
  color   live action   nonverbal
Distributor: Pyramid
Producer: Mike O'Connor
Directors: Claude Chagrin and Julian Chagrin
USA   1976   ages 6 up
Award: First Prize, Kenyon Independent Film-
  makers Festival

Talented mime Julian Chagrin (see also *The Concert,* earlier in this section) portrays a day in the life of a bumbling spider in this clever, funny fantasy. The costumes and special effects are extraordinarily well done, brilliantly evoking the world of an insect. The spider labors to trap a blue fly, and in the course of its day encounters a gang of mosquitoes, a centipede who takes all night to remove its 120 shoes, and a beautiful red spider. Adults as well as children appreciate this masterful piece of mime.

PAUL ROBESON: TRIBUTE TO AN ARTIST

29 min.   16mm, ¾″ U-Matic, ½″ Beta, ½″ VHS
  color   live action
Distributor: Films Inc.
Director: Saul Turell
USA   1979   ages 12 up
Awards: Academy Award; Blue Ribbon, American
  Film Festival; Best in Festival, Montera Film
  Award; CINE Golden Eagle; Gold Medal, Festi-
  val of the Americas; Hemi Trophy, Hemisfilm

Festival; Learning A/V Award, *Learning* Magazine; Bronze Plaque, Columbus Film Festival
Chris Awards

A remarkable documentary on the renowned actor and singer, who died in 1976, narrated by Sidney Poitier. Robeson's powerful performances in such stage and screen productions as *Othello, Show Boat, The Emperor Jones,* and *The Proud Valley* are shown in photographs and film clips, and his magnificent voice is well served by the excellent sound track. Robeson's personal life, however, is passed over completely, and while his championship of human rights and his blacklisting in the 1950s are outlined, this is not a political film. Instead, it is a rare opportunity to appreciate the artistry of an enormously talented man.

PAUL ROBESON: TRIBUTE TO AN ARTIST

ROMEO AND JULIET

138 min.   16mm, 35mm, ¾″ U-Matic, ½″ Beta,
  ½″ VHS   color   live action
Distributor: Films Inc.
Director: Franco Zeffirelli
Italy   1968   ages 12 up

There have been more than a dozen films based on Shakespeare's tragic love story, but Zeffirelli's lush interpretation is the version adolescents like best. It offers exquisite photography, lots of action, and the beautiful young Olivia Hussey and Leonard Whiting to identify with and cry over.

THE SHAKESPEARE PLAYS

37 programs   ¾" U-Matic, ½" Beta II, ½" VHS
   color   live action
Distributor: Time-Life Video
Producers: Cedric Messina and Jonathan Miller, British Broadcasting Corporation and Time-Life Films
Great Britain   1978–1984   ages 12 up

This outstanding series is an ambitious attempt to produce the complete plays of Shakespeare for television. Shown on the British Broadcasting Corporation (BBC) and on the Public Broadcasting Service (PBS), they have been made available for school and home use. The productions completed so far have been of uniformly high quality. Most of the casts are from the Royal Shakespeare troupe or Britain's National Theatre. They feature renowned actors and actresses, including Sir John Gielgud, Anthony Hopkins, Anthony Quayle, and Claire Bloom. The settings and costumes are intended to be those of Shakespeare's time, and by some standards these are conservative interpretations. The aim here, however, is to focus on Shakespeare's words, and they are beautifully spoken. The effective use of closeups takes advantage of the intimacy of television, but in general these presentations have the feeling of plays rather than movies. The productions have been used successfully in classrooms.

Julius Caesar. 161 min.
As You Like It. 150 min.
Romeo and Juliet. 167 min.
Richard II. 157 min.
Measure for Measure. 145 min.

Henry VIII. 165 min.
Henry IV, Part I. 147 min.
Henry IV, Part II. 151 min.
Henry V. 163 min.
Twelfth Night. 124 min.
Hamlet. 222 min.
The Tempest. 150 min.
The Taming of the Shrew. 127 min.
The Merchant of Venice. 157 min.
Antony and Cleopatra. 171 min.
All's Well That Ends Well. 141 min.
Timon of Athens. 128 min.
The Winter's Tale. 173 min.
Othello. Approximately 120 min.
Troilus and Cressida. Approximately 190 min.
Henry VI, Part I. Approximately 120 min.
Henry VI, Part II. Approximately 120 min.
Henry VI, Part III. Approximately 120 min.
A Midsummer Night's Dream. Approximately 120 min.
Richard III. Approximately 120 min.

In 1983

Coriolanus
King Lear
Cymbeline
Love's Labour's Lost
Merry Wives of Windsor
The Two Gentlemen of Verona

In 1984

King John
Macbeth
Pericles
Much Ado about Nothing
Titus Andronicus
Comedy of Errors

WALTER KERR ON THEATER

26 min.   16mm, ¾" U-Matic, ½" Beta, ½" VHS
   color   live action
Distributor: Learning Corporation of America
Producer: Robert Saudek
Director: Joseph Anthony
USA   1970   ages 12 up

The renowned drama critic for *The New York Times* talks easily and informally about how live theater differs from film, illustrating his points with engrossing passages from five plays of varying styles. The excerpts are from *No Place to Be Somebody* by Charles Gordone, Aeschylus's *Prometheus*, Oscar Wilde's *The Importance of Being Earnest*, Joseph Papp's production of Shakespeare's *Richard III*, and Jean-Claude van Itallie's experimental *The Serpent*, performed by the Open Theater. Kerr is informative without being pedantic, and the passages from the plays whet your appetite for more.

3
Literary Arts

Children's Literature

ALICE'S ADVENTURES IN WONDERLAND

101 min.   16mm, 35mm, ¾" U-Matic, ½" Beta,
   ½" VHS   color   live action
Distributor: Films Inc.
Director: William Sterling
Great Britain   1972   ages 9 up

This fine musical version of Lewis Carroll's masterpiece successfully conveys the magic of a young girl's experiences in an outlandish place. The sets are based on the original drawings by Tenniel, and the cast (which includes Sir Ralph Richardson, Peter Sellers, Dudley Moore, and Spike Milligan) has been called the "honor roll of the movie industry."

ALLIGATORS ALL AROUND

2 min.   16mm, ¾" U-Matic, ½" Beta, ½" VHS
   color   animation
Distributor: Weston Woods
Producer: Sheldon Riss
Director: Maurice Sendak
USA   1978   ages 2–8

A lively little alligator pulls a rhyming alphabet out of a paper bag and clowns his way from "alligators all around" all the way to "zippity zound," illustrating an activity for each letter. Based on the book by Maurice Sendak, with jolly music composed and sung by Carole King. Part of the film *Really Rosie* (see later in this section).

THE AMAZING COSMIC AWARENESS OF DUFFY MOON

32 min.   16mm, ¾" U-Matic, ½" Beta II, ½" VHS
   color   live action
Distributor: Time-Life Video
Producer: Daniel Wilson
Director: Larry Elikann
USA   1979   ages 9 up
Awards: Red Ribbon, American Film Festival; Chris
   Statuette, Columbus Film Festival Chris Awards

Sixth-grader Duffy Moon, the "shrimp" of his class, enrolls in a mail-order course that promises to boost his cosmic abilities. Bolstered with new-found morale, Duffy and his friend Peter set up an odd-job business that competes all too successfully with the odd-job business of the town bully. Trouble results, but Duffy finally learns to rely on his own abilities and not on his cosmic course to solve it. Aired as an "ABC Afterschool Special," this realistic and touching comedy adventure is based on Jean Robinson's novel *The Strange but Wonderful Cosmic Awareness of Duffy Moon.*

THE AMERICAN SHORT STORY

18 programs   16mm, ¾" U-Matic   color   live
  action
Distributor: Perspective Films
Producer: Robert Geller
USA   ages 12 up
Award: Peabody Award

This set of 17 short stories on film, plus an introductory film, is superb for classroom use, and it is also terrific entertainment. The films were first shown on the Public Broadcasting Service (PBS). The production values and acting are excellent throughout. The films are faithful to the style and spirit of the authors, who range over a century of American literature from Hawthorne to Updike. Teachers may be interested to know that paperback books entitled *The American Short Story*, volumes 1 and 2 (edited by Calvin Skaggs, published by Dell Publishing in New York) are available. They include the stories, plus critical essays, screenplays, interviews with writers and directors, bibliographies, and photographs.

The American Short Story. 23½ min. 1977. An interview with Robert Geller, executive producer of the series. He discusses the short story as a literary genre, and excerpts from the films in the series are shown.

Rappaccini's Daughter. 57 min. 1980. Nathaniel Hawthorne's romantic story of a young man's involvement with a strangely beautiful young woman who tends a poisonous garden in medieval Italy. Slow paced, but visually captivating. *Director:* Dexso Magyar. *Award:* Golden Babe, Chicagoland Educational Film Festival.

The Golden Honeymoon. 57 min. 1980. To celebrate their fiftieth wedding anniversary, an elderly couple journeys to St. Petersburg, Florida, in the 1920s. Jealousy mars their marriage when they run into the wife's old suitor vacationing with his spouse. Ring Lardner's comic, ironic tale is well acted. *Director:* Noel Black

Bernice Bobs Her Hair. 47 min. 1977. A lovely production of the short story by F. Scott Fitzgerald. Shelley Duvall stars as Bernice, a shy teenager who does not know how to attract boys until her cousin Marjorie teaches her how to flirt. Then she outshines her mentor, to Marjorie's dismay, and Marjorie goads her into cutting her long, beautiful hair. Bud Cort plays the love interest. Although Bernice is of the preflapper generation, the film will seem perfectly up-to-date to teenagers and they will relish Bernice's revenge at the end. *Director:* Joan Micklin Silver. *Awards:* Bronze Plaque, Columbus Film Film Festival Chris Awards; CINE Golden Eagle; International Short and Documentary Film Festival; Red Ribbon, American Film Festival

The Jilting of Granny Weatherall. 57 min. 1980. Geraldine Fitzgerald plays a dying matriarch in this adaptation of Katherine Anne Porter's story. Old resentments come to the surface as the woman realizes that she is fading. Past and present blend in a surreal fashion as she relives being jilted by her first love. Unusual visual effects are employed to give the viewer a sense of Granny Weatherall's confused mind but still-strong spirit. *Director:* Randa Haines

The Sky Is Gray. 46 min. 1980. A young black boy goes to town to visit the dentist with his mother and learns about racism and pride in this subtle film based on Ernest Gaines's short story. *Director:* Stan Lathan. *Awards:* Blue Ribbon and Emily, American Film Festival; Best of Festival, Birmingham International Educational Film Festival; ALA Selected Film for Young Adults; Top Twenty, Cleveland Instructional Film Festival

The Displaced Person. 57½ min. 1977. A Polish refugee creates havoc on a Georgia farm in the late 1940s when an elderly priest tries to integrate him into the community. The fine cast of this tragedy by Flannery O'Connor includes John Houseman and Irene Worth. *Director:* Glenn Jordan

The Music School. 30 min. 1977. John Updike's story concerns 24 hours in the life of a writer as he struggles to find a focus. The writer's wrestlings with religion, technology, violence, and social change are vividly portrayed, and contrast with the order and harmony of his daughter's music lessons. *Director:* John Korty. *Awards:* CINE Golden Eagle; Golden Gate, San Francisco International Film Festival

The Greatest Man in the World. 51 min. 1980. In this clever satire by James Thurber, a very unheroic character becomes the first man to fly nonstop around the world. The government and the press do their best to present him as they would like him to be, and cynically dispose of him when they realize what he is really like. The film features exciting sequences

THE AMERICAN SHORT STORY SERIES: THE GREATEST MAN IN THE WORLD

in the air and on the ground, and some good acting by Brad Davis in the title role and by Carol Kane as his girlfriend, an ex-stripper. *Director:* Ralph Rosenblum

Almos' a Man. 39 min. 1977. Richard Wright's poignant look at adolescence is a moving film. LeVar Burton, star of "Roots," plays David, a teenage farmworker living in the rural South in the 1930s. David convinces his mother to let him buy a gun, and accidentally shoots a mule. He owns up to the deed, but resents the fact that no one will treat him as the almost-adult he feels himself to be. He retrieves his gun and takes off on a passing freight train, to begin life again far away from the bonds of home. *Director:* Stan Lathan. *Award:* Bronze Plaque, Columbus Film Festival Chris Awards

Parker Adderson, Philosopher. 39 min. 1977. Parker Adderson, a Union spy who is captured behind enemy lines at the end of the Civil War, is surprisingly flippant in the face of death, to the annoyance of the Confederate general who nabs him. But when their roles are reversed and the general is mortally wounded, he changes his view of dying. Based on Ambrose Bierce's short story. *Director:* Arthur Barron

The Jolly Corner. 43 min. 1977. An expatriate American who fled the United States during the Civil War returns after 35 years. In an effort to find out what he might have become had he stayed, he revisits the house of his youth, the Jolly Corner, and meets the woman he might have married. Based on the short story by Henry James, the film features Fritz Weaver and Salome Jens. *Director:* Arthur Barron

Barn Burning. 41 min. 1980. A beautifully filmed adaptation of William Faulkner's story of the relationship between father and son. Abner Snopes, a nasty man and one quick to anger and to seek revenge, provokes the wealthy southern land-owners for whom he works. When they punish him, he burns their barns. His son, torn between family duty and his sense of what is right, finally decides that he must speak up. *Director:* Peter Werner

The Blue Hotel. 55 min. 1977. An eerie and effective film based on Stephen Crane's story. A strange Swede in the hotel of a small Nebraska town in the 1880s foretells his own murder, and it comes to pass just as he says it will. *Director:* Jan Kadar

The Man That Corrupted Hadleyburg. 40 min. 1980. A well-paced satire featuring Robert Preston. Mark Twain's tale concerns a man who comes to unfriendly Hadleyburg, which prides itself on staying honest by resisting temptation. The stranger cannot resist the opportunity to show up Hadleyburg's self-righteous citizens, and he succeeds in proving that even honesty has its price. *Director:* Ralph Rosenblum. *Award:* Golden Medallion, Pacific Film Festival

Paul's Case. 55 min. 1980. A young man in turn-of-the-century Philadelphia longs to lead an upper-class life-style and immerse himself in culture. He lives for his after-school job as an usher in a concert hall, but his father takes him out of school and puts him in a full-time job that will not "heat his brain." Paul retaliates by stealing money and running off to lead the life he wants in New York, until his father comes after him. Fine cinematography and period settings and costumes enhance this production, which is based on Willa Cather's story. *Director:* Lamont Jackson. *Awards:* Red Ribbon, American Film Festival; ALA Selected Film for Young Adults

I'm a Fool. 38 min. 1977. Andy, a young man who works on the Ohio racetrack circuit in the 1900s, meets the girl of his dreams and lies himself into a corner in an attempt to win her. Andy is played by Ron

Howard (of TV's "Happy Days"), and both he and the situation he gets himself into will be familiar to young viewers. Based on a Sherwood Anderson story. *Director:* Noel Black. *Award:* Golden Babe, Chicagoland Educational Film Festival

Soldier's Home. 42 min. 1977. A soldier returns from World War I and cannot seem to reenter the life he left. His friends and family try to help him find himself, but he discovers that he has outgrown his past and must look somewhere else for his future. This sensitive production is based on Ernest Hemingway's story. *Director:* Robert Young. *Award:* Silver Hugo, Chicago International Film Festival

AND NOW MIGUEL

95 min.   16mm   color   live action
Distributor: Twyman
Producer: Robert B. Radnitz
Director: James B. Clark
USA   1966   ages 6–11

Eleven-year-old Miguel Chavez is part of a family of Chicano sheep ranchers living in New Mexico. Miguel wants to herd the sheep into the mountains over the summer along with his father and his uncles, but his parents feel that he is still too young. Left on the ranch, Miguel proves his maturity by rescuing a stray flock from attacking wolves. This dramatic and well-produced film is based on the Newbery Medal book by Joseph Krumgold.

THE BEAST OF MONSIEUR RACINE

9 min.   16mm, ¾" U-Matic, ½" Beta, ½" VHS
  color   animation
Distributor: Weston Woods
Director: Gene Deitch
Czechoslovakia   1975   ages 6–8
Awards: First Prize, Children's Category, International Film & TV Festival; Red Ribbon, American Film Festival; Bronze Plaque, Columbus Film Festival Chris Awards; Bronze Hugo, Chicago International Film Festival

When Monsieur Racine's prize pears are stolen, he sets a trap and captures a lumpy, funny-looking creature. He proudly brings his catch to the Academy of Sciences in Paris, only to discover the true nature of the beast while he is making his presentation. A mad riot results, to children's delight. Tomi Ungerer's book translates well to the screen, although the narrator's heavy French accent is a problem for some children. Available in Danish, Dutch, French, German, and Swedish.

THE BEST OF COVER TO COVER

32 programs, 15 min. each   ¾" U-Matic
  color   live action
Distributor: Children's Television International
Producer: Greater Washington Educational Tele-
  communications Association, Inc.
USA   1974–75

Cover to Cover is a reading motivation series that really works, according to teachers and librarians. In each program, host John Robbins introduces one or two popular children's books and tells part of the story. A first reading is illustrated with a series of drawings. During the second reading, Robbins sketches a single picture. Enough of the story is told to leave children hungry for more, and eager to go to the library to read about "what happens next." Children enjoy the format, and the programs fit well into most curricula. These programs were selected from the 64 programs in the Cover to Cover series. (For Part I, a 56-page teacher's guide and a fact sheet are available, and for Part II, a 24-page teacher's guide is available.)

Part I: Ages 6–8

Alphonse, That Bearded One by Natalie Savage Carlson; The Talking Cat and Other Stories of French Canada by Natalie Savage Carlson. A bear who becomes a soldier and a mischievous talking cat outwit gullible humans in these French Canadian folktales.

J.T. by Jane Wagner. A one-eyed cat wins the heart of a young boy, who learns about the pain of caring.

Duffy and the Devil by Harve Zemach and Margot Zemach; Baba Yaga by Ernest Small. Two folktales, one Cornish, the other Russian.

Socks by Beverly Cleary; Gorilla Gorilla by Carol Fenner. A cat and a gorilla narrate these stories about interruptions in their normally peaceful lives.

McBroom's Zoo by Sid Fleischman; The Finches' Fabulous Furnace by Roger W. Drury. A tornado hits McBrooms' menagerie; the Finches have a secret volcano in their basement.

Tales the People Tell in China by Robert Wyndham; Favorite Fairy Tales Told in Japan by Virginia Haviland. Two collections that reveal both countries' cultures.

The White Archer by James Houston; At the Mouth of the Luckiest River by Arnold A. Griese. Tales of Eskimo and Indian boys.

Owls in the Family by Farley Mowat. A true story about how two boys raised two owls.

The Squirrel Wife by Philippa Pearce; The Moonball by Ursula Williams. Stories of fantasy and science fiction.

And Then What Happened, Paul Revere? by Jean Fritz; Poor Richard in France by F. N. Monjo. Two pieces of historical fiction.

The Sea Egg by L. M. Boston. A magical underwater journey with seal pups. Award: Ohio State Award

Jennifer, Hecate, Macbeth, William McKinley, and Me, Elizabeth by E. L. Konigsburg; Little Witch by Anna E. Bennett. Stories of witches.

The Night Watchmen by Helen Cresswell. Henry wonders if the mysterious creatures he sees are imaginary or real.

Freckle Juice by Judy Blume; *Uncle Fonzo's Ford* by Miska Miles. Andrew wants freckles like his friend Nicky; Effie worries about people laughing at his eccentric uncle.

The 18th Emergency by Betsy Byars. A boy named Mouse insults the local bully. *Award:* Ohio State Award

The Best Christmas Pageant Ever by Barbara Robinson. The five Herdman children take over the annual Sunday School Christmas play.

Part II: Ages 9–11

Trouble River by Betsy Byars. A story set in the prairies.

Windmill Summer by Hila Feil. A story of a young girl with more animal friends than human ones.

A Stranger at Green Knowe by Lucy Boston. This tale concerns a young boy's friendship with a gorilla that escapes from the London Zoo.

The Spirit Is Willing by Betty Baker. A period story that contrasts a down-to-earth girl with a romantic.

Akavak by James Houston; *Tikta Liktak* by James Houston. Two stories about Eskimo culture.

The Upstairs Room by Johanna Reiss. A true story of two Jewish girls who hide to escape the Nazis during World War II. *Award:* Ohio State Award

The Nargun and the Stars by Patricia Wrightson. The natural and the supernatural blend in this tale of fantasy.

The Marrow of the World by Ruth Nichols. A classic struggle between good and evil.

The Wolves of Willoughby Chase by Joan Aiken. A parody of a Victorian novel.

A Darkness of Giants by J. Allan Bos-

worth. An adventure about two boys camping in the wilderness.

The Headless Cupid by Zilpha K. Snyder. A girl struggles to deal with her parents' divorce and her mother's remarriage.

The Summer of the Swans by Betsy Byars. A girl grows up and learns to accept herself and others. *Award:* Bronze Medal, Virgin Islands International Film Festival

How to Eat Fried Worms by Thomas Rockwell; *The Ransom of Red Chief* by O. Henry. Two funny stories, one about a boy who eats worms to win a bet, the other about the kidnapping of a very difficult kid.

Moon Eyes by Josephine Poole. An exciting, suspenseful tale.

Against Time by Roderic Jeffries. A detective story about a kidnapping.

A Wizard of Earthsea by Ursula K. Le-Guin. An adventure about a boy's coming of age. *Award:* Gold Hugo, Chicago International Film Festival

BIG HENRY AND THE POLKA DOT KID

51 min. (full version), 33 min. (edited version)
16mm, ¾" U-Matic, ½" Beta, ½" VHS
color   live action
Distributor: Learning Corporation of America
Producer: Linda Gottlieb
Director: Richard Marquand
USA   1976   ages 6 up
Awards: Emmy Award; Birmingham International
Educational Film Festival; Chicago International
Film Festival; Childfilm Festival; Columbus Film
Festival Chris Awards; Learning A/V Award,
Learning Magazine

Based on Morley Callaghan's story "Luke Baldwin's Vow," this sensitive, appealing drama concerns a ten-year-old orphan named Luke who is adopted by his Uncle Henry. Henry (played by Ned Beatty) is a gruff, practical man who runs a small sawmill in the Canadian woods. Luke (played by Chris Barnes) becomes fond of an old, blind dog that his uncle wants to destroy, and with the help of a neighbor (played by Estelle Parsons) Luke works to save the dog's life. This "NBC Special Treat" offers a gripping plot and excellent acting, as well as the refreshing message that there is more to life than just being practical.

THE BLACK STALLION

125 min.   16mm   color   live action
Distributor: United Artists
Producer: Francis Ford Coppola
Director: Carroll Ballard
USA   1979   ages 6 up

Based on Walter Farley's adventure novel about a boy and his horse, this is a gorgeously filmed fantasy that people of all ages can enjoy. Eleven-year-old Alex (played by Kelly Reno) is on a cruise ship that goes down. The black stallion saves his life and the two are washed ashore on a deserted island. There the boy learns to ride the magnificent animal, in exquisite, dreamlike sequences. When they are rescued, the boy and the horse return to America where a horse trainer (Mickey Rooney) helps Alex turn the stallion into a racehorse and ride him in the big race. The cinematography, by Caleb Deschanel, is what makes this movie special, but the plot is engaging and the acting is terrific.

THE CASE OF THE COSMIC COMIC

28 min.   16mm, ¾" U-Matic, ½" Beta, ½" VHS
   color   live action
Distributor: Weston Woods
Director: Gary Templeton
USA   1976   ages 6–11

Based on the book *Homer Price* by Robert McCloskey. Homer's friend Freddy idolizes Super-Duper, a comic strip hero and movie star who flies through space and breaks up battleships as if they were toothpicks. One day the boys unexpectedly have the opportunity to meet Super-Duper in person. Told from a child's viewpoint and set in small-town America

of 50 years ago, this is an engaging and involving story about illusion and reality.

THE CASE OF THE ELEVATOR DUCK

17 min.   16mm, ¾" U-Matic, ½" Beta, ½" VHS
   color   live action
Distributor: Learning Corporation of America
Producer: Linda Gottlieb
Director: Joan Silver
USA   1974   ages 6–11
Awards: Chicago International Film Festival; American Film Festival; Sinking Creek Film Festival; ALA Notable Film for Children; *Preview's* Best Films; selected for EFLA Children's Films Festival

An 11-year-old "detective" who lives in an urban housing project discovers a lost duck in the elevator. His clever and funny attempts to find the duck's owner while concealing the forbidden animal from the housing authorities are thoroughly enjoyable, although some children prefer the book (by Polly Berrien Berends). This is a professional production, with interesting camera work and a nice musical score.

THE CASE OF THE ELEVATOR DUCK

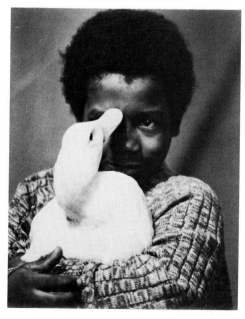

CHARLOTTE'S WEB

90 min.   16mm, 35mm, ¾" U-Matic, ½" Beta,
 ½" VHS   color   animation
Distributor: Films Inc.
Producers: Joseph Barbera and William Hanna
Directors: Charles A. Nichols and Iwao Takamoto
USA   1972   ages 6 up

E. B. White's classic novel has been turned into a delightful animated musical featuring the voices of Debbie Reynolds, Paul Lynde, Henry Gibson, and Agnes Moorehead. The story concerns the friendship between Charlotte, a clever and compassionate spider, and Wilbur the pig, who is in danger of becoming bacon. This production was broadcast as a CBS special presentation.

CHICKEN SOUP WITH RICE

5 min.   16mm, ¾" U-Matic, ½" Beta, ½" VHS
 color   animation
Distributor: Weston Woods
Producer: Sheldon Riss
Director: Maurice Sendak
USA   1978   ages 2–8

An adventurous group of children have fantastic experiences in exotic locales, all involving a certain delectable broth. Maurice Sendak's verse, set to music composed and sung by Carole King, provides an introduction to the months of the year, proving that any time is nice for eating chicken soup with rice. Part of the film *Really Rosie* (see later in this section).

THE COW WHO FELL IN THE CANAL

9 min.   16mm, ¾" U-Matic, ½" Beta, ½" VHS
 color   animation
Distributor: Weston Woods
Director: Cynthia Freitag
USA   1972   ages 2–5

A warm and humorous story set in Holland. One day a cow slips into a canal and floats on a raft down to the city. She creates quite a stir as she gallops through the cobblestoned streets, and she manages to completely disrupt the cheese market before being returned home sporting a straw hat. This film is done in iconographic animation from the book by Phyllis Krasilovsky, illustrated by Peter Spier. Available in Danish, Dutch, and Swedish.

DINKY HOCKER

30 min.   16mm, ¾" U-Matic, ½" Beta, ½" VHS
 color   live action
Distributor: Learning Corporation of America
Producers: Paul Asselin and Diane Asselin
Director: Tom Blank
USA   1979   ages 9 up

Dinky's hooked on food, but her mother is too involved in charity work at a drug-rehabilitation center to notice her daughter's problem. With the help of P. John, an overweight friend, Dinky makes progress, but her mother does not seem to see it until Dinky makes a desperate bid for attention. Somewhat sentimental at the end, this is nevertheless an affecting and believable story, told from the teenager's point of view. Based on M. E. Kerr's novel *Dinky Hocker Shoots Smack,* this production was presented as an "ABC Afterschool Special."

DRAGON STEW

13¼ min.   16mm, ¾" U-Matic, ½" Beta, ½" VHS
 color   animation
Distributor: BFA
Producer: BFA
USA   1972   ages 6–11

King Chubby loves to eat, but he has trouble holding on to a royal cook because he cannot resist giving advice in the kitchen. Then a bright young man named Klaus comes along and wins the job by telling the king of his secret recipe for dragon stew. He does well as a chef by tricking the king into preparing his own meals, until the king presents him with a little dragon to be made into stew. Klaus's clever solution to this quandary is amusing and satisfying to all. This production was adapted from the book by Tom McGovern.

THE ELECTRIC GRANDMOTHER

49 min. (full version), 32 min. (edited version)
  16mm, ¾" U-Matic, ½" Beta, ½" VHS
  color   live action
Distributor: Learning Corporation of America
Producer: Doro Bachrach
Director: Noel Black
USA   1982   ages 6 up

An outstanding performance by Maureen Stapleton as the grandmother of the title highlights this adaptation of "I Sing the Body Electric," a short story by science fiction writer Ray Bradbury. When the mother of three young children dies, their father leases a loving electric grandmother to help out. She proves to have all sorts of wonderful talents, but more important, she is always there when the children need her. This fine production was presented on NBC's "Project Peacock" series, and its dual themes of the positive potential of some machines and the importance of grandparents have great appeal for children.

EVAN'S CORNER

23 min.   16mm, ¾" U-Matic, ½" Beta, ½" VHS
  color   live action
Distributor: BFA
Producer: Stephen Bosustow Productions
USA   1970   ages 6–8

This is the involving story of Evan, a young black boy who is one of six children living in a crowded apartment in an urban ghetto. Evan decides he needs some space to himself, and his mother allows him to select a corner of the apartment to be his very own. He furnishes it with a box, a picture, a plant, and a pet but eventually discovers that sharing can be as rewarding as privacy. The warm portrayal of a family holds children's attention despite the slow pace of the film, which is based on the book by Elizabeth Starr Hill.

THE GOLD BUG

43 min. (full version), 31 min. (edited version)
  16mm, ¾" U-Matic, ½" Beta, ½" VHS
  color   live action
Distributor: Learning Corporation of America
Producer: Doro Bachrach
Director: Robert Fuest
USA   1979   ages 9 up
Awards: Emmy Award; Chicagoland Educational
  Film Festival; Columbus Film Festival Chris
  Awards; Learning A/V Award, Learning Magazine

This excellent, well-acted adaptation of Edgar Allan Poe's suspenseful short story was filmed on location on Sullivan's Island, off the coast of South Carolina. The story, set in 1866, concerns an adventurous young boy hunting butterflies on a supposedly deserted island. He comes across a gold bug and meets a strange hermit and his mute, hulking servant. The boy finds Captain Kidd's map and gets swept up in a wild hunt to find his treasure. This exciting production was broadcast as an "ABC Weekend Special."

THE HORRIBLE HONCHOS

31 min.   16mm, ¾" U-Matic, ½" Beta II, ½" VHS
  color   live action
Distributor: Time-Life Video
Producer: Daniel Wilson
Director: Larry Elikann
USA   1977   ages 9 up

The Horrible Honchos, a small gang of children led by a tough little girl, vow to stick together no matter what and play pranks to prove their loyalty. Hollis, a new boy in the neighborhood, becomes the target of their teasing even though individually the gang members like him. When they play a practical joke on Hollis that nearly has serious consequences, they reevaluate being Horrible Honchos. This realistic and involving production is based on Emily Cheney Neville's Seventeenth Street Gang.

THE HUNDRED PENNY BOX

18 min.   16mm, ¾" U-Matic, ½" Beta, ½" VHS
  color   live action
Distributor: Churchill
Producers: Pieter Van Deusen and Leah Miller
Director: Pieter Van Deusen
USA   1979   ages 9 up
Awards: American Film Festival; Chicago Interna-
  tional Film Festival

The hundred penny box is an old wooden
crate that contains a penny for each year
of Aunt Dew's life. It is also her only
possession, and her young nephew understands why she does not want to give it
up, despite his mother's pleas. Fine performances and interesting camera work
bring to life this slow-paced, atmospheric
adaptation of Sharon Bell Mathis's Newbery Honor book.

THE INCREDIBLE BOOK ESCAPE

45 min. (complete version)   16mm, ¾" U-Matic,
  ½" Beta, ½" VHS   color   live action and
  animation
Distributor: Churchill Films
Producer: Nick Bosustow
USA   1980   ages 6–11

This thoroughly entertaining production
was designed to stimulate reading and
library use; it is also just plain fun to
watch. The complete version was presented as a children's special on CBS, but
each short animated story is available
separately. The film concerns a young
girl named P. J., who accidentally gets
locked in the library after closing time.
Four animated storybook characters appear to offer suggestions on how to get
out. The imaginative stories they tell are
taken from popular children's books. The
film is engaging and well produced, and
emphasizes taking action in all sorts of
different ways. A teacher's guide is available.

Myra. 3 min. Myra has such an active
imagination that when her dance teacher
tells the class to leap like frogs or swim

THE INCREDIBLE BOOK ESCAPE

like fish, Myra actually becomes the
animal mentioned, much to the conster-
nation of the class. From the book by
Barbara Bottner.

Ghost in the Shed. 8 min. This spooky
story concerns the persistent ghost of a
murdered peddler, who will not stop
slamming the kitchen door until his bones
are properly buried. From the book *Encounters with the Invisible World* by
Marilynne K. Roach.

The Practical Princess. 10 min. Princess
Bedelia was given three gifts by the fairies
when she was born: beauty, grace, and
common sense. She foils a dragon, dis-
poses of an unwanted suitor, and rescues
a handsome prince. From the book by Jay
Williams. (Also distributed by Coe.)

The Furious Flycycle. 12 min. Melvin
Spitznagel, boy inventor and mechanical
genius, creates a flying bicycle that helps
him become a hero. From the book by Jan
Wahl.

THE ISLAND OF THE BLUE DOLPHINS

99 min.   16mm   color   live action
Distributor: Twyman
Producer: Robert B. Radnitz
Director: James B. Clark
USA   1964   ages 6 up
Awards: *Parents'* Magazine Family Medal Award;
    Venice Film Festival

Based on Scott O'Dell's Newbery Medal-winning book, this is the beautifully filmed story of a girl and her dog. Karana, an Indian girl from a Pacific Northwest tribe, is stranded on an island off California. She and the dog start out as enemies and gradually become inseparable friends.

IT'S SO NICE TO HAVE A WOLF AROUND THE HOUSE

12 min.   16mm, ¾" U-Matic, ½" Beta, ½" VHS
    color   animation
Distributor: Learning Corporation of America
Producer/director: Paul Fierlinger
USA   1979   ages 6 up
Awards: CINE Golden Eagle; Chicago International
    Film Festival; Ottawa International Animated
    Film Festival; National Educational Film Festival

This funny fantasy is based on Harry Allard's popular book. An old man advertises for someone to take care of him and his pets. His ad is answered by a furry stranger with a dazzling smile named Cuthbert J. Devine, who soon proves indispensable. But one day the old man discovers to his horror that his new companion is really a wolf. Cuthbert begs to be allowed to stay, and all ends well. While some children prefer the book, all enjoy the detailed animation and hilarious characterizations of the film and appreciate its goofy humor.

JACOB TWO-TWO MEETS THE HOODED FANG

90 min.   16mm   color   live action
Distributor: Cinema Shares
Producer: Harry Gulkin
Director: Theodore J. Flicker

Canada   1978   ages 6 up
Award: Gold Medal, Greater Miami International
    Film Festival

Six-year-old Jacob Two-Two has to say everything twice because he and other children are seldom noticed by adults. He dreams a wonderful fantasy about two young champions of "Child Power," who help him out when he is arrested for repeating himself. They slip Jacob a homing device by which they can trace him to the secret prison run by the dreaded Hooded Fang (played by Alex Karras), and in a climactic scene they help him free all the children. This funny, suspenseful film about grown-up tyranny is based on the children's book by Mordecai Richler.

LAFCADIO, THE LION WHO SHOT BACK

24 min.   16mm, ¾" U-Matic, ½" Beta, ½" VHS
    color   animation
Distributor: Learning Corporation of America
Producer/director: Larry Moyer
USA   1979   ages 6 up

LAFCADIO, THE LION WHO SHOT BACK

A lion becomes the world's greatest marksman, joins the circus, and grows famous, but in the process he loses his identity. Author Shel Silverstein narrates this humorous but thought-provoking fable with great wit and style, and his simple line drawings are full of character. This is one of those rare films that works equally well for viewers of different ages, because it can be enjoyed at many different levels.

THE LITTLE PRINCE

27 min.   16mm   color   animation
Distributor: Billy Budd
Producer/director: Will Vinton
USA   1979   all ages
Awards: Aspen Film Festival; Northwest International Film Festival; Jacksonville International Film Festival; Chicago International Film Festival

A clay-animated version of Antoine de Saint-Exupéry's classic allegory about a little boy who comes down from his tiny planet to spend a year on earth and learns the secret of happiness. The film, faithful to Saint-Exupéry's poetic prose, is narrated by Cliff Robertson, and the animation is extraordinary.

THE LITTLE PRINCE

LUKE WAS THERE

47 min. (full version), 32 min. (edited version)
   16mm, ¾" U-Matic, ½" Beta, ½" VHS
   color   live action
Distributor: Learning Corporation of America
Director: Richard Marquand
USA   1977   ages 6–11
Awards: Columbus Film Festival Chris Awards; Learning A/V Award, *Learning* Magazine; ALA Notable Film for Children

This warm and realistic film was shown on television as an "NBC Special Treat." It is based on the book of the same title by Eleanor Clymer, which won the Children's Book Award of the Child Study Association. Julius, a young boy who lives in New York City with his mother, must go to live in a children's shelter while his mother is in the hospital: At the shelter he is befriended by a perceptive black counselor named Luke. When Luke has to go away for a while, Julius is angry and gets in trouble, until Luke teaches him the meaning of trust. The acting is good, and the production values are excellent.

MADELINE

7 min.   16mm, ¾" U-Matic, ½" Beta, ½" VHS
   color   live action
Distributor: Learning Corporation of America
Filmmaker: Stephen Bosustow
USA   1969   ages 2–8

This entrancing story, told in rhyming verse, concerns the smallest and boldest of 12 girls at a boarding school in Paris. When Madeline has to have her appendix removed, the other girls are so impressed that they want theirs out too. Ludwig Bemelmans's Caldecott Medal winner translates beautifully to the screen.

MANDY'S GRANDMOTHER

30 min.   16mm, ¾" U-Matic, ½" Beta, ½" VHS
   color   live action
Distributor: Phoenix
Producer/director: Andrew Sugarman
USA   1978   ages 9–11

When Mandy's grandmother comes to visit from England, Mandy expects the kind of grandmother she has read about in books. For her part, Mandy's grandmother had not expected Mandy to be the kind of girl who prefers cowboy boots to a frilly dress. Based on Liesel Moak Skorpen's book, this is the story of how Mandy and her grandmother overcome their false expectations and learn to love each other as they really are. Maureen O'Sullivan gives a wonderful performance as the fastidious, beautifully dressed grand- mother who is willing to participate in Mandy's world, even to the extent of helping Mandy chase escaped chickens. This is a thoroughly enjoyable, well- produced film that is both humorous and affecting. It was presented on TV as a "Young People's Special." Available with captions for the hearing impaired.

MARTIN THE COBBLER

28 min.   16mm   color   animation
Distributor: Billy Budd
Producer: Frank Moynihan
Director: Will Vinton
USA   1978   ages 6 up
Awards: CINE Golden Eagle; Golden Image Grand
   Prize Statuette, Long Island International Film
   Festival; Council of Europe Award; Mayor's
   Chris Award, Columbus International Film Festi-
   val; Best in Show, Annual Motion Picture Semi-
   nar of the Northwest; Best in Show, Best in
   Category, Golden Gate International Film Festi-
   val; First Prize, Linz (Austria) Festival of Interna-
   tional Children's Films

An old Russian shoemaker who has lost his faith as a result of losing his family regains it by learning to care for others. Using wonderfully detailed clay anima- tion, the film is based on a Leo Tolstoy folktale, "Where Love Is, God Is." Alex- andra Tolstoy, Leo Tolstoy's daughter, narrates. This production is particularly nice for Christmastime programming.

MOON MAN

8 min.   16mm, ¾" U-Matic, ½" Beta, ½" VHS
   color   animation
Distributor: Weston Woods
Producer: Kratky Films
Director: Gene Deitch
Czechoslovakia   1981   ages 2–8

This fanciful, colorful film is based on the book of the same title, written and illus- trated by Tomi Ungerer. It concerns the man in the moon, who is bored with life in the sky. He catches a shooting star and rockets down to earth, only to be jailed as an invader. As the moon wanes, he shrinks and is able to slip between the bars of his cell. He runs off to frolic at a costume party, but when the police chase him he takes refuge with a scientist. Disillusioned with life on earth, the Moon Man returns to the moon in the scientist's rocket ship. Rhythmic blues music ac- companies the animation of Tomi Ungerer's delightful illustrations.

MOWGLI'S BROTHERS

26 min.   16mm, ¾" U-Matic, ½" Beta, ½" VHS
   color   animation
Distributor: Xerox
Producer/director: Chuck Jones
USA   1977   ages 6–11
Awards: CINE Golden Eagle; Bronze Plaque, Co-
   lumbus Film Festival Chris Awards

Rudyard Kipling's exciting tale of Mowgli, a boy brought up by wolves in the jungles of India, is interpreted here in vivid animation. The story concerns Mowgli's loyalty to an aging wolf and his bravery in fighting off a vicious tiger. This TV pro- duction is riveting and moves along at a fast pace, with well-developed characters. Voices are supplied by Roddy McDowall and June Foray.

NATE THE GREAT GOES UNDERCOVER

10 min.   16mm, ¾" U-Matic, ½" Beta, ½" VHS
   color   animation
Distributor: Churchill Films

Producers: Mitchell Seltzer Productions and Nick
　Bosustow
Director: Sam Weiss
USA　1978　ages 6–11
Awards: American Film Festival; Ruby Slipper, Los
　Angeles International Children's Film Festival

Young Nate takes on the case of the overturned garbage can, accompanied by his dog, Sludge. This is Nate's first night job, and after a dark and smelly stakeout, he finally captures what seems to be the culprit. Children enjoy the humor and the suspense of this imaginative mystery. They also get a kick out of seeing children (and animals) as the central characters. Based on the book by Marjorie Weinman Sharmat.

THE NOTORIOUS JUMPING FROG OF CALAVERAS COUNTY

24 min.　16mm, ¾″ U-Matic, ½″ Beta, ½″ VHS
　color　live action and animation
Distributor: Barr Films
Producer: Severo Pérez
Directors: Bill Davis and Dan Bessie
USA　1980　ages 9 up

Mark Twain recalls his first published story, about a jumping frog, in an interview with a reporter. The story itself is told in droll animation. It concerns a man who cannot turn down a bet and his frog, who has never lost a jumping contest—that is, until a stranger comes to town and plays a trick on them both. An entertaining tale, well served by this film version.

OLIVER!

146 min.　16mm　color　live action
Distributor: Twyman
Director: Sir Carol Reed
Great Britain　1968　ages 6 up
Awards: Five Academy Awards, including Best
　Picture and Best Director; two Golden Globe
　awards

A superbly entertaining musical version of Charles Dickens's *Oliver Twist*, adapted from Lionel Bart's play. The lavish sets and the energetic song-and-dance numbers are outstanding. So is Ron Moody as Fagin, and he just about steals the show. Mark Lester plays poor Oliver, the orphan who runs away, and Jack Wild is a terrific Artful Dodger.

ONE WAS JOHNNY

3 min.　16mm, ¾″ U-Matic, ½″ Beta, ½″ VHS
　color　animation
Distributor: Weston Woods
Producer: Sheldon Riss
Director: Maurice Sendak
USA　1978　ages 2–8

Rhyming verses sung by Carole King tell the counting tale of young Johnny, alone at first but gradually besieged by a growing houseful of unwanted company. Intrepid Johnny solves his problem in a most satisfying way. A pretty tune and a funny tale, based on the book by Maurice Sendak, and part of the film *Really Rosie* (see later in this section).

PADDINGTON BEAR

57 programs　16mm, ¾″ U-Matic, ½″ Beta,
　½″ VHS　color　animation
Distributors: Coe, FilmFair Communications
Producer: FilmFair Communications
Great Britain　ages 2–8

The delightful Paddington, a curious teddy bear from Darkest Peru, has become a classic character in children's literature. Paddington lives in London with his adopted human family, the Browns, and gets into various predicaments such as might befall a naive but well-intentioned bear. Younger children love his misadventures. This series of films, which has been presented on PBS, combines two- and three-dimensional animation. The films are faithful to the look and the spirit of the books by Michael Bond. The narration is by English actor Michael Hordean.

Series I—1977

Please Look After This Bear; A Bear in Hot Water; Paddington Goes Underground. 16½ min. Three episodes adapted from the first three chapters of *A Bear Called Paddington*.

A Shopping Expedition; Paddington and the "Old Master"; A Disappearing Trick. 16½ min. From chapters 4, 5, and 8 of *A Bear Called Paddington*.

A Family Group; A Spot of Decorating; Paddington Turns Detective. 16½ min. From chapters 1, 2, and 3 of the book *More about Paddington*.

Trouble at Number Thirty-Two; Paddington and the Christmas Shopping; Christmas. 16½ min. From chapters 5, 6, and 7 of *More about Paddington*.

Too Much Off the Top. 5½ min. From chapter 6 of the book *Paddington at Work*.

A Visit to the Dentist; Paddington Recommended. 11 min. From chapters 1 and 6 of *Paddington Takes the Air*.

Paddington and the "Cold Snap"; Paddington Makes a Clean Sweep; Mr. Gruber's Mystery Tour; An Unexpected Party. 22 min. From chapters 1, 3, 4, and 7 of *Paddington Marches On*.

Paddington Hits the Jackpot; A Sticky Time. 11 min. From chapters 4 and 5 of *Paddington at Large*.

Paddington Hits Out; A Visit to the Hospital. 11 min. From chapters 2 and 3 of *Paddington Goes to Town*.

Paddington Makes a Bid; Do-It-Yourself; Something Nasty in the Kitchen; Trouble at the Launderette. 22 min. From chapters 2, 3, 5, and 6 of *Paddington Helps Out*.

Paddington Cleans Up. 5½ min. From chapter 2 of *Paddington on Top*.

Mr. Curry Takes a Bath; Fortune Telling. 11 min. New Paddington episodes.

Series II—1980

Paddington in Court; Keeping Fit; Paddington in Touch; Comings and Goings at Number Thirty-Two. 21½ min. From chapters 3, 5, 6, and 7 of *Paddington on Top*.

Paddington Bakes a Cake; Paddington Clears the Coach; Paddington Weighs In. 16 min. From chapters 1, 3, and 6 of *Paddington Takes to TV*.

A Picnic on the River; Paddington Dines Out. 10 ¾ min. From chapters 1 and 7 of *Paddington Helps Out*.

Picture Trouble; Trouble on the Beach; A Visit to the Theatre. 16 min. From chapters 6 and 7 of *A Bear Called Paddington*.

Paddington Buys a Share; Paddington in a Hole. 11 min. From chapters 3 and 5 of *Paddington at Work*.

An Outing in the Park; Trouble in the Bargain Basement; Paddington Takes the Stage. 15 min. From chapters 2, 6, and 7 of *Paddington at Large*.

A Visit to the Bank. 22 min. From chapter 2 of *Paddington Abroad*.

Paddington's Patch. 22 min. From the book *Paddington's Patch*.

In and Out of Trouble. 22 min. From chapter 2 of *Paddington Takes the Test*.

Paddington at the Tower. 22 min. From the book *Paddington at the Tower*.

Paddington and the "Finishing Touch." 11 min. From chapter 5 of *Paddington Goes to Town*.

Paddington and the Mystery Box. 11 min. From *The Great Big Paddington Book*.

Paddington in the Hot Seat; Paddington's Puzzle; Paddington Takes a Snip. 16½ min. New Paddington episodes.

PADDLE TO THE SEA

28 min.   16mm, ¾" U-Matic, ½" Beta, ½" VHS
  color   live action
Distributor: National Film Board of Canada
Producer: Julian Biggs
Director: Bill Mason
Canada   1966   ages 6 up
Award: Salerno International Festival of Cinema for
  Children and Youth

This children's favorite is based on a story by Holling C. Holling. Paddle to the Sea is a toy canoe that an Indian boy whittles from a cedar log. He carves on it the words "I am Paddle to the Sea. Please put me back in the water," and starts it on its journey from the north shores of Lake Superior. Beautiful cinematography traces the canoe's adventures as it travels to the ocean.

PIERRE

6 min.   16mm, ¾" U-Matic, ½" Beta, ½" VHS
   color   animation
Distributor: Weston Woods
Producer: Sheldon Riss
Director: Maurice Sendak
USA   1978   ages 2–5

Pierre, a thoroughly rotten little boy who snarls "I don't care" to everyone and everything, changes his attitude after he has a run-in with a lion. Maurice Sendak's animated tale, from his children's book of the same title, is told in song by Carole King. An amusing story with a catchy tune. Part of *Really Rosie* (see later in this section).

PONIES OF MIKLAENGI

25 min.   16mm, ¾" U-Matic, ½" Beta, ½" VHS
   color   live action
Distributor: Phoenix
Producers: Daniel G. Smith and Gary Templeton
Director: Gary Templeton
Iceland   1979   ages 6–11

Shot on location in Iceland, this film's greatest asset is its breathtaking cinematography, with views of impressive waterfalls and glaciers. The slow-paced story, based on the book by Lonzo Anderson, concerns young Gumi and his sister Annie. The two children set out on horseback to look for three lost sheep, but they must go slowly because Annie's horse is about to foal. Then they get trapped in an earthquake, and the horse foals prematurely. The slim plot is needlessly drawn out, but the animals capture children's attention, and the exotic, rugged setting is appealing.

THE RANSOM OF RED CHIEF

27 min.   16mm, ¾" U-Matic, ½" Beta, ½" VHS
   color   live action
Distributor: Learning Corporation of America
Producer: Marian Rosenberg
Director: Tony Bill
USA   1978   ages 9 up
Awards: CINE Golden Eagle; ALA Selected Film for Young Adults; Columbus Film Festival Chris Awards

Based on the famous O. Henry short story of the same title, this amusing film is set in the 1920s. Two shabby and rather incompetent con men think that their fortune is made when they kidnap the son of a wealthy family. But they soon find Johnny (alias "Red Chief, Terror of the Plains") more trouble than he is worth and realize with dismay that Johnny's family thinks so, too. This production was a popular "ABC Weekend Special."

REALLY ROSIE

26 min.   16mm, ¾" U-Matic, ½" Beta, ½" VHS
   color   animation
Distributor: Weston Woods
Producer: Sheldon Riss
Director: Maurice Sendak
USA   1976   ages 2–8
Awards: Blue Ribbon, American Film Festival; CINE Golden Eagle; Gold Venus Medallion, Virgin Islands International Film Festival; ALA Notable Film; Learning A/V Award, *Learning* Magazine

Rosie, self-proclaimed star of the neighborhood, auditions her tenement-dwelling friends for a movie about her life. First presented on CBS, this film incorporates characters from five of Maurice Sendak's books. The lilting, pleasant music was composed and sung by Carole King. Fine entertainment, although some younger children find it a little long. Four of the segments in the film are available as separate films: *Alligators All Around, Chicken Soup with Rice, One Was Johnny,* and *Pierre* (see earlier in this section).

RIKKI-TIKKI-TAVI

26 min.   16mm, ¾" U-Matic, ½" Beta, ½" VHS
  color   animation
Distributor: Xerox
Producer/director: Chuck Jones
USA   1976   ages 6–11
Awards: President's Award, Columbus Film Festival
  Chris Awards; CINE Golden Eagle; Silver Hugo,
  Chicago International Film Festival

A mongoose saves a British family from two terrible cobras in this thrilling tale by Rudyard Kipling. The animation (by Chuck Jones, responsible for such TV characters as Wile E. Coyote and Tom and Jerry) is slick, colorful, and well suited to this kind of storytelling. Orson Welles narrates.

RODEO RED AND THE RUNAWAY

46 min. (full version), 33 min. (edited version)
  16mm, ¾" U-Matic, ½" Beta, ½" VHS
  color   live action
Distributor: Learning Corporation of America
Producer: Doro Bachrach
Director: Bert Salsman
USA   1979   ages 6 up
Awards: Emmy Award; Christopher Award; Mental
  Health Film Festival

This sensitive, well-acted "NBC Special Treat" was adapted from Marion Dane Bauer's novel *Shelter from the Wind*. Shot on location in Montana, the story concerns Stacey, a young girl who cannot accept her new stepmother and runs away from home. She takes refuge with a prairie woman named Ella (beautifully portrayed by Geraldine Fitzgerald) and becomes attached to Ella's old rodeo horse, Big Red. When Big Red becomes ill and must be shot, Stacey learns about compassion and responsibility from Ella and finally returns home.

ROLL OF THUNDER, HEAR MY CRY

110 min.   16mm, ¾" U-Matic, ½" Beta, ½" VHS
  color   live action
Distributor: Learning Corporation of America
Director: Jack Smight
USA   1977   ages 9 up

A powerfully affecting story about a black family's struggle to hold on to the land they have owned for three generations. Set in the impoverished and racist Mississippi of the 1930s, the film is based on episodes from Mildred D. Taylor's Newbery Medal–winning book. The performances are outstanding, and authentic settings and dialogue help to make this an exceptional experience.

ROOKIE OF THE YEAR

47 min.   16mm, ¾" U-Matic, ½" Beta II, ½" VHS
  color   live action
Distributor: Time-Life Video
Producer: Daniel Wilson
Director: Larry Elikann
USA   1975   ages 9 up
Awards: Blue Ribbon, American Film Festival;
  Emmy, Outstanding Children's Entertainment;
  Christopher Award; Gold Plaque, Chicago International Film Festival; Ohio State Award; Learning A/V Award, *Learning* Magazine

Sports-loving 11-year-old Sharon Lee (well played by Jodie Foster) triggers a controversy among players, parents, and game officials when she wins a place on her brother's all-boy baseball team. The coach and her parents are supportive, but Sharon's brother and friends shun her and other parents furiously pull their sons off the team. Sharon saves the day and wins the final game, of course, and the audience along with the team will cheer for her. From the book *Not Bad for a Girl* by Isabella Taves; presented as an "ABC Afterschool Special."

THE SEVEN WISHES OF JOANNA PEABODY

27 min.   16mm, ¾" U-Matic, ½" Beta, ½" VHS
  color   live action
Distributor: Learning Corporation of America
Producer: Doro Bachrach
Director: Stephen Foreman
USA   1980   ages 6 up
Award: National Educational Film Festival

Spunky young Joanna turns on TV one day and miraculously meets a lively video-age

ROOKIE OF THE YEAR

fairy godmother (played by Butterfly McQueen), who offers her seven wishes. This upbeat modern fairy tale is realistic and humorous, and it draws an authentic portrait of urban ghetto life. Excellent production values enhance an entertaining story. Based on the book by Genevieve Gray, this program was shown on television as an "ABC Afterschool Special."

SILVER BLAZE

31 min.   16mm, ¾" U-Matic, ½" Beta, ½" VHS
   color   live action
Distributor: Learning Corporation of America
Producer: William Deneen
Director: Jon Davies
Great Britain   1977   ages 9 up

A famous racehorse is stolen and his manager murdered, but have no fear: Sherlock Holmes (played by Christopher Plummer) is hot on the trail. This is one of Sir Arthur Conan Doyle's most famous tales, and it is authentically filmed in the English countryside. Suspenseful music and excellent cinematography contribute to an exciting adventure. Part of Learning

Corporation of America's "Classics Dark and Dangerous" series; a teacher's manual and guide, as well as the story and the script, are available.

SMILE FOR AUNTIE

5 min.   16mm, ¾" U-Matic, ½" Beta, ½" VHS
   color   animation
Distributor: Weston Woods
Producer: Morton Schindel
Director: Gene Deitch
USA   1979   ages 6 up

A delightful adaptation of Diane Paterson's picture book. Auntie waddles over to baby and tries every trick in the book to elicit a grin, but only when Auntie declares in frustration that she will go away and never come back does baby at last respond. Younger children may not understand baby's rejection of ice cream and other appealing bribes, but older children appreciate the irony.

SNOWBOUND

50 min. (full version), 32 min. (edited version)
   color   live action
Distributor: Learning Corporation of America

Producer: Linda Gottlieb
Director: Andrew Young
USA   1978   ages 12 up
Awards: American Film Festival; Birmingham International Educational Film Festival; Columbus Film Festival Chris Awards; ALA Selected Film for Young Adults

After an argument with his girlfriend, Tony, the high school heartthrob, insists on giving a lift to plain, unpopular Cindy during a storm that develops into a terrible blizzard. The car breaks down in a wilderness area and the ill-matched pair confronts all sorts of dangers in the struggle for survival. In the process, they learn more about life and about each other. Good performances, excellent cinematography, and authentic settings save this gripping adventure story from becoming too melodramatic. Shown as part of the "NBC Special Treat" series, the film is based on Harry Mazer's book of the same title.

THE SNOWY DAY

6 min.   16mm, ¾" U-Matic, ½" Beta, ½" VHS
   color   animation
Distributor: Weston Woods
Producer: Morton Schindel
Director: Mal Wittman
USA   1964   ages 2–5

Based on the Caldecott Award—winning book by Ezra Jack Keats, this is the quiet, gentle tale of a little black boy joyfully playing in the snow. Cel animation depicts Peter's frolics, with the accompaniment of classical guitar music. This is a favorite film of young children. Available in Spanish, Swedish, Turkish, and captioned versions. See also *Whistle for Willie* (later in this section) for another film about Peter.

THE STREET

10 min.   16mm, ¾" U-Matic, ½" Beta, ½" VHS
   color   animation
Distributors: Coe, National Film Board of Canada
Producers: Guy Glover and Wolf Koenig
Director: Caroline Leaf

Canada   1976   ages 12 up
Awards: Blue Ribbon, American Film Festival; Gold Hugo, Chicago International Film Festival; Grand Prix, International Animation Festival, Ottawa; Etrog, Canadian Film Awards; "Outstanding Achievement" Certificate, San Francisco International Film Festival

Caroline Leaf's animation perfectly illustrates this selection from Mordecai Richler's novel of the same name. Leaf's technique involves tempera and oils on glass, and the flowing lines and washes that result give the film the feeling of a dream. The story concerns the death of a grandmother and how it affects the different members of a family, as seen from the viewpoint of a young boy. It is also a nostalgic recollection of childhood in the Jewish neighborhood of Montreal in the late 1940s, and a thought-provoking, exquisitely rendered work.

SUMMER OF MY GERMAN SOLDIER

98 min.   16mm, ¾" U-Matic, ½" Beta, ½" VHS
   color   live action
Distributor: Learning Corporation of America
Producer: Linda Gottlieb

SUMMER OF MY GERMAN SOLDIER

Director: Michael Tuchner
USA   1978   ages 12 up

An engrossing and powerful drama based on the novel by Bette Greene. The setting is a small southern town during World War II, and the story concerns the ill-fated friendship between a lonely Jewish girl and an escaped German prisoner of war. The performances by Kristy McNichol, Bruce Davison, and Esther Rolle are superb. A teacher's guide is available.

SUPERLATIVE HORSE

36 min.   16mm, ¾" U-Matic, ½" Beta, ½" VHS
   color   live action
Distributor: Phoenix
Producers: Urs Furrer and Yanna Brandt
Director: Yanna Brandt
USA   1975   ages 9–15
Award: American Film Festival

This excellent adaptation of Jean Merrill's story has great appeal for children. In ancient China, a powerful ruler assigns an important task to Han Kan, an aspiring young groom. He must find a "superlative horse" as a test of his ability to judge horses. Han Kan's choice is unusual but exactly right, proving that inner qualities can be more important than outward appearances.

THE THREE ROBBERS

6 min.   16mm, ¾" U-Matic, ½" Beta, ½" VHS
   color   animation
Distributor: Weston Woods
Producer: Morton Schindel
Director: Gene Deitch
Czechoslovakia   1972   ages 2–8
Awards: Emily Award and Blue Ribbon, American Film Festival; Bronze Medal, Atlanta International Film Festival; Bronze Award, International Film & TV Festival of New York; Jack London Award, National Educational Film Festival

"Once upon a time there were three fierce robbers. They went about hidden under large black capes and tall black hats. . . ." So begins this pleasurably scary story by Tomi Ungerer. The three bad guys plunder the countryside until they capture a stagecoach containing a little orphan girl named Tiffany. Tiffany convinces the robbers to use their gold to do good, and they turn to running an orphanage in an old castle. Bold visuals and unusual sound effects, done with voices, help make this film a big hit with younger children. Available in Danish, Dutch, French, German, and Swedish.

THE UGLY LITTLE BOY

26 min.   16mm, ¾" U-Matic, ½" Beta, ½" VHS
   color   live action
Distributor: Learning Corporation of America
Producer: William Deneen
Directors: Barry Morse and Don Thompson
USA   1977   ages 9 up
Awards: Science-Fiction Film Festival; Chicago International Film Festival; Gabriel Award; ALA Notable Film for Children and Young Adults

An eerie, effective, and affecting science fiction film, based on a story by Isaac Asimov. A Neanderthal boy is transported into the present time as an experimental subject. Kate Reid plays the nurse in charge of the boy. She is told to remain completely detached. Instead, a bond forms between the two, and she makes a climactic decision when the scientists prepare to send the boy back in time. The high quality of the production and the controversial issue of science versus morality make this film appealing to non–science fiction fans as well as to Asimov admirers. Part of Learning Corporation of America's "Classics Dark and Dangerous" series; a teacher's manual and guide are available, as well as the story and the script.

VERY GOOD FRIENDS

29 min.   16mm, ¾" U-Matic, ½" Beta, ½" VHS
   color   live action
Distributor: Learning Corporation of America
Producer: Martin Tahse
Director: Richard Bennett
USA   1977   ages 9 up

Awards: Chicago International Film Festival; Learning A/V Award, *Learning* Magazine; Gabriel Award

Based on the novel *Beat the Turtle Drum* by Constance Greene, this is the story of the close relationship between 13-year-old Kate and her 11-year-old sister, Joss. Flashback sequences focus on the week of Joss's eleventh birthday, when she excitedly rents a horse, and on Joss's sudden death in a fall from a tree shortly afterward. This touching "ABC After-school Special" deals skillfully with the difficult topic of death.

WHERE THE WILD THINGS ARE

8 min.   16mm, ¾" U-Matic, ½" Beta, ½" VHS
   color   animation
Distributor: Weston Woods
Producer: Morton Schindel
Director: Gene Deitch
Czechoslovakia   1973   ages 2–8
Awards: CINE Golden Eagle; Bronze Plaque, Virgin Islands International Film Festival

WHERE THE WILD THINGS ARE

Based on Maurice Sendak's well-known Caldecott Medal–winning book, this is the delightful story of mischievous Max. Sent to his room for misbehaving, Max sails off in his imagination to a land of bizarre monsters. He tames them and becomes their king, then grows hungry and tired and returns to the security of home. This fantasy of power over the dread Wild Things really appeals to children, as does the film's elaborate soundtrack, with its many unusual effects. Available in Dutch, French, German, and Spanish.

WHISTLE FOR WILLIE

6 min.   16mm, ¾" U-Matic, ½" Beta, ½" VHS
   color   animation
Distributor: Weston Woods
Producer: Morton Schindel
Director: Mal Wittman
USA   1965   ages 2–5

Based on the American Library Association Notable Book by Ezra Jack Keats, this is one in a series of stories about a young black boy named Peter. The plot concerns Peter's attempt to learn how to whistle for his dachshund, Willie, the way the older boys do. Simple cutout animation is the technique used. Young children enjoy the story and are often moved to whistle, too. Available in Danish, Dutch, Spanish, and Swedish. See *The Snowy Day* (earlier in this section) for another film about Keats's character Peter.

THE WHITE HERON

26 min.   16mm, ¾" U-Matic, ½" Beta, ½" VHS
   color   live action
Distributor: Learning Corporation of America
Filmmaker: Jane Morrison
USA   1978   ages 9 up
Award: Columbus Film Festival Chris Awards

Sylvy, a shy young girl, lives alone with her grandmother in the Maine woods in 1896. When a handsome young hunter asks her to help him find a rare white heron, Sylvy is torn between her desire to please him and her love for the wild birds he kills. This is a slow-moving, beautifully filmed production that captures the rhythms of nature and the spirit of another time and place. Adapted from the short story of the same title by Sarah Orne Jewett.

Poetry

CASEY AT THE BAT

9 min.   16mm   color   animation
Distributor: Walt Disney
USA   1971   ages 2–11

The poetic saga of Casey, the batting star of the Mudville Nine, in an entertaining animated musical version. E. L. Thayer's poem first appeared in 1888 and has been popular ever since. Disney's interpretation is lively and funny.

THE CAT IN THE HAT

24 min.   16mm, ¾" U-Matic, ½" Beta, ½" VHS
   color   animation
Distributor: BFA
Producer: DePatie-Freleng Productions
USA   1973   ages 2–11

A talking cat with a top hat wreaks hilarious havoc when he visits a brother and sister one rainy afternoon while their mother is out. Based on Dr. Seuss's delightful book, this CBS presentation features the infamous cat singing some of Seuss's marvelous rhymes. Available in a captioned version.

THE CREATION

9 min.   16mm   color   animation
Distributor: Billy Budd
Producer/director: Will Vinton
USA   1981   all ages

"The Creation" was written by James Weldon Johnson in 1919, and like the other pieces in his collection called *God's Trombones*, it is in the tradition of black spirituals and old-time preachers. This powerful poem tells the story of how God created the earth, the animals, and humans, and the deep, rich voice of James Earl Jones as the narrator suits the poem's dramatic style perfectly. Visually, this is a unique film, executed in a "clay painting" technique by Joan Gratz. Strongly colored images flow into each other unceasingly to the pulsing rhythm of jazz music, and the effect is mesmerizing. The problems inherent in translating "and God created man in His own image" are handled neatly by depicting an array of faces of both sexes and all races.

HAILSTONES AND HALIBUT BONES (PARTS I and II)

Part I: 6 min., Part II: 7 min.   16mm, ¾" U-Matic,
   ½" Beta, ½" VHS   color   animation
Distributors: Coe, Sterling
USA   1964   ages 2–8

Two Mary O'Neill poems (one per film) about colors are narrated by Celeste Holm and illustrated with appropriate, often funny, drawings by Robert Curtis. Percussion music in the background augments these lively, lovely explorations of how colors can convey feelings.

IN A SPRING GARDEN

6 min.   16mm, ¾" U-Matic, ½" Beta, ½" VHS
   color   animation
Distributor: Weston Woods
Producer/director: Morton Schindel
USA   1967   all ages

Ezra Jack Keats's beautiful illustrations, animated iconographically, complement the delicate mood of Japanese haiku poetry read by Richard Lewis. The verses follow the progress of a spring day in a garden from early dawn through dusk. There is no plot, just evocative images of animals going about their activities in the course of a day. Classical music in the background adds to the peaceful feeling created by the words and the artwork. This film can be appreciated by any age level, but it is especially nice for preschoolers.

THE OWL AND THE PUSSYCAT and LITTLE BIRDS

8 min.   16mm, ¾" U-Matic, ½" Beta, ½" VHS
   color   animation
Distributor: Texture
Filmmaker: Deborah Healy
USA   1980   ages 2–8

Two films that tickle the funnybone. Edward Lear's nonsense rhyme "The Owl and the Pussycat" is interpreted in pretty *Yellow Submarine*–influenced animation by Deborah Healy. The images and the music match the lighthearted mood of the verses, but the narration is less inspired. "Little Birds," from *Sylvie and Bruno* by Lewis Carroll, is more successful. The same imaginative animation, involving metamorphoses, is accompanied by classical harpsichord music and a more spirited recital of the poem.

POETRY FOR FUN: DARES AND DREAMS

13 min.   16mm, ¾" U-Matic, ½" Beta, ½" VHS
   color   live action and animation
Distributor: Centron
Producer: Centron Corporation
USA   1974   ages 6–11

This outstanding production imaginatively presents six poems selected by over 100 fourth, fifth, and sixth graders as their favorites. Each poem is read and depicted in a style suiting its theme. "Pirate Don Dirk of Dowdee" is particularly good, a funny, rollicking poem narrated in a London dockyard accent with colorful cutout animation.

POETRY FOR FUN: POEMS ABOUT ANIMALS

13 min.   16mm, ¾" U-Matic, ½" Beta, ½" VHS
   color   live action and animation
Distributor: Centron
Producer: Centron Corporation
USA   1972   ages 6–11
Award: Certificate of Excellence, U.S. Industrial
   Film Festival

The eight poems included here alternate between animated and live-action presentations. The best is Ogden Nash's "An Introduction to Dogs," which shows dogs doing all the things they delight in and humans hate. The other poems are less successful, but children always seem to enjoy seeing animals.

POETRY FOR FUN: TROOLIER COOLIER

11 min.   16mm, ¾" U-Matic, ½" Beta, ½" VHS
   color   live action and animation
Distributor: Centron
Producer: Centron Corporation
USA   1978   ages 6–11
Award: Bronze Plaque, Columbus Film Festival
   Chris Awards

This is the best of the three *Poetry for Fun* films (see previous two entries). It offers a child's view of the world in its eight humorous poems, which were chosen by children. Three are by the hilarious Shel Silverstein, but perhaps the most enjoyable is Zilpha K. Snyder's "Poem to Mud," which features children rolling in the stuff to their hearts' content.

POETRY FOR PEOPLE WHO HATE POETRY WITH ROGER STEFFENS

3 films   16mm, ¾" U-Matic, ½" Beta, ½" VHS
   color   live action
Distributor: Churchill Films
Producer: Steffens/Shedd Poetry Films
Director: Ben A. Shedd
USA   1979   ages 12 up

Roger Steffens, a lecturer, performer, and poet, communicates his enthusiasm for poetry in these three presentations. Steffens's dramatic readings, his expressive gestures, and his infectious love for his material, augmented by lively anecdotes and personal commentary, compensate for the bare-bones look of these productions. Steffens is shown alone on a bare stage, but he manages nevertheless to hold viewers' attention by sheer force of personality. His performances might make even confirmed poetry-hating students think twice about poetry.

About Words. 16 min. Steffens examines the way in which contemporary poets use language to create surprise and to express emotions.

e. e. cummings. 17 min. A look at the range of e. e. cummings's work and at its unusual structure. Steffens emphasizes the emotional, spiritual side of the master poet.

Shakespeare. 12 min. By acting out some of the characters in *Julius Caesar* in a contemporary style, Steffens communicates a sense of the timeless, universal quality of Shakespeare.

THE RAVEN

11 min.   16mm, ¾" U-Matic, ½" Beta, ½" VHS
   color   animation
Distributor: Texture
Filmmaker: Lewis Jacobs
Awards: Silver Medallion, Durban (South Africa)
   International Film Festival; Bronze Plaque, Sa-
   lerno (Italy) International Festival of Cinema for
   Children and Youth; Award of Merit, Photo-
   graphic Society of America

A dramatic rendition of Edgar Allan Poe's classic poem. Actor Gregg Morton gives an outstanding reading over music by Ravel. The visuals, engravings of Gustave Doré, which are animated iconographically and highlighted with color, match the somber, nightmarish mood.

ROBERT FROST'S NEW ENGLAND

22 min.   16mm, ¾" U-Matic, ½" Beta, ½" VHS
   color   live action
Distributor: Churchill Films
Filmmaker: Dewitt Jones
USA   1976   ages 12 up
Award: Columbus Film Festival Chris Awards

Splendid photography of the beautiful New England landscape illustrates a selection of Frost's poetry. Unseen narrators discuss Frost and his work briefly and read his poems aloud clearly and sensitively.

Background guitar music contributes to create a lovely, if somewhat slow-paced, experience.

SEA DREAM

6 min.   16mm, ¾" U-Matic, ½" Beta, ½" VHS
   color   animation
Distributors: Coe, Phoenix
Producer: Kathleen Shannon
Director: Ellen Besen
Canada   1979   ages 2–8
Awards: Blue Ribbon, American Film Festival;
   Ottawa International Animated Film Festival

A little girl who has had a bad day falls asleep and dreams a wonderful, watery fantasy. She dives down into the ocean and has a tea party with a charming octopus. They dance together to the music of fish and starfish, play cards and baseball, and in general have a terrific time before the little girl rises up to her bed and the real world again. This film is based on a poem by Debora Bojman. The words conjure up a world of gentle nonsense, and the fanciful animation matches the feeling.

TALES OF HIAWATHA

19 min.   16mm, ¾" U-Matic, ½" Beta, ½" VHS
   color   animation
Distributor: Sterling
Producer: Filmpolski
Poland   1968   ages 6–11

Henry Wadsworth Longfellow's famous epic poem is performed by beautifully handled puppets. Narration alternates with sections of the poem to relate the exploits of the American Indian hero Hiawatha, who was sent as a prophet to bring prosperity and peace to his people. The puppets, by Waclaw Kondek, are amazingly detailed and move realistically.

WYNKEN, BLYNKEN AND NOD

4 min.   16mm, ¾" U-Matic, ½" Beta, ½" VHS
   color   animation
Distributor: Weston Woods

Producer/director: Morton Schindel
USA   1971   ages 2–5

Three children sail off in a wooden shoe to find adventures in the night sky. Based on Eugene Field's well-known poem, this is a lovely lullaby for younger children. The iconographic animation uses illustrations by Barbara Cooney, and soft piano music contributes to the gentle mood.

Fairy Tales, Folktales, Legends, and Myths

ANANSI THE SPIDER

10 min.   16mm, ¾" U-Matic, ½" Beta, ½" VHS
   color   animation
Distributors: Coe, Texture
Filmmaker: Gerald McDermott
USA   1969   ages 6 up
Awards: CINE Golden Eagle; Blue Ribbon, American Film Festival; White House Conference on Children; Tehran Film Festival; Edinburgh Film Festival; Venice Film Festival; Exceptional Merit, Philadelphia Film Festival

Beautiful, bold, colorful animation with an abstract African look is the real star of this story about the cunning folk hero of the Ashanti people of Ghana. Anansi the Spider has six sons who keep busy rescu-ing their father from trouble. When Anansi finds a silver globe of light, he cannot decide which son is most deserving of the prize. Nyame, the Ashanti God, helps him by placing the globe in the sky for all to share; it is the moon. Gerald McDermott's Caldecott Honor book, *Anansi the Spider*, is also available through Texture. See *A Story, A Story* later in this section for another tale about Anansi.

ARROW TO THE SUN

12 min.   16mm, ¾" U-Matic, ½" Beta, ½" VHS
   color   animation
Distributors: Coe, Texture

ARROW TO THE SUN

Filmmaker: Gerald McDermott
USA   1973   ages 6 up
Awards: CINE Golden Eagle; First Prize, Birmingham International Educational Film Festival; National Educational Film Festival; Berlin Film Festival; Zagreb (Yugoslavia) Festival of World Animation; Silver Mermaid, Fairytale Film Festival; American Film Festival

This tale from the Acoma Pueblo Indians of the southwestern United States is exquisitely visualized. A young boy goes on a fantastic voyage in search of his father, and the images essentially tell the story, since the narration is minimal. The striking animation is based on the designs and colors of Pueblo art. Gerald McDermott's Caldecott Medal book, *Arrow to the Sun,* is also available through Texture.

AUCASSIN AND NICOLETTE

16 min.   16mm, ¾" U-Matic, ½" Beta, ½" VHS
   color   animation
Distributor: National Film Board of Canada
Director: Lotte Reiniger
Producers: Guy Glover and Wolf Koenig
Canada   1975   ages 6–11

An exquisite animated version of a medieval French *chantefable,* or ballad. German animator Lotte Reiniger uses wonderfully detailed black cutout silhouettes against strongly colored backgrounds to tell the tale of two lovers who are separated and must overcome formidable obstacles to find each other and finally marry. Nicolette, an orphan girl, emerges as the heroine. Disguised as a minstrel, she is the one who sets out to find her pining, handsome prince. Renaissance music by Canada's Huggett family matches the story's mood. A French version, *Aucassin et Nicolette,* is available from the International Film Bureau.

THE BEAR AND THE MOUSE

8 min.   16mm, ¾" U-Matic, ½" Beta, ½" VHS
   color   live action
Distributors: Coe, National Film Board of Canada
Producer: Nicholas Balla

Director: Michael Rubbo
Canada   1966   ages 2–8

This variation of Aesop's famous fable of the lion and the mouse takes place in colonial America and features real animals. The bear catches and then frees a mouse, who later helps the bear escape from a trap. The use of live creatures with human voices makes this tale exceptionally appealing to younger children.

BEAUTY AND THE BEAST

19 min.   16mm, ¾" U-Matic, ½" Beta, ½" VHS
   color   animation
Distributor: Coronet
Producer: Gakken Film
Japan   1978   ages 6–11

De Beaumont's classic tale about a young girl's love for a handsome prince who is under an evil spell is beautifully enacted by detailed puppets. The quality of the voice-over narration is not up to the high standard of the animation, sets, and costumes, but nevertheless this is an enchanting romance for young viewers.

THE BIG BANG AND OTHER CREATION MYTHS

11 min.   16mm, ¾" U-Matic, ½" Beta, ½" VHS
   color   animation
Distributor: Pyramid
Filmmaker: Faith Hubley
USA   1981   ages 9 up

Creation myths from around the world are interpreted in appealing animation, with original music by Elizabeth Swados. The film begins by depicting scientific theory (the "big bang") about the origins of the universe, and then presents African, Finnish, Chinese, native American, Australian, and Indian myths. Both the visuals and the music for each myth are done in a style influenced by the culture of the land where the myth originated. Minimal narration and the rather abstract style of the animation make this lovely film more appropriate for older children.

THE BIG BANG AND OTHER CREATION MYTHS

THE BIRD, THE FOX AND THE FULL MOON

11 min.   16mm, ¾″ U-Matic, ½″ Beta, ½″ VHS
  color   animation
Distributor: Texture
Producer/director: Eduardo Darino
USA   1976   ages 6–11

A creatively animated South American folktale enhanced by guitar and percussion music, as well as sound effects. A lazy fox persuades a hard-working bird to farm his land, expecting that he will get to keep the best crops for himself. Each spring, the fox proposes a different scheme for dividing the harvest, and each fall he finds himself outwitted by the bird and left to howl in frustration at the moon. Available in Spanish as well, as *El hornero, el zorro, y la luna llena.*

BREMEN TOWN MUSICIANS

16 min.   16mm, ¾″ U-Matic   color   animation
Distributors: Coe, Films Inc.

Filmmaker: Institut für Film und Bild
West Germany   1972   ages 6–8

This funny folktale features appealing puppets. Donkey, Dog, Cat, and Rooster are getting too old to be useful to their masters, so they run away to become famous musicians in the town of Bremen. Along the way they run into a trio of robbers and succeed in tricking them into giving up their food. Encouraged by their success, the animals give up their musical ambitions and settle down to live happily ever after. For a similar production, see *The Shoemaker and the Elves*, later in this section.

CLEVER HIKO-ICHI (A JAPANESE TALE)

12 min.   16mm, ¾″ U-Matic   color   animation
Distributor: Coronet
Producer: Gakken Film
Japan   1974   ages 2–8

This enchanting folktale from medieval Japan is told with animated wooden puppets. It concerns a young boy, Hiko-Ichi, who comes to the rescue when a giant threatens his country, using scientific principles to overcome the enemy and save the kingdom. Children enjoy seeing other children in heroic roles, and Hiko-Ichi is a true hero, both clever and brave. What is more, he solves his problems without resorting to violence.

COWHERD MARKO

10 min.   16mm, ¾" U-Matic, ½" Beta, ½" VHS
   color   animation
Distributor: International Film Bureau
Producer: Zagreb Film
Directors: Aleksandar Marks and Neven Petričić
Yugoslavia   1978   ages 6–8

Done in lovely cel animation, this Eastern European folktale concerns a little cowherd who runs away from his home and his mean stepmother. After many adventures involving satyrs, dragons, and false friends, he wins a treasure and the hand of a beautiful princess.

THE FISHERMAN AND HIS WIFE

20 min.   16mm, ¾" U-Matic, ½" Beta, ½" VHS
   color   animation
Distributor: Weston Woods
Producer: Minimal Produkter, Stockholm
Sweden   1978   ages 6–8

In this stylized adaptation of a Grimm fairy tale, cutout animation is used to tell the story of a poor fisherman who catches a magic fish. The fisherman's greedy wife makes the fisherman ask increasingly outrageous wishes of the fish, until she demands to be made ruler of the universe and the fish puts her in her place—back where she started from. The effective use of music, sound effects, and strong colors in this somewhat long version of the tale helps keep children's interest.

THE FOLK BOOK

15 programs, 20 min. each   ¾" U-Matic, ½" Beta,
   ½" VHS   color   live action and animation

Distributor: Agency for Instructional Television
Producer: Eileen Littig, NEWIST, University of Wisconsin at Green Bay, in association with AIT
USA   1980   ages 6–8
Awards: Central Educational Network Award for Excellence in Elementary Programming; Silver Medal, International Film & TV Festival of New York; Special Merit Award, 1979 Athens (Ohio) Video Festival

This lively series of programs on ethnic folklore was designed to promote interracial, intercultural, and interethnic understanding among young children. Each program is organized around a universal theme, and the program segments illustrate this theme as it has been interpreted in different cultures. Legends, myths, fables, and fairy tales from around the world are presented in a variety of forms; dance, drama, puppets, and animation are employed as well as storytelling. A 56-page teacher's guide providing program summaries, cultural notes, and bibliographies and suggesting classroom activities is available.

Hodge Podge: a potpourri of the oral tradition
   Children's Games, Riddles and Jokes. Claudia Schmidt sings "The Unicorn" and "Ode to Joy."
   Ote. A Puerto Rican folktale performed by Robin Reed Puppets and storyteller Pura Belpre.

Stories of Stories: stories about the origins of storytelling
   How Anansi the Spider Stole the Sky God's Stories. A tale from the Ashanti tribe of Ghana, West Africa, done in creative improvisation by students of the Urban Day School, Milwaukee.
   Feather Toes. A Seneca Indian story told by native American storyteller Ernie Stevens.

In the Beginning: stories explaining how the world began
   The Earth Is on a Fish's Back. A poem by Natalia Belting, performed by The Other Theatre, Chicago.

P'an Ku. A Chinese creation story told with animated tangrams.

In the Beginning. A tale from the Australian aborigines, performed by the Powderhorn Puppets, Minneapolis.

Serpent of Eternity. A fable from Benin, West Africa, danced by the Ko-Thi Dance Company, Milwaukee.

How and Why: stories that explain natural phenomena

The Sun Man. Storyteller Linda Goss of Philadelphia narrates this tale from the Bushmen of South-West Africa's Kalahari Desert.

The Sun and Moon. A Netsilik Eskimo legend, performed by The Other Theatre, Chicago.

The First Zebra. Children at the Museum of African Art, Washington, D.C., interpret this folktale from Malawi, South West Africa, in dramatic improvisation.

Why Men Have to Work. An Afro-American story performed by the Mixed Blood Theatre, Minneapolis.

Whirlwind Is a Ghost Dancing. Four short native American explanations of natural occurrences, dramatized by The Other Theatre, Chicago, and interpreted in illustrations by Leo Dillon and Diane Dillon.

How and Why—II

How the Snake Lost His Voice. Chicago storyteller Bill Holmes tells this Japanese folktale.

The Bear Dance. A legend from the Mountain Indians, performed by the Echo Hawk Theatre, Oneida.

Trickster Tales: stories of sly pranksters

Señor Coyote and the Tricked Trickster. A Mexican folktale done in animation.

Brer Rabbit and the Tar Baby. A story from the black American South, enacted by students of the Prairie School, Racine.

The Trial of the Stone. Actors from Madison, Wisconsin's Oriental Theatre perform this Burmese Shan tale.

Award: NAEB Graphic Design Award

Learning to Be: stories that have morals

The Monkey and the Crocodile. A Jataka tale from India dramatized by The Other Theatre, Chicago.

It Couldn't Be Worse. An Eastern European Jewish folktale, interpreted by The Other Theatre, Chicago.

Deep Down in the Jungle. An urban folktale from Philadelphia, told by storyteller Linda Goss of Philadelphia.

Learning to Be in East Africa: more stories with morals

Arap Sang and the Cranes. Children at the Museum of African Art, Washington, D.C., wear masks and act out this story from the Lake Nyanza region.

Digging for Water. An East African legend narrated by storyteller Linda Goss of Philadelphia.

The Fire on the Mountain. An Ethiopian story performed by the Mixed Blood Theatre of Minneapolis.

Monsters and Magic: supernatural tales

Baba Yaga. The Makaroff Dance Company of Appleton, Wisconsin, performs this Russian folktale.

Wicked John and the Devil. An Appalachian story, done by The Chimera Theatre, St. Paul.

Wonderful Womenfolk: stories about clever women

Scheherazade. A famous story from the Middle East, illustrated with Persian miniatures from the collection of the Art Institute of Chicago.

Three Strong Women. A Japanese legend, told with puppets by Doug Lieberman of Chicago.

Just for Fun: stories to enjoy

Juan Bobo and the Caldron. A Puerto Rican tale, performed by members of Arts Development, University of Wisconsin Extension—Milwaukee.

Two of Everything. The Oriental Theatre, Madison, Wisconsin, performs this Chinese story.

The Silver Bell. Puppets by Doug Lieberman of Chicago are the actors in this Japanese legend.

Just for Fun—II

The King with the Horse's Ears. An Irish folktale told by Irish storyteller Batt Burns and illustrated with children's art.

The Clever Wife. Actors from the Oriental Theatre of Madison, Wisconsin, perform this Chinese tale.

Mark Twain and Huckleberry Finn. Parker Drew, aboard the Delta Queen, portrays both Mark Twain and Huckleberry Finn in this American story.

Who Is the Real Cinderella?: variations on the traditional fairy tale

Turkey Girl. A version from the Pueblo Indians of the American Southwest, told with the puppets of Chicago's Doug Lieberman.

Nitokris and the Gilded Sandals. An ancient Egyptian variation, told using Doug Lieberman's puppets.

Kari Woodencoat. A version from the Norwegian Vikings, told with Doug Lieberman's puppets.

At the Back of Beyond: stories about how different cultures deal with death

Death of Kigtak. An Eskimo tale performed by The Other Theatre, Chicago.

The Descent of Ishtar. An ancient Sumerian legend told with the Powderhorn Puppets, Minneapolis.

Barrington Bunny. A contemporary American Christmas story by Martin Bell, performed by the theater department of the University of Wisconsin at Green Bay.

Reflections: tales to think about

Two Highwaymen. The Oriental Theatre of Madison, Wisconsin, acts out this Japanese folktale.

Princess of the Full Moon. A story from the Upper Volta of West Africa, performed by students of the Urban Day School, Milwaukee.

The Tiger's Whisker. A Korean fable

enacted by the Oriental Theatre of Madison, Wisconsin.

FROM THE BROTHERS GRIMM: AMERICAN VERSIONS OF FAIRYTALE CLASSICS

3 films   16mm, ¾" U-Matic, ½" Beta, ½" VHS
   color   live action
Distributor: Tom Davenport Films
Producer/director: Tom Davenport
USA   ages 6–11

HANSEL AND GRETEL: AN APPALACHIAN VERSION

These unique, powerful dramas are true to the spirit of the original tales. Some adults feel that their realism is potentially disturbing, but most children find them exciting, engrossing, and highly satisfying. The tales are set in various eras of America's past. Shot on location in the Virginia countryside, they feature authentic-looking settings and costumes. The three films are part of a series of eight similar adaptations of fairy tales scheduled for broadcast on public television. Each is available separately.

Hansel and Gretel: An Appalachian Version. 16 min. 1975. This version of the famous fairy tale is set in the Blue Ridge Mountains of Virginia in the Depression years. It is well photographed and wonderfully effective and involving. Children sit through it perched on the edge of their chairs. *Award:* CINE Golden Eagle

Rapunzel, Rapunzel. 15 min. 1978. This austere, beautifully filmed version of the tale is set in the Victorian era. The prince's fall into the thorns may worry younger children, but the happy ending is reassuring. (Also distributed by Coe.) *Awards:* Learning A/V Award, *Learning* Magazine; CINE Golden Eagle

The Frog King or Faithful Henry. 15 min. 1980. This tale is set in Victorian times. The antics of the talking live frog in the film give it an offbeat comic touch. A nine-minute documentary film entitled *The Making of "The Frog King"* (1980) is available. Narrated by Tom Davenport and the film's young star, it explains how this fairy tale was brought to life. *Award:* Blue Ribbon, American Film Festival

THE GINGERBREAD MAN

10 min.   16mm, ¾" U-Matic, ½" Beta, ½" VHS
   color   animation
Distributor: Coronet
Producer: Pajon Arts
Directors: Lillian Somersaulter and J. P. Somersaulter
USA   1980   ages 2–8
Awards: Gijon (Spain) International Cinema Contest for Children and Teenagers; CINE Golden Eagle; Honor Film Award, Pacific Film Festival

A captivating version of the traditional folktale about a gingerbread man who comes to life and runs away from all the people and animals who chase him. It seems as if he will escape everyone's appetite, until he runs into a sly fox. The animation is executed in line drawings, with the words of the story shown on the screen and incorporated as elements of the tale. Funny sound effects help make this a huge success with children.

THE HAPPY PRINCE

25 min.   16mm, ¾" U-Matic, ½" Beta, ½" VHS
   color   animation
Distributor: Pyramid
Producers: Murray Shostak and Michael Mills
Director: Michael Mills
USA   1974   ages 6 up
Awards: Best Children's Film, Australian World Animation Festival; Learning A/V Award, *Learning* Magazine; Gold Medal, Atlanta Film Festival

This imaginatively animated version of Oscar Wilde's fairy tale features narration by Glynis Johns and Christopher Plummer. A gold-covered, jewel-encrusted statue of a prince feels pity for the poor and convinces a swallow to pluck out his jewels and distribute the riches to the needy. The animation is colorful, and the camera work captures the swooping feeling of a swallow in flight.

THE HARE AND THE TORTOISE (2ND EDITION)

10 min.   16mm, ¾" U-Matic, ½" Beta, ½" VHS
   color   animation
Distributor: Encyclopaedia Britannica
Producer/director: Paul Buchbinder
USA   1979   ages 2–8

This cel-animated adaptation of one of the most popular of Aesop's fables features lovely watercolor backgrounds. The story of the slow-but-steady tortoise who wins his race with the overconfident hare is told mostly through action, music, and sound effects. Children enjoy this attractive version of a familiar tale.

THE LEGEND OF SLEEPY HOLLOW

13 min.   16mm, ¾" U-Matic, ½" Beta, ½" VHS
   color   animation
Distributors: Coe, Pyramid
Filmmaker: Nick Bosustow
USA   1972   ages 6 up
Awards: Blue Ribbon, American Film Festival; Gold Hugo, Chicago International Film Festival

Lanky, superstitious Ichabod Crane courts a lady but gets chased away by a headless horseman in this funny, well-animated version of Washington Irving's famous tale. The visuals are eye-catching, with strong colors and expressive, humorously drawn characters. The narration is by John

Carradine, who does justice to Irving's splendid prose. Also available in Spanish.

THE LION AND THE MOUSE

5 min.   16mm   color   animation   nonverbal
Distributors: Benchmark, Coe
Producer: Wolf Koenig
Director: Evelyn Lambart
Canada   1976   ages 2–6

A brilliantly colored, cutout animation film by an award-winning director from the National Film Board of Canada. In this classic Aesop's fable, a compassionate lion catches and then releases a grateful mouse. Later, when the lion is trapped in a net, the mouse chews through the rope to free him. Music and sound effects carry the simple story line along successfully.

LITTLE RED RIDING HOOD

13 min.   16mm, ¾″ U-Matic, ½″ Beta, ½″ VHS
   color   animation
Distributor: Learning Corporation of America
Producer: DEFA Studios for Trick Films, Dresden
Director: Otto Sacher
East Germany   1979   ages 6–8

Vivid colors and animation with the quality of paintings or superior picture book illustrations highlight this famous fairy tale. Based on the original Brothers Grimm story, this version is authentically grim in places. Little Red Riding Hood strays off the trail on the way to Grandmother's house and meets a hungry wolf, who bounds ahead and gobbles up Grandmother and then Little Red herself. A hunter saves them by cutting open the wolf's belly. The happy ending reassures children that all is well, and the quality of the animation makes this a particularly enjoyable version of the story.

LITTLE RED RIDING HOOD: A BALINESE-OREGON ADAPTATION

17 min.   16mm, ¾″ U-Matic, ½″ Beta, ½″ VHS
   color   live action   nonverbal
Distributor: Texture
Filmmaker: David Sonnenschein

USA   1979   ages 9 up
Awards: CINE Golden Eagle; Bronze CINEMAN Trophy, Melbourne Film Festival; San Francisco International Film Festival; Four Star Certificate, New Zealand Festival

A unique version of an old favorite, in which masked actors in Balinese costumes play out the story in mime against the background of an Oregon state forest. Time-lapse photography shows the carving of the wooden masks for each character—the mask for the wolf is most ferocious!—and the actors then don the masks and mime the story to the accompaniment of an exotic-sounding woodwind quintet. An unusual and excitingly different experience.

LITTLE RED RIDING HOOD:
A BALINESE-OREGON ADAPTATION

THE LOON'S NECKLACE

11 min.   16mm, ¾″ U-Matic, ½″ Beta, ½″ VHS
   color   live action
Distributor: Encyclopaedia Britannica
Producer: Crawley Films
Canada   1949   ages 9 up

A distinctive and dramatic enactment of a Canadian Indian legend about how the loon got a white ring of feathers around its neck. Strikingly beautiful ceremonial masks carved by British Columbian Indians are worn by the actors, who perform against painted backdrops. This authentic and powerful presentation is now available in a restored version.

THE MAGIC TREE

10 min.   16mm, ¾" U-Matic, ½" Beta, ½" VHS
   color   animation
Distributors: Coe, Texture
Filmmaker: Gerald McDermott
USA   1970   ages 6 up
Awards: CINE Golden Eagle; Red Ribbon, American Film Festival; White House Conference on Children

A tale from the Congo about a homely, unloved boy who runs off and finds a secret paradise, only to lose it when he reveals its mystery. The glowing animation is based on African design motifs. Filmmaker Gerald McDermott has written and illustrated a companion book to the film, available from Texture.

THE MAN, THE SNAKE AND THE FOX

12 min.   16mm, ¾" U-Matic, ½" Beta, ½" VHS
   color   live action
Distributors: Arthur Mokin, Coe
Producer/director: Tony Snowsill
Canada   1979   ages 6–11

Storyteller Basil Johnston relates this Ojibway legend to a group of children in a forest setting, as beautifully handled puppets act out the roles of the main characters. The tale concerns an Indian hunter who comes upon a snake with the head of a wolf, which is trapped in a hole. When the hunter gives in to the creature's pleas and frees it, the monster goes back on its promise not to attack him. A fox comes along and tricks the snake back into the hole. The grateful man promises he will give food to the fox if ever it is hungry. Years later, the Indian inadvertently

shoots the fox when he finds it in his food stores. The narration, setting, and sound effects create a suspenseful mood, and the appealing puppets help make this an effective presentation of a native American fable.

MEDOONAK, THE STORMMAKER

13 min.   16mm   color   live action
Distributors: Coe, International Film Bureau
Producers: Ian McLaren and Rex Tasker, National Film Board of Canada
Director: Les Krizsan
Canada   1975   ages 6–11

This Micmac Indian legend concerns an Indian brave who traps the mighty Medoonak, a bird whose great wings cause storms, and makes him promise to rest between storms so that the Micmac people can catch fish. The legend is interpreted in mime, dance, and narration by the Mermaid Puppet Theater of Wolfville, Nova Scotia. The dancers wear wonderful masks, and the production is unusual, dramatic, and effective.

MY MOTHER IS THE MOST BEAUTIFUL WOMAN IN THE WORLD

9 min.   16mm, ¾" U-Matic, ½" Beta, ½" VHS
   color   animation
Distributor: BFA
Producer: Stephen Bosustow Productions
USA   1968   ages 6–8

A wordy but appealing folktale from the Ukraine about a young girl who is lost. She looks for her mother through wheat fields and villages, describing her as "the most beautiful woman in the world." And when the mother is finally found, that is just what she proves to be—if only in her daughter's eyes. Done mostly in cutout animation, with decorative touches in warm tones that match the warm mood of the tale, this production was adapted from the book by Rebecca Reyher and Ruth Gannet.

THE NUTCRACKER

26 min. 16mm color animation
Distributor: Barr
Producer: Soyuzmult Film Studio
USSR 1978 ages 6 up

Hoffmann's classic tale of magic is interpreted here in colorful animation, with stirring music from Tchaikovsky's score for *The Nutcracker.* On Christmas Eve, a servant girl finds a wooden nutcracker under the tree. When she kisses it, the nutcracker comes to life and explains that he is really a prince who is under an evil spell cast by the Mouse Queen. Then the nutcracker leads an army of Christmas ornaments and toys into battle against the terrible three-headed Mouse King and his troops. After the mouse hordes have been vanquished, the nutcracker becomes a prince again, the servant girl becomes a princess, and they live happily ever after in their magical kingdom. The animation features some unusual special effects, giving the film a magical quality. This is a fine choice for Christmastime programming.

THE OWL WHO MARRIED A GOOSE

8 min. 16mm, ¾" U-Matic, ½" Beta, ½" VHS
  b&w animation
Distributors: Coe, National Film Board of Canada
Producer: Pierre Moretti
Director: Caroline Leaf
Canada 1976 ages 6 up
Awards: ASIFA; Information Film Producers of
  America; American Film Festival; Canadian Film
  Award

Extraordinary sand animation by Caroline Leaf is used to tell this Eskimo legend about an ill-matched pair. The sound track is in Eskimo, but the story is perfectly clear without words. An owl and a goose meet and fall in love, and the owl attempts to keep up with the goose and her goslings. But an owl is not a goose, and when the goose and the goslings land on a lake the owl plummets to the bottom. The sad ending of the film may upset younger children, so it is important to preview this before showing it to decide if it is appropriate for a particular audience.

THE PRINCESS AND THE PEARLS

15 min. 16mm, ¾" U-Matic, ½" Beta, ½" VHS
  color animation
Distributor: Learning Corporation of America
Producer/director: Karel Zeman
Czechoslovakia 1973 ages 6–11
Award: Fairytale Film Festival

Unusual animation and exotic music highlight this tale from the *Arabian Nights.* Sinbad the Sailor is shipwrecked, rescued by a magical fish, and set ashore in a hostile land. Various adventures lead him to the Sultan's Court and a happy ending. The artwork has the exquisitely detailed, two-dimensional look of Persian miniatures. Children find the film "pretty" and enjoy the story despite its slow pace.

RIP VAN WINKLE

27 min. 16mm color animation
Distributor: Billy Budd
Producer/director: Will Vinton
USA 1978 ages 6 up
Awards: Ottawa International Animated Film Festi-
  val; Bronze Award, International Film & TV Fes-
  tival of New York; Gold Hugo, Grand Prix of
  Festival; Norman McLaren Award, Best Film in
  Short Subject Animation, Chicago International
  Film Festival; Gold Venus Medallion, First Place,
  Children's Films, Miami International Film Festi-
  val; Best Educational Film, *Instructor* Magazine;
  Chrome Reel Award, Best in Festival, Indiana
  Film Festival; Ruby Slipper, Best Short, Los An-
  geles International Children's Film Festival; Best
  in Show, Motion Picture Seminar of the North-
  west; CINE Golden Eagle; Gold Cindy Award,
  Information Film Festival of America

An adaptation of Washington Irving's classic tale about a good-natured but lazy dreamer who falls asleep for 20 years after drinking a mysterious potion. Will Vinton Productions' clay animation is wonderfully detailed. A fanciful dream sequence has been added that shows off the animators' skills. The film is somewhat drawn out, but the technique holds the audience's attention.

THE SEVEN RAVENS

21 min.   16mm, ¾" U-Matic, ½" Beta, ½" VHS
  color   animation
Distributor: Learning Corporation of America
Producer: DEFA Studios
Director: Christel Wiemer
East Germany   1971   ages 2–8
Award: Fairytale Film Festival

A courageous little girl sets out to find her seven long-lost brothers, turned into ravens seven years before by a vengeful witch. The film is rather long, but the colorful animation and the background flute music are appealing. This is one of the few Grimm fairy tales that features a female in a heroic role.

THE SHOEMAKER AND THE ELVES

15 min.   16mm, ¾" U-Matic   color   animation
Distributors: Coe, Films Inc.
Filmmaker: Institut für Film und Bild
West Germany   1972   ages 6–8
Award: Bronze Plaque, Columbus Film Festival
  Chris Awards

This beautifully produced film features charmingly detailed puppets. Based on the Grimm tale, it is the story of two tiny cobbler elves who slip into a poor shoemaker's shop at night and make shoes for him. In gratitude, the cobbler and his wife make new clothes for their little helpers, surprising and delighting them. For a similar production, see *Bremen Town Musicians,* earlier in this section.

SLEEPING BEAUTY

75 min.   16mm, 35mm   color   animation
Distributor: Films Inc.
Producer: Walt Disney
Director: Clyde Geromini
USA   1959   ages 6–11

One of the finest examples of Disney animation; the rich colors and detailed artwork of the production put Saturday morning cartoons to shame. The beautiful young princess Briar Rose, who has been cursed with an evil spell, is raised in a forest by three good fairies. She meets a handsome young prince and falls in love. But then the wicked witch Maleficent leads Briar Rose to prick her finger on a spinning wheel spindle, and she falls into a deep sleep. Only the prince can save her, but first he must fight a fearsome dragon.

THE SORCERER'S APPRENTICE

27 min.   16mm, ¾" U-Matic, ½" Beta, ½" VHS
  color   animation
Distributor: Pyramid
Filmmakers: Robertsco/Aeicor/Sorcery Films
USA   1980   ages 6–11

This version of the Brothers Grimm tale is pleasurably spooky and imaginatively animated. The sound and visual effects are unusual; they show the influence of the special effects used in such films as *Star Wars.* The story concerns young Hans, who sets out to seek his fortune. He meets Spellbinder the Sorcerer, who mistakenly believes that Hans cannot read or write and takes him on as his apprentice. Hans befriends Spellbinder's servant, Greta, and the two soon discover the true, evil nature of the sorcerer. Hans and Greta find Spellbinder's book of magic and Hans reads it and practices his magic. When Spellbinder discovers what is happening, he challenges Hans to a fantastic duel. Good, naturally, triumphs over evil, and the two children march off together in a most satisfying ending. Also available in French and Spanish.

A STORY—A STORY

10 min.   16mm, ¾" U-Matic, ½" Beta, ½" VHS
  color   animation
Distributor: Weston Woods
Producer: Morton Schindel
Director: Gene Deitch
Czechoslovakia   1973   ages 6–8

A STORY—A STORY

This engaging African tale is based on the Caldecott Medal book by Gail E. Haley. It concerns the sly folk hero, Anansi the Spider Man, who climbs up to the sky to buy stories from the Sky God. In return for the stories, Anansi agrees to capture three creatures for the Sky God: the leopard-of-the-terrible-teeth, the hornet-who-stings-like-fire, and the fairy-whom-men-never-see. Anansi's clever ruses make for a winning story, enhanced by excellent narration (by John Akar), African music, and unusual animation based on woodcut illustrations. Words carry the plot more than the visuals do, making this film more appropriate for six- to eight-year-olds than for younger children. Available in Danish as well. For another of Anansi's adventures, see *Anansi the Spider,* earlier in this section.

THE STORY OF GOOD KING HUEMAC

21 min.   16mm, ¾" U-Matic, ½" Beta, ½" VHS
   color   animation

Distributor: Films Inc.
Filmmaker: Richard Fichter
USA   1979   ages 6–11

Creative puppet animation is used to tell this ancient Mexican legend. King Huemac of the Toltecs is a wise and kind ruler until an evil prince of the underworld poisons him. Then the king becomes cruel and wicked, and his kingdom suffers. Finally a kindly goddess steps in and restores his goodness, bringing happiness back to his people again. Children enjoy watching the expressive puppets.

STREGA NONNA

7 min.   16mm, ¾" U-Matic, ½" Beta, ½" VHS
   color   animation
Distributor: Weston Woods
Producer: Morton Schindel
Director: Gene Deitch
Czechoslovakia   1978   ages 2–8
Awards: Silver Medal, Greater Miami International
   Film Festival; Silver Plaque, Chicago Interna-
   tional Film Festival; Silver Award, International
   Film & TV Festival of New York; Thorbjorn
   Egner Prize, Fairytale Film Festival; Blue Ribbon,

American Film Festival; CINE Golden Eagle; Learning A/V Award, *Learning* Magazine

Strega Nonna ("Grandmother Witch") has a magic pasta pot. Her helper, Big Anthony, thinks he can make it produce pasta too, but his experiment with the pot nearly spells the end for their little medieval town and for Big Anthony himself. Children call this film "the spaghetti movie," and they adore it. The animation of Tomie de Paola's Caldecott Honor book is lovely and funny. The production has the feeling of an Italian operetta, enhanced by the sound track, which combines dramatic narration with choral singing and the music of a Jew's harp and an accordion. Available in Danish and Swedish, and with captions.

STREGA NONNA

THE SWINEHERD

13 min.   16mm, ¾" U-Matic, ½" Beta, ½" VHS
   color   animation
Distributor: Weston Woods
Producer: Paul Hammerich
Director: Gene Deitch

Czechoslovakia   1975   ages 2–8
Awards: Gold Plaque, Chicago International Film Festival; Silver Mermaid, Fairytale Film Festival; ALA Notable Film for Children

A sly prince shows up a spoiled princess in this appealingly animated version of a Hans Christian Andersen tale. The princess scorns the beautiful gifts of a rose and a nightingale offered by the prince, but she is willing to kiss a swineherd (the prince in disguise) in exchange for a silly musical toy. Available in Afrikaans and Danish.

A TALE OF TILL

11¼ min.   16mm, ¾" U-Matic, ½" Beta, ½" VHS
   color   live action
Distributor: FilmFair Communications
Producer/director: Marianne Meyerhoff
West Germany   1975   ages 6–14

Till Eulenspiegel is a famous character from medieval German folk literature. This production, set in Mölln, Schleswig-Holstein, Germany, introduces Till and then focuses on an outdoor puppet show of a story about him. An engrossed audience of children looks on as marionettes act out a tale about a merchant who has lost a purse containing 800 pieces of gold and a carpenter who has found a purse containing 700 pieces of gold. The two come before the king to settle their quarrel, and Till, as the king's jester, proposes a solution that leaves the audience thinking.

TALEB AND HIS LAMB

16 min.   16mm, ¾" U-Matic, ½" Beta, ½" VHS
   color   live action
Distributor: Barr
Filmmaker: Ami Amitai
Israel   1975   ages 6–15
Award: Best of the Year, Learning A/V Award, *Learning* Magazine

A modern retelling of an ancient Bedouin folktale about a young shepherd and his pet lamb. When the lamb must be taken to the marketplace to be slaughtered, Taleb steals it and runs away to the desert. After several days, Taleb's angry father finds them. The film offers two possible endings and invites the viewer to decide which solution would be best. Beautiful photography of Israel's Negev Desert and the thought-provoking choice to be made at the end make for a special experience.

TEENY-TINY AND THE WITCH-WOMAN

14 min.   16mm, ¾" U-Matic, ½" Beta, ½" VHS
   color   animation
Distributor: Weston Woods
Producer: Morton Schindel
Director: Gene Deitch
Czechoslovakia   1979   ages 6–11
Awards: CINE Golden Eagle; Gold Award, International Film & TV Festival of New York; Bronze Award, Houston International Film Festival of the Americas; Special Mention, Milan Film Festival

This enjoyably scary, suspenseful film is based on an old Turkish folktale, retold in Barbara K. Walker's book. It is a variation on the Hansel and Gretel story: Teeny-Tiny and his two older brothers, lost in a forest, are enticed into an evil witch's house. Only Teeny-Tiny realizes the witch's sinister intentions, and it is up to him to save himself and his brothers. The animation is beautifully done, highlighting all the awful details of the forest and the witch's house, and the music and sound effects contribute to the spooky mood. Most children like to be a bit scared, as long as the ending is happy, but since some children may be truly frightened, it is advisable to prescreen this film. Available in Swedish.

TI-JEAN GOES LUMBERING

16 min.   16mm, ¾" U-Matic, ½" Beta, ½". VHS
   color   live action
Distributors: Coe, International Film Bureau
Producer: Jean Palardy
Canada   1953   ages 6–11

This traditional French Canadian folktale is somewhat dated, but it is still a big hit with children. It features a mysterious and amazingly strong boy who appears at a lumber camp and outperforms all the men before riding off again on his big white horse. Daily life at a lumber camp is shown, including some unusual games that lumberjacks play—which our hero wins, naturally, thereby winning respect and admiration from the adults. Children relish Ti-Jean's triumphs and the role reversal. Available in French (*P'tit Jean S'en Va aux Chantiers*) and Spanish (*Ti-Jean leñador*), and with captions.

THE UGLY DUCKLING

15 min.   16mm, ¾" U-Matic, ½" Beta, ½" VHS
   color   animation
Distributor: Weston Woods
Producers: Paul Hammerich and Egan Schmidt
Director: Gene Deitch
Czechoslovakia   1977   ages 2–8

Hans Christian Andersen's enduring tale, an allegory of his own childhood in a Copenhagen slum, is interpreted here in realistically detailed animation. An ugly baby bird, born amidst a group of ducklings, is scorned by other members of barnyard society and flees. He encounters still more prejudice and endures a harsh winter on his own before he accidentally discovers that he has grown into a beautiful swan. Children adore the barnyard scenes, but the film may be a little long for some younger viewers. Based on the book illustrated by Svend Otto. Available in Danish.

WHAZZAT?

10 min.   16mm, ¾" U-Matic, ½" Beta, ½" VHS
   color   animation   nonverbal
Distributor: Encyclopaedia Britannica
Producer: Crocus Productions
Director: Art Pierson
USA   1975   all ages

A jubilant, creative, clay-animation adaptation of the eleventh-century folktale from India about the six blind men and the elephant. Six colorful clay figures bumble along exploring their environment and helping each other out as they surmount obstacles in their path. When they come upon an elephant, each arrives at a different notion of what this strange new object might be, based on feeling only one part of it at a time. They excitedly describe their versions of the beast to each other in a wonderful wordless sequence, and finally figure it out together.

ZLATEH THE GOAT

20 min.   16mm, ¾" U-Matic, ½" Beta, ½" VHS
    color   live action
Distributor: Weston Woods
Producer: Morton Schindel
Director: Gene Deitch
Czechoslovakia   1974   ages 6–11
Awards: Gold Medal, Atlanta International Film
    Festival; Silver Award, International Film & TV
    Festival of New York; Silver Plaque, Chicago In-
    ternational Film Festival; Bronze Plaque, Colum-
    bus Film Festival Chris Awards

A young boy in prewar Poland sets out with the family goat to sell it to the butcher for much-needed money to buy supplies for the Jewish holidays. On the way, a fierce snowstorm forces them to take refuge in a haystack for three days, and the boy and the animal must depend on each other to survive. Based on a folktale by Isaac Bashevis Singer, this film is exquisitely photographed in an authentic-

ZLATEH THE GOAT

looking setting. Despite a slow beginning and minimal narration, it is an engrossing story. Available in Danish, French, and German.

Part II
Resources

4
Awards and Festivals

ACADEMY AWARDS

Academy of Motion Picture Arts and Sciences
8949 Wilshire Blvd.
Beverly Hills, CA 90211
  (213) 278-8990

Oscar statuettes are presented for outstanding achievement in connection with
motion pictures. Feature films, foreign
feature films, documentaries, and shorts
(animated and live action) are eligible.
The categories include acting, art direction, cinematography, costume design,
directing, documentaries, film editing,
foreign-language film, music, best picture, short subjects, special visual effects,
and writing. There are also several special
awards recognizing individuals and scientific or technical achievement, with student film awards as well. Entries are due
in December, and the award ceremony
takes place each year in April.

ACHIEVEMENT IN CHILDREN'S
TELEVISION AWARDS

Action for Children's Television (ACT)
46 Austin St.
Newtonville, MA 02160
  (617) 527-7870

ACT is a national nonprofit consumer
organization working to improve broadcasting practices directed to children.

Awards are presented annually for signifi-
cant contributions in children's broadcast
and cable television. To be considered for
an ACT award, programs must be designed for and directed to an audience of
children or young people and broadcast
as part of a series of six or more programs.
Entries are due in February. Award certificates are presented at a ceremony in May.

AMERICAN FILM FESTIVAL

Educational Film Library Association
43 West 61 St.
New York, NY 10023
  (212) 246-4533

This festival of recent 16mm and video
releases is held annually to give recognition to film- and videomakers and to
promote the use of film and video in
schools, libraries, museums, and community groups. Categories include children's
entertainment, fine arts and performing
arts, social documentaries, and business
and industry, health and safety, and instructional films. A Blue Ribbon is
awarded to the winner in each category
and a Red Ribbon to the runner-up. The
highest rated of the Blue Ribbon winners
receives an Emily Award. The John Grier-
son Award goes to a new filmmaker in the
social documentary category. Entries are

due in January, and the festival is held in June, when the awards are presented.

ANNECY INTERNATIONAL ANIMATED FILM FESTIVAL

21 rue de la Tour d'Auvergne
Paris 75009
France

This festival is sponsored by the Ministry of Foreign Affairs, French National Center of Cinema. An award is given for the best children's film, and there are also two grand prizes, three juried special prizes, and prizes for a first work by a director, a commercial film, and a TV film. The festival is held biennially in odd-numbered years. Entries are due in January, and the festival is held in June.

ASOLO INTERNATIONAL FESTIVAL OF FILMS ON ART AND BIOGRAPHIES OF ARTISTS

Calle Avogaria 1633
30123 Venice
Italy

Feature-length and short films on arts and artists, including painting, sculpture, and architecture, compete for the Asolo Grand Prize and awards for best-filmed biography, best creatively done art film, and best TV film. The festival is held each year in May and June, and entries are due in April.

AUSTRALIAN INTERNATIONAL FILM FESTIVAL FOR CHILDREN

Australian Council for Children's Films and Television
Film Study Section
Education Department of South Australia
164 O'Connell St.
North Adelaide, South Australia 5006
Australia

This is an international noncompetitive screening of children's feature and short films. Entries are due in February, and the festival tours six Australian state capitals annually through April and May.

AWARDS FOR CABLECASTING EXCELLENCE (ACE)

National Cable Television Association (NCTA)
1724 Massachusetts Ave. N.W.
Washington, DC 20036
  (202) 775-3611

Categories in this annual competition include overall excellence in community programming and excellence in single community-oriented programs, educational and children's community programming, and national service series and programs. NCTA members are eligible to submit entries, which are due in April. The winners are announced in November.

BESANÇON INTERNATIONAL MUSICAL AND CHOREOGRAPHIC FILM FESTIVAL

Parc des Expositions
B.P. 1913
25020 Besançon Cedex
France

Feature-length and short films that focus on music and choreography compete for a Festival Prize and a Public Prize. The festival, sponsored by the National Center of French Cinematography and the City of Besançon, is held during the annual International Music Festival of Besançon in September. Entries are due in July.

BILBOA INTERNATIONAL FESTIVAL OF DOCUMENTARY AND SHORT FILMS

Instituto Vascongado de Cultura Hispanica
Box 1198
Gran Via 17, #3
Bilbao 1
Spain

Short 16 and 35mm films (30 minutes or less) in three categories—fiction, documentary, and animation—compete in this international festival held in late November through early December. Entries must be received by October.

BIRMINGHAM INTERNATIONAL EDUCATIONAL FILM FESTIVAL

Box 78-SDB
University Station
Birmingham, AL 35294
  (205) 934-3884

Educational 16mm films and videocassettes compete annually for Gold and Silver Electra statuettes, certificates, and cash prizes. Categories include applied and performing arts and language arts, as well as subjects in the sciences and the social sciences, and there is a special category of student productions. Entries are due in January, and the festival takes place in March.

CHICAGO INTERNATIONAL FILM FESTIVAL

Cinema/Chicago
415 North Dearborn St.
Chicago, IL 60610
  (312) 644-3400

Cinema/Chicago is a nonprofit arts and culture organization; 35mm, 16mm, and super 8 films, as well as 35mm filmstrips and ¾" videocassettes, compete annually for gold, silver, and bronze Hugos, gold and silver plaques, certificates, and cash. Categories include animation, TV productions, video arts, and student productions, among other subjects. Entries are due in September, and awards are presented in November.

CHICAGOLAND EDUCATIONAL FILM FESTIVAL

Chicago Board of Education
Division of Visual Education
4215 West 45 St.
Chicago, IL 60632
  (312) 641-8300

Competing for Golden Babe statuettes are

16mm educational films from around the world. Levels are from kindergarten to twelfth grade, and the categories are science, mathematics, social studies, language arts, fine arts, careers, guidance, consumer education, vocational education, health/safety, physical education, and practical arts. The judging is done by teachers, parents, and students. Entries are due in May, and the festival is held each year in October.

THE CHRISTOPHER AWARDS

The Christophers
12 East 48 St.
New York, NY 10017
  (212) 759-4050

The Christopher Awards annually honor writers, producers, and directors of TV specials, feature films, and books for children and adults. The prize is a bronze medallion. Productions of the previous calendar year are eligible, and the winners are announced in January.

CINE GOLDEN EAGLE CERTIFICATES

Council of International Nontheatrical Events
  (CINE)
1201 16 St. N.W.
Washington, DC 20036
  (202) 785-1136

CINE is the official United States organization for accrediting American entries in foreign film festivals. Amateur and professional 8mm, 16mm, and 35mm films in a wide range of categories (including arts and crafts, architecture, animation, and entertainment/short subject) are judged semiannually. Professional productions compete for the CINE Golden Eagle Certificate, and amateur productions compete for the CINE Eagle Certificate. Entries are due in February and in August, and the awards are presented in December.

CLEVELAND INSTRUCTIONAL FILM FESTIVAL

Metropolitan Cleveland Educational Resources
  Center
4300 Brookpark Rd.
Cleveland, OH 44134
  (216) 398-2800

This international festival of curriculum-related 16mm classroom films is held each year in October. The categories include language arts and art/music, as well as science and social science topics, for both the elementary and secondary levels. Films are given star ratings. Entries are due in August.

COLUMBUS FILM FESTIVAL
CHRIS AWARDS

Film Council of Greater Columbus
257 South Brinker Ave.
Columbus, OH 43204
  (614) 274-1826

Filmstrips, 16mm films, videotapes, and TV spot announcements are eligible to compete for Chris statuettes. The categories are art and culture, business and industry, education, social studies, health and medicine, religion and ethics, and travel. There is also a Student Chris Award for the best 16mm film made by a student. Entries are due in June, and the award ceremony takes place each year in October at the film festival.

DANCE FILM AND VIDEO FESTIVAL

Dance Films Association, Inc.
125 East 23 St., Room 401-A
New York, NY 10010
  (212) 598-9138

Videocassettes and 16mm films on various kinds of dance and on mime compete for Gold Seal Awards. There is a category for TV spots that feature dance elements. Entries are due in February, and the festival takes place each year in April.

DANUBE PRIZE

International Festival of Television Programs for
  Children and Youth
Ceskoslovenska Televizia
Osmolovova Ul.C. 24
893 19 Bratislava
Czechoslovakia

This international festival of entertainment programs for young people is sponsored by Czechoslovak Television. The motto of the festival is "In furtherance of a progressive relationship of children and youth to life." Entries are selected by official broadcasting organizations in each country. Danube Prizes and Honorable Mentions are awarded. The festival takes place annually in September.

FAIRYTALE FILM FESTIVAL

Rådhuset, Flakhaven
5000 Odense
Denmark

This international festival is for films based on fairy tales or folklore. The categories are short cartoons and puppet films. Winners receive Gold Tin Soldiers for superior art quality, and silver trophies are awarded for best treatment of a story by Andersen, technical achievement, creative imagination, and color composition. Entries are due each year in May, and the festival takes place in August.

GABRIEL AWARDS

National Association of Catholic Broadcasters &
  Allied Communicators (UNDA-USA)
136 West Georgia St.
Indianapolis, IN 46225
  (317) 635-3586

Network and local radio and television programs compete each year in the categories of youth, information/education, religion, entertainment, public service announcements, station performance, and personal achievement. Entries are due in August, and the awards are presented in November.

GEORGE FOSTER PEABODY BROADCASTING AWARDS

Henry W. Grady School of Journalism and Mass
  Communication
University of Georgia
Athens, GA 30602
  (404) 542-3785

Radio and television programs broadcast during the previous calendar year are eligible for Peabody Awards. The categories are news, entertainment, education, programs for children, documentaries, public service, and individuals or organizations. Entries are due in January, and the award winners are announced in April.

GIJON INTERNATIONAL CINEMA CONTEST FOR CHILDREN AND TEENAGERS

Paseo de Begona, 24 Entlo
Gijon
Spain

Feature-length and short films for youth are eligible for various prizes given by an international jury, a jury of children, and a jury of teenagers. This annual festival takes place in July; entries are due in May.

GOLDEN HARP TELEVISION FESTIVAL

Radio Telfis Eireann
Donnybrook
Dublin 4
Ireland

Folklore and folk music television films and videotapes compete for Harp Awards. Entries must be submitted by official broadcast organizations in each country. The festival is held annually in August and September.

GREATER MIAMI INTERNATIONAL FILM FESTIVAL

Box 01-4861 Flagler
Miami, FL 33101
  (305) 673-5700

Features, shorts, documentaries, TV films and commercials, student films and experimental films, as well as videotapes and filmstrips, compete in this annual international festival. There is a large number of categories. In the documentary division, these include arts, children, and educational. There is also a large number of different awards, including Gold, Silver, and Bronze Venus awards, and Medallions. A $1,000 Children's Film Award is made as well. Entries are due in September, and the festival takes place in November.

INTERNATIONAL CRAFT FILM FESTIVAL

New York State Craftsmen Inc.
27 West 53 St.
New York, NY 10019
  (212) 586-0026

Held in December, this annual noncompetitive festival is for 16mm films that treat any aspect of traditional or contemporary crafts. Entries are due in September, and the festival is held in October.

INTERNATIONAL FILM & TV FESTIVAL OF NEW YORK

51 West 57 St.
New York, NY 10019
  (212) 246-5133

Trophy cups and gold, silver, and bronze medals go to winners in a wide range of categories that include art and music, animation, and syndicated TV series for children; 16mm films, videocassettes, filmstrips, and slide programs are eligible. Entries are due in August, and the awards are presented each year in November.

INTERNATIONAL MEETING OF FILM AND YOUTH (RIFJ)

B.P. 796
38017 Grenoble Cedex
France

This biennial festival is held in odd-numbered years. Feature films for youth are eligible for a jury grand prize, a special jury prize, a public grand prize, and the public's choice of the ten best films. Entries are due in September, and the festival takes place in December and January.

INTERNATIONAL REVIEWS OF EDUCATIONAL, CULTURAL, DIDACTIC FILMS, TELEVISION FILMS, AND FILMS FOR VIDEOCASSETTE

Didactic Film Service
Via Savoia 78
001978 Rome
Italy

Cups, medals, and certificates are awarded for 16mm educational films from around the world that compete in the categories of educational/cultural films, educational TV films, and didactic/educational films for videocassette. Entries are due in March, and the festival takes place each year in June.

INTERNATIONAL TOURNÉE OF ANIMATION

4530 18 St.
San Francisco, CA 94114
  (415) 863-6100

This is an annual feature-length exhibit of short animated films gathered from festivals and screenings of animation from around the world. It tours museums, universities, and art centers in the United States and Canada. Entries are due in February, and the touring exhibition begins in April.

IRIS AWARDS

National Association of Television Program Executives (NATPE)
310 Madison Ave., Suite 1207
New York, NY 10017
  (212) 661-0270

Children's programming is one of the categories in these awards for excellence in individual local TV station program efforts. NATPE member stations are eligible. Entries are due in December, and the awards are presented in the spring.

ITALIA PRIZE

Radiotelevisione Italiana
Viale Mazzini 14
00195 Rome
Italy

This international competition for radio and television programs is held each year in September. Television films, videotapes, and radio audiotapes in the categories of drama, documentary, and music must be submitted by broadcast organizations in each country. Italia cash prizes and special prizes are awarded.

JAPAN PRIZE CONTEST

NHK/Nippon Hoso Kyokai
2-2-1, Jinnan, Shibuya-ku
Tokyo 150
Japan

This international annual competition for educational television and radio series aims to promote educational and instructional broadcasting and to further cooperation among broadcast organizations. The Japan Broadcasting Corporation sponsors the contest. The categories are Educational for Primary/Kindergarten/Nursery, Secondary Educational, and Adult Educational. Cash prizes are awarded. Entries are due in November, and the contest takes place in February.

LOS ANGELES INTERNATIONAL CHILDREN'S FILM FESTIVAL

The American Center of Films for Children
School of Library Science
University of Southern California
Los Angeles, CA 90007
  (213) 746-6071

This annual festival shows recent American and foreign films for children. Feature films and short subjects are screened, and the winning films receive Ruby Slipper Awards. Awards are also given to those individuals who have most helped enrich the lives of children with quality film and television productions. The festival is held in April and May.

MANNHEIM INTERNATIONAL YOUTH FILM CONTEST

Stadt Mannheim
Rathaus E-5
D-6800 Mannheim 1
Federal Republic of Germany

This noncompetitive festival is held each year in October during Mannheim International Film Week. Films and television productions for children and young adults are eligible. Entries are due in September.

THE MIDWEST FILM CONFERENCE

Box 1665
Evanston, IL 60204
  (312) 869-0600

This conference is an annual showcase for creative short films, feature films, and video. The categories are films for children, energy, business, films for business meetings, general, and video. Entries are due in September, and the conference takes place in February.

NATIONAL EDUCATIONAL FILM FESTIVAL

Montera Educational Film Foundation
5555 Ascot Dr.
Oakland, CA 94611
  (415) 530-9250

Educational feature films and short films compete for awards and cash prizes in this international festival. The categories include language arts and fine arts, and film as art, as well as the sciences and social sciences. There is also a category for student films. Judging is done by students, educators, film professionals, and parents.

Entries are due in February, and the festival is held annually in April.

NATIONAL EMMY AWARDS

National Academy of Television Arts and Sciences
110 West 57 St.
New York, NY 10019
  (212) 586-8424

The National Emmy Awards are given for excellence in daytime shows, children's programming, religious programming, and sports. Winners receive gold Emmy statuettes. Entries are due in February, and the awards are presented in September.

NEW YORK WORLD TELEVISION FESTIVAL

Box 1232
Madison Square Station
New York, NY 10010
  (212) 684-1047

This annual festival, held in November, showcases award-winning television programs from around the world. The programs screened are award winners in such international competitions as the Golden Harp, the Golden Rose of Montreux, the International Emmy Awards, Monte Carlo, Prague D'Or, Premios Ondas, and Prix Futura.

OHIO STATE AWARDS

Institute for Education by Radio-Television
Ohio State University
Telecommunications Center
2400 Olentangy River Rd.
Columbus, OH 43210
  (614) 422-9678

These annual awards are presented in the spring to local and network radio and television programs to recognize achievement in educational, informational, and public affairs broadcasting. The categories are performing arts/humanities, natural/physical sciences, social sciences/public affairs. Entries are due in July.

OTTAWA INTERNATIONAL ANIMATED FILM FESTIVAL

75 Albert St., Suite 1105
Ottawa, Ontario K1P 5E7
Canada
   (613) 238-6748

This festival is sponsored by the Canadian Film Institute. Animated films compete in the categories of animation, promotional, and instructional, first film by student/independent filmmaker, and children's films. The grand prize is a Silver Owl Trophy. There are also prizes in each category and special jury prizes. The festival is held in even-numbered years. Entries are due in June, and the festival takes place in August.

POETRY FILM FESTIVAL

Poetry Film Theater
Fort Mason Cultural Center
San Francisco, CA 94123
   (415) 921-4470

Films and videotapes on poetry are eligible to compete in this international festival, which takes place in odd-numbered years. Cash prizes and honorable-mention awards go to films selected by the festival audience. Entries are due in April, and the festival takes place in May.

PRAGUE D'OR INTERNATIONAL TELEVISION FESTIVAL

Ceskoslovenska Televize
29-30 Gorkeho Nam
11150 Prague 1
Czechoslovakia

Entries in this festival must be submitted by official broadcast organizations in each country. TV drama films and videotapes and TV music films and videotapes are eligible for Prague D'Or awards and prizes. The festival is held annually in June.

PRIX JEUNESSE INTERNATIONAL

Bayerischer Rundfunk
Rundfunkplatz 1
D-8000 Munich 2
Federal Republic of Germany

This biennial television contest (held in even-numbered years) for children and young people is intended to deepen understanding between nations and to increase the exchange of television programs on an international level. Six prizes are awarded in three categories: storytelling, information, and music/light entertainment. A special prize is awarded to an outstanding program produced by a television station with restricted means of production. UNICEF and the German UNESCO Commission also award special prizes. Entries are due in April, and the awards are presented in June.

SALERNO INTERNATIONAL FESTIVAL OF CINEMA FOR CHILDREN AND YOUTH

84095 Giffoni Valle Piana
Salerno
Italy

This annual showcase of feature and short films for young people is sponsored by the Italian Ministry of Tourism and Recreation. Films are judged in several categories, including best young filmmaker and best treatment of problems of youth. A Silver Grifone goes to the best film for children. The best film in each category gets a Bronze Grifone. The judging is done by a jury of children and teens. Entries are due in May, and the festival takes place in July and August.

SAN FRANCISCO INTERNATIONAL FILM FESTIVAL

3501 California St., Suite 201
San Francisco, CA 94118
   (415) 221-9055

Nontheatrical 16mm films, in categories

including classroom films and fine arts, compete for Golden Gate and Silver or Bronze Reel Awards. There are also best-of-category and special jury certificates. Theatrical features and short films are shown as well. Entries are due in August, and the festival is held annually in October.

VANCOUVER INTERNATIONAL FILM FESTIVAL FOR CHILDREN AND YOUNG PEOPLE

c/o Pacific Cinematheque
1616 West Third Ave.
Vancouver, BC V6J 1K2
Canada
  (604) 732-9012

This annual film exhibition aims to promote international understanding of the welfare of children and young people, to arouse concern and love for their well-being, and ultimately to encourage film-making in this field. Cash prizes are given on the recommendation of an international jury panel in the following categories: best live feature film over 60 minutes; best live medium-length film (31 to 60 minutes); best live short film (3 to 30 minutes); best animated film; and best performance by a child or young adult, or to any one film or filmmaker. Entries are due in May, and the festival takes place in October.

ZAGREB FESTIVAL OF WORLD ANIMATION

Zagreb Film
Nova Ves 18
P.B. 915
41000 Zagreb
Yugoslavia

This international competition has been held every four years since 1970. Animated 35mm and 16mm films 30 minutes in length or less compete in the following categories: longer than 3 minutes, shorter than 3 minutes, educational, for children, television series, first work. A Zagreb Grand Prize and prizes in each category are awarded. Entries are due in February, and the festival takes place in June.

5
Organizations

Public libraries and museums often have excellent film programs for children, as well as free or inexpensive film-loan services. University film libraries are another source for renting films. In addition to the organizations listed below, these institutions can provide helpful information about film and video for young viewers.

ACTION FOR CHILDREN'S TELEVISION (ACT)

46 Austin St.
Newtonville, MA 02160
  (617) 527-7870

ACT is a national, nonprofit consumer organization working to improve television practices related to children. Through legal action, education, and research, ACT aims to encourage diversity and eliminate commercial abuses in children's television. Publications include a news magazine, *re:act,* and a series of resource books, films, and handbooks. Annual awards are given for achievement in children's programming.

AMERICAN ASSOCIATION OF SCHOOL LIBRARIANS (AASL)

50 East Huron St.
Chicago, IL 60611
  (312) 944-6780 ext. 306

This division of the American Library Association is concerned with improving school library media services for children and young people. AASL offers guidelines for the selection and use of media, and offers educational programs for school library media specialists and school administrators. It publishes *School Media Quarterly.*

THE AMERICAN CENTER OF FILMS FOR CHILDREN (ACFC)

School of Library Science
University of Southern California
Los Angeles, CA 90007
  (213) 743-8632

ACFC sponsors the annual Los Angeles International Children's Film Festival, serves as a research center on children's film, and hosts seminars and symposia on children's films. It is a national organization of parents, children, librarians, educators, and film producers and distributors who work to encourage the production, distribution, and exhibition of outstanding children's films.

AMERICAN COUNCIL FOR BETTER BROADCASTS (ACBB)

120 East Wilson St.
Madison, WI 53703
  (608) 257-7712

A consumer group that seeks to promote quality in broadcasting, ACBB is concerned with teaching critical TV viewing skills to children. It evaluates programs, using an annual Look-Listen Poll, and publishes *Better Broadcast News,* a bimonthly newsletter.

THE AMERICAN FEDERATION OF ARTS (AFA)

41 East 65 St.
New York, NY 10021
  (212) 988-7700

AFA is a national, nonprofit cultural service agency that organizes art exhibitions and film programs and circulates them through the United States and abroad. The AFA Film Department distributes series of films on art and films as art, designed for presentation in schools, libraries, media art centers, museums, and universities. Besides offering assistance in planning film programs, the Film Department has program notes, study guides, press kits, and program guides of new films available through AFA, which publishes a newsletter, a variety of art magazines, and books on art.

THE AMERICAN FILM INSTITUTE (AFI)

The John F. Kennedy Center
  for the Performing Arts
Washington, DC 20566
  (202) 828-4000

This national organization was established by the National Endowment for the Arts to "preserve and advance the art of film." AFI assists filmmakers, provides clearinghouse information on media organizations and publications, and operates a national film repertory exhibition program. Publications include *American Film, AFI Education Newsletter,* and *Factfile,* a series of reference lists on film and television topics.

AMERICAN LIBRARY ASSOCIATION (ALA)

50 East Huron St.
Chicago, IL 60611
  (312) 944-6780

This national organization of librarians works to promote the use of books and information services. The Children's Services Division and the Young Adult Services Division both have committees that evaluate films for these age levels. ALA publications include *American Libraries, Booklist, Choice,* and *Top of the News,* as well as books and pamphlets related to library service.

ARTS, EDUCATION AND AMERICANS, INC.

Box 5297
Grand Central Station
New York, NY 10163
  (212) 582-2074

This national arts advocacy group offers arts information services and a quarterly bulletin to members. It also publishes monographs, and has produced a slide-tape presentation and public service announcements to promote arts education.

ASSOCIATION FOR EDUCATIONAL COMMUNICATIONS AND TECHNOLOGY (AECT)

1126 16 St. N.W.
Washington, DC 20036
  (202) 833-4180

AECT works to improve instruction through the effective use of media and technology. It compiles data and prepares recommendations to establish guidelines and standards for media programs and personnel. It also monitors and reports on government activities of interest to the membership. AECT sponsors an annual Student Film Festival and a Student Media Showcase, and publishes books, magazines, pamphlets, films, and filmstrips.

ASSOCIATION OF MEDIA PRODUCERS (AMP)

1707 L St. N.W., Suite 515
Washington, DC 20036
  (202) 296-4710

AMP is a national organization of producers and distributors of educational media. It works to promote the use of media in education, through involvement in copyright issues, media evaluation, government lobbying, and sales statistics. It holds conferences and meetings and publishes surveys, policy statements, and newsletters.

CANADIAN CENTRE FOR FILMS ON ART (CCFA)

75 Albert St., Suite B-20
Ottawa, Ontario K1P 5E7
Canada
  (613) 232-2495

CCFA is part of the Canadian Film Institute. It is a national center for information and assistance in programming films on art.

CANADIAN CENTRE OF FILMS FOR CHILDREN (CCFC)

227 Bloor St. East
Toronto, Ontario M4W 1C8
Canada
  (416) 961-8119

CCFC serves as a clearinghouse for information on films for, by, and about children. It sponsors film programs for children, organizes international meetings and film exchanges, and publishes a newsletter.

CENTER FOR ARTS INFORMATION

615 Broadway
New York, NY 10012
  (212) 677-7548

An information clearinghouse for and about the arts in New York State and the nation, the center offers special services for independent film- and videomakers, film and video service organizations, and organizations interested in using film and videotapes.

CENTER FOR MEDIA AWARENESS (CMA)

Box 86
Millburn, NJ 07041
  (201) 379-3781

The publications and training sessions of the Center for Media Awareness are designed to provide educators, parents, and media professionals with practical ways to use media—especially television—as constructive learning tools. CMA works on a consultant basis, offering workshops on critical TV viewing skills.

CENTER FOR UNDERSTANDING MEDIA

69 Horatio St.
New York, NY 10014
  (212) 929-1448

The center is a nonprofit organization that engages in research and projects in communications, the arts, and education. It specializes in projects involving children and media and has produced various publications, including *Doing the Media*, to help people working with children and media.

CHICAGO CHILDREN'S FILM CENTER

Facets Multimedia, Inc.
1517 West Fullerton Ave.
Chicago, IL 60614
  (312) 281-9075

Facets presents free screenings of films for children and offers its low-cost, nationwide Children's Film Distribution Network of selected, child-tested films to schools, libraries, and children's and parents' groups. It also conducts workshops on children's films, offers a film-study program for students, and undertakes studies on films for minority and ethnic audiences.

THE CHILDREN'S BROADCAST INSTITUTE

160 Eglinton Ave. East, Suite 207
Toronto, Ontario M4P 1G3
Canada
  (416) 482-0321

The primary goal of this national organization is to improve the quality and quantity of children's programming in Canada. The institute sponsors festivals of children's programming and distributes information on children and television.

CHILDREN'S TELEVISION WORKSHOP (CTW)

1 Lincoln Plaza
New York, NY 10023
  (212) 595-3456

Best known as the producer of "Sesame Street," CTW is a research and development laboratory that researches ways to use television as a teaching tool. It produces educational children's programming and publishes newsletters and research notes.

EDUCATIONAL FILM LIBRARY ASSOCIATION (EFLA)

43 West 61 St.
New York, NY 10023
  (212) 246-4533

EFLA promotes the production, distribution, and use of films and other audiovisual materials in education and community programs. It serves as a national clearinghouse for information on 16mm nontheatrical film and video. Its information center is open to the public by appointment. EFLA sponsors the annual American Film Festival of outstanding 16mm nontheatrical documentary, short film, and video releases of the preceding year. Its publications include *EFLA Bulletin, Festival Guide,* and *Sightlines,* as well as bibliographies, filmographies, directories, and manuals.

FILM LIBRARY INFORMATION COUNCIL (FLIC)

Box 348
Radio City Station
New York, NY 10019
  (212) 790-6418

FLIC aims to promote the wider and more effective use of films and other nonprint media by public libraries and the communities they serve. It helps librarians evaluate nonprint media and encourages the exchange of information among film librarians, distributors, and film producers. It also sponsors workshops on topics relating to the use of film and publishes *Film Library Quarterly.*

FILM SOCIETY OF LINCOLN CENTER

140 West 65 St.
New York, NY 10023
  (212) 877-1800

This arts organization sponsors film programs and the New York Film Festival, and also publishes *Film Comment Magazine.*

FILM USERS' NETWORK

Cine Information
Box 449
Planetarium Station
New York, NY 10024
  (212) 686-9897

Film Users' Network is a service for film users and distributors. Prospective members fill out a form identifying their areas of interest. The form is forwarded to filmmakers and distributors, who then send on information about new releases, festivals, conferences, and telecasts.

MEDIA CENTER FOR CHILDREN (MCC)

3 West 29 St.
New York, NY 10001
  (212) 679-9620

MCC works on behalf of children and film users to provide information about children's responses to short 16mm films. It publishes *Young Viewers,* a quarterly magazine, and sponsors national conferences and workshops.

MEDIA NETWORK

208 West 13 St.
New York, NY 10011
  (212) 620-0878

Media Network is a national organization of community, labor, and social activists, librarians, teachers, and others who use media for organizing and education. Media Network's Information Center is a clearinghouse for information on films, videotapes, and slide shows that deal with social issues.

THE MUSEUM OF BROADCASTING

One East 53 St.
New York, NY 10022
  (212) 752-7684

The museum is dedicated to the study and preservation of the history of American radio and television broadcasting. A large collection of programs from the 1920s to the present is available for viewing. The museum has a library of books and periodicals and presents films and lectures.

NATIONAL ART EDUCATION ASSOCIATION (NAEA)

1916 Association Dr.
Reston, VA 22091
  (703) 860-8000

NAEA is a national nonprofit organization of art educators. Its aim is to improve the quality of visual art instruction, and it conducts research, holds conferences and conventions, and publishes journals to achieve this aim.

NATIONAL ENDOWMENT FOR THE ARTS (NEA)

2401 E St. N.W.
Washington, DC 20506
  (202) 382-6085

NEA is an independent agency of the federal government that makes grants to organizations and individuals concerned with the arts throughout the United States. Its Public Media Program provides support in arts programming, regional development, and media studies.

PTA TV ACTION CENTER

700 North Rush St.
Chicago, IL 60611
  (800) 621-4114

The TV Review Panel of the National Congress of Parents and Teachers (PTA) rates and approves shows for family viewing. PTA also holds workshops around the country to teach children to think critically about what they see on television.

PACIFIC FILM ARCHIVE

University Art Museum
2625 Durant Ave.
Berkeley, CA 94720
  (415) 642-1412

This international resource for film exhibition and scholarship shows films and maintains an archive of 6,000 prints. Its Public Service Media Program [(415) 642-1437] provides a media-information service, a film-study center, and a children's film program that shows short films on art and other subjects, offers programs for high school students, and holds public matinees for families.

TELEVISION INFORMATION OFFICE (TIO)

745 Fifth Ave.
New York, NY 10022
  (212) 579-6800

An industry organization funded by TV networks and stations and the National

Association of Broadcasters, TIO seeks to promote understanding between the audience and the television industry. It undertakes research and publications, maintains a public library and information center, and provides program information.

VIDEO RAINBOW

98 Mercer Ave.
Hartsdale, NY 10530
  (914) 948-0114

This national clearinghouse locates, evaluates, and distributes independent video for children.

6
Periodicals

AFI EDUCATION NEWSLETTER

The American Film Institute National Education
  Services
The John F. Kennedy Center for the Performing
  Arts
Washington, DC 20566
  bimonthly; free with membership in The Ameri-
  can Film Institute ($16)

News, announcements, and a calendar of
events relating to film and video education are included. "Course File," a series
of model syllabi, is a regular feature, as is
"Profile," a series of articles focusing on
selected media organizations. "Media
Messages," articles on children's media,
appears twice a year.

AGENCY FOR INSTRUCTIONAL
TELEVISION NEWSLETTER

Agency for Instructional Television (AIT)
Box A
Bloomington, IN 47402
  quarterly; free

This newsletter describes how educational
TV series distributed by AIT are being used
in classrooms. It also provides information
on series in production.

AMERICAN FILM

The American Film Institute
The John F. Kennedy Center for the Performing Arts
Washington, DC 20566
  10 issues; $16 a year

The subtitle of this periodical is "Magazine of the film and television arts."
Feature articles treat recent films and
issues and personalities in film and video,
with photographs and illustrations.

ART & MAN

902 Sylvan Ave.
Englewood Cliffs, NJ 07632
  6 issues; student edition, $7.90 each for 1–9
  subscriptions, $3.95 each for 10 or more sub-
  scriptions; teaching guide, $16

Published by Scholastic, Inc., under the
direction of the National Gallery of Art,
this is a beautifully illustrated magazine
for grades 7–12. Each issue focuses on a
different theme and artist. The teaching
guide contains curriculum and project
ideas, and lists recommended books and
films.

ARTS & ACTIVITIES

591 Camino de la Reina, Suite 200
San Diego, CA 92108
  10 issues; $15 a year

Articles on art education offer ideas for
teachers of grades K–12. A regular column, "A/V Reviews," evaluates 16mm
films on art.

BOOKLIST

American Library Association
50 East Huron St.
Chicago, IL 60611
   biweekly; $24 a year

This review journal recommends materials for library purchase to librarians and teachers. Books are its focus, but it reviews films, filmstrips, recordings, slides, and video as well.

CHILDREN'S FILM INTERNATIONAL

School of Library Science
University of Southern California
University Park
Los Angeles, CA 90007
   annual; $2.00

This report on the annual Los Angeles International Children's Film Festival is published cooperatively by the American Center of Films for Children and the University of Southern California School of Library Science. It is illustrated and has brief articles and reviews as well as coverage of the festival.

EFLA BULLETIN

Educational Film Library Association
43 West 61 St.
New York, NY 10023
   quarterly; free with membership in EFLA ($35)

This newsletter reports on festivals, filmmakers and videomakers, and news items relating to 16mm films. A calendar of upcoming festivals, conferences, and symposia is included.

EFLA EVALUATIONS

Educational Film Library Association
43 West 61 St.
New York, NY 10023
   bimonthly except July/August; price is based on
   size of film collection

Newly released 16mm films entered in the annual American Film Festival are described and rated in each issue by reviewers from colleges, libraries, and community organizations nationwide. Reviews include a plot synopsis, comments, age level, and suggested uses.

FILM COMMENT

140 West 65 St.
New York, NY 10023
   bimonthly; $10 a year

Published by the Film Society of Lincoln Center, this illustrated magazine examines international film and television. Long feature articles focus on individual films and filmmakers.

FILM LIBRARY QUARTERLY

Film Library Information Council
Box 348
Radio City Station
New York, NY 10019
   quarterly; $12 a year

Articles on the use of 16mm film in libraries are supplemented by video, film, and book reviews. This is a basic film journal for public, school, or academic libraries.

FILM LITERATURE INDEX

Filmdex, Inc.
Box 22672 Suny-A
Albany, NY 10019
   quarterly, with annual cumulation; $175 a year

International periodical literature about film is the subject of this index. About 300 periodicals are scanned for relevant articles, and there are entries for individual film titles as well as for personal names and subjects.

FILM NEWS

Box 619
La Salle, IL 61301
   quarterly; $10 a year

This international illustrated review of audiovisual software and hardware is intended for teachers, librarians, and community organizations. It offers feature articles on current film activities, including reports on film festivals; 16mm films are reviewed under appropriate subject headings.

FILMS IN REVIEW

National Board of Review of Motion Pictures
209 East 66 St., #4C
New York, NY 10021
    10 issues; $14 a year

Articles on directors and actors and feature film reviews are the focus of this publication. There are also columns on the TV scene, book reviews, and films in release, with ratings.

G P NEWSLETTER

Great Plains National Instructional Television
    Library
Box 80669
Lincoln, NE 68501
    monthly, September–May; free

News about activities at and new instructional television programs acquired by Great Plains National is provided in this newsletter.

THE HORN BOOK MAGAZINE

Park Square Building
31 St. James Ave.
Boston, MA 02116
    bimonthly; $21 a year

Aimed at teachers, children's librarians, and parents, this magazine features book and audiovisual reviews as well as articles about children's literature.

INSTRUCTIONAL INNOVATOR

Association for Educational Communications and
    Technology
1126 16 St. N.W.
Washington, DC 20036
    monthly, August–May; $18 a year

This publication focuses on the use of

media and technology in education. The section "New Products" contains reviews of various media, including films, filmstrips, and videocassettes.

INTERNATIONAL INDEX TO FILM PERIODICALS

St. Martin's Press, Inc.
175 Fifth Ave.
New York, NY 10010
    annual; $35 a year

This index is a project of the International Federation of Film Archives. About 60 periodicals on film, selected as being representative of the countries in which they are published, are indexed. Entries are organized by subject, and there is an index of subject headings used. There are separate sections for reviews, studies of individual films, and biographies.

JOURNAL OF BROADCASTING

Broadcast Education Association (BEA)
1171 N St. N.W.
Washington, DC 20036
    quarterly; $17.50 a year, $9 for students

Research articles and book reviews on all aspects of broadcasting and related fields are featured in this scholarly journal. Articles on children and television often appear.

JOURNAL OF POPULAR FILM AND TELEVISION

Heldref Publications
4000 Albemarle St. N.W.
Washington, DC 20016
    quarterly; $10 for individuals, $12 for institutions

This journal focuses on commercial cinema and television. It offers articles on film and television theory and criticism as well as interviews, filmographies, and bibliographies.

LANDERS FILM REVIEWS

Landers Associates
Box 69760
Los Angeles, CA 90069
  5 issues; $45 a year

A large number of nontheatrical 16mm films and multimedia materials are described in each issue, making this a valuable resource for teachers and librarians. The films are indexed by subject.

LEARNING: THE MAGAZINE FOR CREATIVE TEACHING

Pitman Learning, Inc.
530 University Ave.
Palo Alto, CA 94301
  9 issues; $14 a year

New trends in education and ideas for teachers are the subjects of this magazine, which gives annual Learning A/V Awards for the best films and filmstrips of the year.

MEDIA & METHODS

American Society of Educators
1511 Walnut St.
Philadelphia, PA 19102
  9 issues; $24 a year

This stimulating journal is written by teachers for teachers. Aimed at elementary through high school educators, it offers creative ideas for teaching that incorporate various media. "Study Guide Previews" of PBS programs are included, and films, filmstrips, audiocassettes, and books are regularly reviewed.

MEDIA REVIEW

343 Manville Rd.
Pleasantville, NY 10570
  10 issues; $149 (K–college) for commercial subscriptions, $99 (K–college) for educational or nonprofit institutions, $69 (K–8 or 9–college) for educational or nonprofit institutions

Educational audiovisual materials are described and rated in this resource intended for school media librarians. The service includes a newsletter that discusses the selection and use of nonprint media.

MEDIA REVIEW DIGEST

Pierian Press
5000 Washtenaw
Ann Arbor, MI 48106
  quarterly; $65 a year

Excerpts of reviews of films, videotapes, filmstrips, and records that have appeared in about 200 periodicals are included in this index, along with indications as to whether the item has been recommended. Annual cumulations offer special features including lists of award-winning films, mediagraphies, and book reviews.

PARENTS' CHOICE

Parents' Choice Foundation
Box 185
Waban, MA 02168
  quarterly; $10 a year

This periodical reviews children's media, including books, television, movies, music, story records, and toys and games. Brief articles discuss children's media and short reviews highlight recommended material.

PRIME TIME SCHOOL TELEVISION (PTST)

120 South LaSalle St., Suite 810
Chicago, IL 60603
  monthly; $10 a year

PTST is a nonprofit organization formed to encourage teachers to assign and use television programs in social studies classes. Its flyers and newsletters are a source of information for high school teachers about prime-time network programs and their uses as educational resources.

re:act

Action for Children's Television (ACT)
46 Austin St.
Newtonville, MA 02160
  biannual; $15 a year or free with membership in ACT ($20)

This news magazine treats social, cultural, and legal issues in children's television; it also reports on ACT's activities. ACT's annual achievement awards for children's programming receive coverage and books and other materials on children's television are regularly reviewed.

SCHOOL ARTS

50 Portland St.
Worcester, MA 01608
   9 issues; $14 a year

Intended for art teachers at the elementary and secondary levels, this magazine features ideas for projects, advice on equipment and teaching techniques, and audiovisual and book reviews, with high-quality color illustrations.

SCHOOL LIBRARY JOURNAL

R. R. Bowker
1180 Ave. of the Americas
New York, NY 10036
   10 issues; $25 a year

Feature articles and columns on issues of interest to children's, young adult, and school librarians are the focus of this journal, which also reviews books and audiovisual materials.

SCHOOL MEDIA QUARTERLY

American Library Association
50 East Huron St.
Chicago, IL 60611
   quarterly; $15 a year

This journal is the official publication of the American Association of School Librarians, a division of the American Library Association. Its intended audience is librarians and teachers. Feature articles focus on issues in the school library media field and there are regular columns on news, current research, media reviews, and idea exchange.

SIGHT AND SOUND

British Film Institute
111 Eighth Ave.
New York, NY 10011
   quarterly; $10 a year

This international critical magazine is published by the British Film Institute. It offers intellectual articles on film and television, film reviews, and book reviews.

SIGHTLINES

Educational Film Library Association (EFLA)
43 West 61 St.
New York, NY 10023
   quarterly; $15 a year

The focus here is on 16mm films and their use in programs. The magazine is intended for libraries, schools, colleges, and young filmmakers. Each issue offers feature articles, interviews, and filmographies. There is a regular list of recent film/video releases, and each issue contains a supplement to the book. *Feature Films on 8mm, 16mm and Videotape.*

TEACHERS GUIDES TO TELEVISION

699 Madison Ave.
New York, NY 10021
   biannual; $4 a year

This publication of the National Association of Broadcasters is intended to encourage teachers to use commercial television programs for educational purposes. A synopsis of programs is given, along with lists of related materials such as books, articles, and films, and suggestions "For Further Exploration."

TELEVISION & CHILDREN

National Council for Children and Television (NCCT)
20 Nassau St., Suite 215
Princeton, NJ 08540
   quarterly; $25 a year for institutions, $16 a year for individuals

The subtitle of this periodical is "A forum for information, research and opinion." Articles discuss aspects of children's experiences with television, and interviews and book reviews are included.

VIDEO REVIEW

325 East 75 St.
New York, NY 10021
  monthly; $18 a year

Several hundred capsule reviews of video programming appear in each issue. Feature articles examine video equipment and programming. Previews of upcoming TV and cable programs are a regular feature.

WILSON LIBRARY BULLETIN

The H. W. Wilson Company
950 University Ave.
Bronx, NY 10452
  10 issues; $14 a year

This magazine reports and comments on the world of librarianship, with feature articles and news about children and media. A regular audiovisual column reviews films for library use.

YOUNG VIEWERS

Media Center for Children
3 West 29 St.
New York, NY 10001
  quarterly; $15 a year

Articles on 16mm films for children and ideas on programming films are featured. Film reviews report on children's reactions and suggest possible uses for films.

7
Books and Articles

Children, Arts, and Media

Abelson, Alison. "Programs on the Visual Arts." *Televisions* 7, no. 1 (Winter 1979): 7–10. Aims, pitfalls, audience, and funding for visual arts programs are discussed.

"ACT on the Arts." *re:act* 8, no. 3 (Spring 1979): 16–17. A report on a symposium on television, the arts, and young people held by Action for Children's Television.

"ACT on the Arts in Minneapolis." *re:act* 9, nos. 1 and 2 (Fall/Winter 1979): 14–16. A report on Action for Children's Television's second symposium on television, the arts, and young people, designed to encourage arts programming on local children's television.

Action for Children's Television. *Editors' Choice.* Newtonville, Mass.: ACT, 1982. Editors of children's books select from their companies' lists titles that would make exciting television programs for young viewers. Plot summaries for the books are given, and the editors tell why each would translate well to the small screen.

Alper, Mara. "Lotte Reiniger." *Film Library Quarterly* 10, nos. 1 and 2 (1977): 40–44. Filmmaker Lotte Reiniger was famous for her silhouette animation. This article focuses on an animation workshop held by Reiniger, and includes a filmography of her work.

Alperowicz, Cynthia. *Arts for Young Audiences: An ACT Handbook.* Newtonville, Mass.: Action for Children's Television, 1982. 24 pp. A discussion of problems, solutions, and suggestions for bringing the arts to children through television.

American Council for the Arts in Education. Arts, Education and Americans Panel. *Coming to Our Senses: The Significance of the Arts for American Education.* New York: McGraw-Hill, 1977. 334 pp. Essays focus on the role the arts can play in education, including the promises and the problems of the media.

Berger, Pam. "Children's Video: A Beginning." *Film Library Quarterly* 13, no. 1

(1980): 36–38. The potential of video for children is the subject of this article, which points out that children's video must take into account children's experience and be respectful of their sensibilities. It also mentions some examples of art tapes for children.

Bourne, Anne Munzer. "Fear and Elation in P.S. 105: A Film/Poetry Activity." *Young Viewers* 4, nos. 3 and 4 (Summer/Fall 1981): 9–10. A report on using films in the classroom as a means of stimulating language arts activity.

Camp, Brian. "Jazz on Film: A Living Legacy." *Sightlines* 14, no. 3 (Spring 1981): 15–18. Discusses jazz films and lists sources for finding them.

Coe, Bernice. "A Gold Mine for Programmers." *Television & Children* 4, no. 3 (Summer 1981): 37–40. Alternative programming for children in the form of independent short films is the focus of this article.

Community Television Review 4, no. 2 (1981). This issue focuses on the arts, and includes articles about conferences on cable TV and the arts, producing art for television, and television by artists.

Crowley, John. "Interview with Robert Geller." *Film Library Quarterly* 10, nos. 3 and 4 (1977): 41–47. Geller is the producer of "The American Short Story" series. Here he talks about which films of the series he feels are best suited for young people. Student and teacher comments on "I'm a Fool" are given.

De Fossard, Esta. "Children's Film: An Art Form in Its Own Right." *AFI Education Newsletter* 4, no. 4 (March/April 1981): 8–9. Compares the potential of film with the potential of literature, and argues that film has "as much ability as books to enrich and ennoble the minds of the young."

DiPerna, Paula. "Conference on Films for Children." *Sightlines* 12, no. 3 (Spring 1979): 11–13. A report on a conference that focused on evaluation and production of children's films.

Egan, Catherine. "Putting the Bard on the Small Screen." *Sightlines* 11, no. 1 (Fall 1977): 8–13. A discussion of the use of film adaptations of Shakespeare's plays in the classroom, with a bibliography and a filmography.

Egan, Catherine, and Egan, John. "Films about Artists and Their Audiences." *Sightlines* 14, no. 3 (Spring 1981): 7–10. Describes what constitutes a good film about an artist, with examples.

Eisner, Elliot W., ed. *The Arts, Human Development, and Education*. Berkeley, Calif.: McCutchan, 1976. 226 pp. Essays on the arts and the course of human development, and on the arts and the social context of schooling.

"Far from Grim: Bruce Marson Discusses His Folktale Series." *Sightlines* 12, no. 1 (Fall 1978): 7–8 (*Young Viewers* supplement). An interview with the producer of "Catch a Rainbow," a children's series of folktales adapted for television.

Film Library Quarterly 9, no. 3 (1976). This is a special issue: "Children's Films: Orphans of the Industry."

Freeman, Debra. "A New Use for Television: Leading Families to Museums." *Teachers Guides to Television* 14, no. 2 (Spring 1982): 15–19. A report on the nationwide Parent Participation TV Workshop experiment that used television as a springboard for cultural activities with children and parents.

Gaffney, Maureen. "Master Artist, Master Storyteller: An Interview with Gerald McDermott." *Young Viewers* 4, nos. 3 and 4 (Summer–Fall 1981): 7–8, 19–20. Gerald McDermott discusses his unusual animated films based on folktales.

Gaffney, Maureen. "Tom Davenport Discusses His Breakthrough Fairy Tale Films." *Sightlines* 11, no. 3 (Spring 1978): 5–7 (*Young Viewers* supplement). Filmmaker Davenport talks about *Hansel and Gretel—An Appalachian Version* and *Rapunzel, Rapunzel,* two live action fairy tales for children.

Gardner, Howard. *The Arts and Human Development.* New York: Wiley, 1973. 395 pp. A psychological study of the artistic process, which examines the relationship of art to childhood development.

Gaugert, Richard. "Playing with Art Films." *Sightlines* 13, no. 4 (Summer 1980): 14. A report on an American Film Festival workshop on films for children entitled "Using Film as an Art Form."

Green, Kerry. "What's New in Italian Animation: The World of Bruno Bozzetto." *Film Library Quarterly* 13, no. 4 (1980): 30–36. A survey of the work of the well-known Italian animator.

Grover, Robert, and Avant, Julia K. "Selecting Films for Children." *Children's Film International* 2 (1979): 2–3. A report on the selection process used for the Los Angeles International Children's Film Festival. Children's preferences were a major consideration, and some of the elements they enjoyed in films included child and animal characters, action, humor, a fast start, and a good sound track.

Harmetz, Richard, and Grover, Robert. "Trends in Foreign Children's Films: England and Eastern Europe Set Pace." *Children's Film International* 1 (1977): 3–4. Observations on films produced in Eastern Europe, Iran, Japan, Canada, Australia, England, the Netherlands, and France that were screened for the Los Angeles International Children's Film Festival. The authors conclude that at present, the British Children's Film Foundation is most successful at producing films that appeal to children.

Harmonay, Maureen. "Reading: The Mass Media as Motivation." *re:act* 7, nos. 1 and 2 (Fall 1977): 8, 14. Discusses TV reading experiments and the debate over TV's ability to enrich children's reading habits by broadcasting dramas or series based on books.

Harmonay, Maureen, ed. *ACT on the Arts, Volume I: A Symposium on Television, the Arts, and Young People.* Newtonville, Mass.: Action for Children's Television, 1979. 48 pp. Transcripts of a national symposium attended by artists, art educators, government regulators, television producers, and broadcasters. Speeches address the topic of introducing the arts to young people on television, and there are case studies of arts programming for children.

Harmonay, Maureen, ed. *Promise and Performance: ACT's Guide to Television Programming for Children, Vol. II: The Arts.* Cambridge, Mass.: Ballinger, 1977. 225 pp. A collection of 25 essays by artists, educators, producers, and broadcasters on aspects of children's television and the arts.

Iarusso, Marilyn Berg. "Children's Films: Orphans of the Industry." *Film Library Quarterly* 9, no. 3 (1976): 6–15. Discusses why children's films are not as good as adult films, what children like in films, and what goes into making a good children's film.

Johnson, Jean. "Setting the Stage for the Arts: Television Plays a Starring Role." In *Curriculum and Instruction in Arts and Aesthetic Education,* edited by Martin Engel and Jerome J. Hausman. St. Louis, Mo.: CEMREL, 1981. Examines the unfulfilled promise of televised arts programs and their use in education.

Leonard, William Torbert. *Theatre: Stage-To-Screen-To-Television.* Metuchen, N.J.: Scarecrow, 1981. 2 vols. Information is provided on 327 plays that originated as stage productions, were filmed, and then televised. A synopsis of each play and background on the playwrights and the productions is included.

Levinson, Bonnie. "Playing with Film: An Approach to Programming." *Young Viewers* 3, no. 1 (Spring 1980): 4–8. A report on a program of film screenings for children at the Delaware Art Museum, which was followed by related arts activities.

Levinson, Bonnie. "Playing with Film (Part Two): Inventive Children's Programs at the Delaware Museum of Art." *Young Viewers* 3, no. 2 (Summer 1980): 4–10. Lists and describes the films used in ten programs with children, with comments on how the programs worked.

Liepmann, Lise. "An Experiment: Film and Kids and Dance." *Sightlines* 11, no. 3 (Spring 1978): 10 (*Young Viewers* supplement). A report on a film and movement program for children at a New York elementary school, listing the benefits, problems, and films involved.

May, Jill P. "Butchering Children's Literature." *Film Library Quarterly* 11, nos. 1 and 2 (1978): 55–62. A criticism of Disney's adaptations of children's literature and fairy tales.

Morton, Miriam. "TV and the Aesthetic Education of Children: An Interview with Vladimir A. Razumnyi." *Television & Children* 4, no. 4 (Fall 1981/Winter 1982): 45–56. Professor Razumnyi, a Soviet researcher in educational mass media, discusses how exposure to the arts through television can be an important part of children's education.

Moscowitz, Ronnie. "Kids Talk Back." *Film Library Quarterly* 9, no. 3 (1976): 44–45. A short article giving children's comments on films, telling what they like and what they would like to see.

"The Reference Shelf: Arts Bibliography." *Sightlines* 14, no. 3 (Spring 1981): 19. Lists 25 books and articles on films about animation, art, dance, music, and theater.

Rice, Susan, and Mukerji, Rose, eds. *Children Are Centers for Understanding Media.* Washington, D.C.: Association for Childhood Education International, 1973. 89 pp. Details ways in which children can be directly involved with producing, rather than just consuming nonprint media, with ideas for making cameras, flipbooks, animation, films, and other media tools with children.

Ruth, Deborah Dashow. "Expanded Literacy: The New Basic Skill." *AFI Education Newsletter* 4, no. 1 (September/October 1980): 8–9. An argument for including nonprint media in elementary and secondary curricula, because of the increasing importance of visual literacy.

Schecter, Ellen. "A Stimulus—Not a Substitute." *Sightlines* 11, no. 4 (Summer 1978): 7–9 (*Young Viewers* supplement). A report on a workshop at which arts educators demonstrated how they use film with children.

Schenkel, Thelma. "Talking with Caroline Leaf." *Film Library Quarterly* 10, nos. 1 and 2 (1977): 31–39. An interview with an animator who has done films for children, in which she talks about her unusual animation techniques.

Schindel, Morton. "Children's Literature on Film: Through the Audiovisual Era to the Age of Telecommunications." In *Children's Literature: Annual of The Modern Language Association Division on Children's Literature and The Children's Literature Association,* vol. 9, pp. 93–106. New Haven, Conn.: Yale University Press, 1981. Schindel is the founder and president of Weston Woods, which specializes in producing films based on children's books. In this article he discusses adapting children's literature for film and television.

Schwarz, Meg. "Broadcasting Books to Young Audiences." *re:act* 9, nos. 3 and 4 (Spring/Summer 1980): 18–19. A report on a symposium held jointly by Action for Children's Television and the Library of Congress Center for the Book, at which authors, editors, producers, broadcasters, and librarians explored ways to develop more children's television programming based on books.

Semkow, Julie. "Programming New Matinees." *Young Viewers* 1, no. 4 (Summer 1978): 15–17, 19. A report on the workshop "Film Programming for Young People," with a list of resources and a filmography.

Sightlines 14, no. 3 (Spring 1981). This issue focuses on the arts, with feature articles on films about artists and their audiences, musical theater, jazz on film, and filmmaker Michael Blackwood, among other topics.

Singer, Marilyn. "The Originals: Women in Art." *Film Library Quarterly* 11, no. 3 (1978): 17–26. A criticism of Perry Miller Adato's series on women artists, this includes a filmography of the "Women in Art" series and a related filmography of works on women in the visual arts.

Spirt, Diana L. "Imagination and Childhood: A Creative Approach to Film Programming for Children." *Previews* 7, no. 2 (October 1978): 2–3. A discussion of the necessity of capturing the imagination of children when programming films by entertaining and stimulating curiosity, and by understanding children's thoughts and feelings.

Trojan, Judith. "The Documentaries of Perry Miller Adato." *Film Library Quarterly* 11, nos. 1 and 2 (1978): 28–35. An interview with the filmmaker responsible for *Georgia O'Keeffe* and other films about artists and writers.

Trojan, Judith. "Poetry, Film & Kids: An Interview with Janet Sternburg." *Sightlines* 10, no. 1 (Fall 1976): 14–16. An interview with a poet and filmmaker who uses short films to expand the creative consciousness of children.

Trojan, Judith. "Who's Who in Filmmaking: Michael Blackwood." *Sightlines* 14, no. 3 (Spring 1981): 22–26. An interview with a filmmaker whose subjects are art and artists. A filmography of Blackwood's work is included.

Welch, Jeffrey Egan. *Literature and Film: An Annotated Bibliography.* New York: Garland, 1981. 315 pp. Books, articles, and dissertations on the relationship between film and literature are annotated, with indexes by literary author and by name and subject. There are also listings of interviews and screenplays, and articles on teaching film and literature courses. An appendix lists major literary works that have been adapted into films.

Young Viewers 5, nos. 1 and 2 (Winter/Spring 1982). This issue provides a model user's guide for the film *The Frog King or Faithful Henry,* with guides for different grade levels, bibliographies, and a filmography.

Filmographies: Books and Articles Listing Selected Films

"A to Z: A Sampler of Animated Films." *Top of the News* 37, no. 2 (Winter 1981): 202–206. Forty-nine 16mm films that illustrate a wide range of animation techniques are listed and briefly described, with information on the animation techniques used, the length, the distributor, and the year of release. The list was prepared by the Media Selection and Usage Committee of the Young Adult Services Division of the American Library Association.

Artel, Linda. "Films for Very Young Viewers." *Sightlines* 11, no. 3 (Spring 1978): 3–4, 10 (*Young Viewers* supplement). An annotated list of films tested with children at the Pacific Film Archive.

Artel, Linda, and Wengraf, Susan. *Positive Images: A Guide to Non-Sexist Films for Young People.* San Francisco: Bootlegger Press, 1976. 167 pp. An annotated catalogue of over 400 films, videotapes, filmstrips, and slides that promote nonstereotyped images; includes a subject index and a selected bibliography.

Braun, Susan, and Kitching, Jesse, comps. *Dance and Mime: Film and Videotape Catalog.* 2nd ed. New York: Dance Films Association, 1980. 146 pp. Lists and describes more than 1,100 films and videotapes on all aspects of dance. Productions are indexed by name of dancer, dance company, choreographer, composer, dance teacher, narrator, type of dance, film producer, director, and cinematographer.

Brown, Lucy Gregor. *Core Media Collection for Elementary Schools.* 2nd ed. New York: R. R. Bowker, 1978. 224 pp. A guide to over 3,000 nonprint media titles for grades K–6. Materials included "have been favorably reviewed, are award winners, or have been evaluated for their authenticity, technical quality, appropriateness for the subjects being considered, student level, interest and motivation, accuracy in content and validity in treatment." Productions are organized by subject with brief descriptions; a title index and a list of distributors are provided.

Brown, Lucy Gregor. *Core Media Collection for Secondary Schools.* 2nd ed. New York: R. R. Bowker, 1979 (1st ed. 1975). 263 pp. A selection aid for teachers of grades 7–12. Inclusion of materials in the list was based on favorable reviews in professional journals and/or awards won. Productions are organized by subject and briefly annotated with a title index and a producer/distributor directory. The first edition has 2,000 titles; the second has 3,000 titles, with little overlap.

Canadian Centre for Films on Art. *Films on Art.* New York: Watson-Guptill, 1977. 240 pp. An annotated index of 450 films on painting, drawing, prints, sculpture, architecture, photography, and archeology. A subject index, an index by artist, and a distributor directory are included.

Center for Southern Folklore, comp. *American Folklore Films and Videotapes: A Catalog.* Vol. 2. New York: R. R. Bowker, 1982. A list of about 2,200 productions on aspects of the American folk experience and specific folk arts. Entries are briefly described, with distributor information and a subject index.

Children's Films. Madison, Wis.: Wisconsin Library Association, 1979. 20 pp. Recommended short films for children are listed in this booklet, which also includes a bibliography and a section on films for professional use.

Collier, Marilyn, Almy, Millie, and Keller, Barbara. *Films for Children Ages 3 to 5.* Berkeley, Calif.: The Instructional Laboratories, Department of Education, University of California, 1976. Fifty-seven child-tested films are described in detail, with information on children's reactions. Follow-up ac-

tivities for teachers to implement are suggested.

Delson, Susan. *Hispanic Children's Film: Towards a Viewer-Responsive Media.* Chicago: Facets Multimedia, 1979. 41 pp. An evaluation of 20 films oriented to Hispanic children, based on screenings with young audiences.

Emmens, Carol A. "Films to Liven a Language Arts Program." *Previews* 3, no. 6 (February 1975): 5–9. Creative, entertaining short films for ages 3 to 12 are described.

Emmens, Carol A. "Poets and Poetry on Film." *Media & Methods* 13, no. 9 (May/June 1977): 42–46. A discussion and comparison of filmed versions of poems and also films about poets.

Emmens, Carol A. *Short Stories on Film.* Littleton, Colo.: Libraries Unlimited, 1978. 345 pp. Identifies and annotates more than 1,300 films produced from 1920 to 1976 that were based on short stories by American authors or by international authors well known in America.

"Films for Kids in the Minority." *Film Library Quarterly* 9, no. 3 (1976): 46–52. Children's films focusing on blacks, Asian Americans, girls, Hispanic Americans, and native Americans are featured.

Gaffney, Maureen. "Ex Libris: Transforming Literature into Film." *Young Viewers* 4, nos. 3 and 4 (Summer/Fall 1981): 14–15. Short films based on literature and folktales are listed, with a description of sources for locating feature-length film adaptations of literary works.

Gaffney, Maureen. *More Films Kids Like: A Catalog of Short Films for Children.*

Chicago: American Library Association, 1977. 159 pp. An annotated, illustrated list of films successfully tested with children under 13. The author includes suggestions for film activities enjoyed by children, a key to distributors, an appendix of films for ages 3–6, and a subject index.

Gaffney, Maureen, and Laybourne, Gerry. *What to Do When the Lights Go On*. Phoenix, Ariz.: Oryx Press, 1981. 268 pp. Subtitled "A comprehensive guide to 16mm films and related activities for children," this is an illustrated guidebook for film programming featuring "recipes" for activities designed to follow film showings. About 300 child-tested short films are described, and a bibliography, a key to distributors, and indexes of films by distributor, technique, filmmaker, and title are among the appendixes.

Goldstein, Ruth M., and Zornow, Edith. *Movies for Kids: A Guide for Parents and Teachers on the Entertainment Film for Children*. Rev. ed. New York: Ungar, 1980. 268 pp. A catalog of 430 features, featurettes, and documentaries available in 16mm. Entries are annotated, and cast information as well as technical information is provided. Charlie Chaplin Mutual Comedies and Children's Film Foundation features are listed. A directory of film companies and distributors, bibliographies, organization lists, and a title index are also included.

Goldstein, Ruth M., and Zornow, Edith. *The Screen Image of Youth: Movies about Children and Adolescents*. Metuchen, N.J.: Scarecrow, 1980. 384 pp. Annotations on 350 films about youth that are suitable for youth are provided in this book, intended to serve as a guide for parents and teachers.

Greene, Ellin, and Schoenfeld, Madalynne. *Multimedia Approach to Children's Literature: A Selective List of Films, Filmstrips, and Recordings Based on Children's Books*. 2nd ed. Chicago: American Library Association, 1977. 206 pp. Materials to serve the interests of children from preschool to grade eight are catalogued here. Author, subject, film, and record indexes and a directory of distributors are included.

Helfand, Esther, ed. *Films for Young Adults*. New York: Educational Film Library Association, 1970. 54 pp. A selected, annotated list of classic films prepared by the Children's and Young Adult Services Section of the New York Library Association, with a subject index and suggestions on planning film programs.

Iarusso, Marilyn Berg. "Folktales and Legends in Children's Films." *Previews* 7, no. 1 (September 1978): 1–7. Fifty children's films based on folktales, myths, and legends are discussed. The author deals with problems encountered in this film genre, such as racial stereotyping and authenticity of style and spirit.

Kislia, J. A. *Let's See It Again: Free Films for Elementary Schools*. Dayton, Ohio: Pflaum/Standard, 1975. 124 pp. Over 200 films available without charge for classroom viewing are described and evaluated in this catalog, and children's reactions to the films are noted. There is a subject index and a source list.

Mandell, Phyllis Levy, and Rosenthal, Shiri, comps. "Basic Photography and Filmmaking Techniques: A Multimedia Collection." *Previews* 9, no. 4 (December 1980): 14–21. Lists films, filmstrips, videocassettes, and slides on photography, film, and animation, many of which are appropriate for children. Nonevaluative descriptions are provided.

May, Jill. *Films and Filmstrips for Language Arts.* Urbana, Ill.: National Council of Teachers of English, 1981. 103 pp. An annotated bibliography of 296 items, with author and title indexes for children's literature as well as a general subject index.

McCarthy, Connie. "The Special Children Film Project." *Sightlines* 10, no. 2 (Winter 1976/77): 13–16. Films that were successful with hospitalized youngsters and learning-disabled children are described.

MediaLog. New York: Film Fund, 1982. A guide to television, film, and radio programs supported by the National Endowment for the Humanities, *MediaLog* contains information about more than 315 productions on the humanities, including "History, Theory and Criticism of the Arts" and "The Humanities in Literature." The publication is available free by writing to the National Endowment for the Humanities, 806 15th St. N.W., Washington, DC 20506.

Mueller, John. *Dance Film Directory: An Annotative and Evaluative Guide to Films on Ballet and Modern Dance.* Princeton N.J.: Princeton, University Press, 1979. 103 pp. Dance performances and excerpts on 16mm films and videotape are included, with information on distributors, choreographers, dance works, and dance. There are appendixes on mime films, ethnic dance films, Fred Astaire, and Busby Berkeley.

Parlato, Salvatore J., Jr. "Children's Novels on Film." *Previews* 7, no. 9 (May 1979): 3–4. Twenty-four films based on novels for children are listed and briefly outlined.

Parlato, Salvatore J., Jr. *Films Ex Libris: Literature in 16mm and Video.* Jefferson, N.C.: McFarland, 1980. 271 pp. Over 1,000 short 16mm films, videocassettes, and discs based on literary works are annotated. Entries are arranged according to genre, such as children's stories, novels, and poetry, with author and title indexes.

Parlato, Salvatore J., Jr. *Films—Too Good for Words: A Directory of Nonnarrated 16mm Films.* New York: R. R. Bowker, 1972. 209 pp. Nearly 1,000 nonverbal films are listed under broad subject headings, with a title index and a detailed subject index.

Parlato, Salvatore J., Jr. *Superfilms: An International Guide to Award-Winning Educational Films.* Metuchen, N.J.: Scarecrow, 1976. 365 pp. This guide to 1,500 award-winning 16mm educational films contains a subject index, a company title index, and a list of festivals. Sale and rental information is provided.

Parlato, Salvatore J., Jr. "A Tautology of Short Story Films." *Previews* 7, no. 7 (March 1979): 4–7. Fifty-seven films based on short stories are described; many are recommended for children.

Rehrauer, George. *The Short Film: An Evaluative Selection of 500 Recommended Films.* New York: Macmillan, 1975. 199 pp. The films included are those that have been recommended in selected books (and one periodical). Brief descriptions are provided, with illustrations, a subject index, and lists of books and periodicals.

Rice, Susan. *Films Kids Like: A Catalog of Short Films for Children*. Chicago: American Library Association, 1973. 150 pp. An annotated, illustrated list of 219 short 16mm films for children, giving children's reactions.

Salz, Kay. *Craft Films: An Index of International Films on Crafts*. New York: Neal-Schuman, 1979. 178 pp. One thousand 16mm films are listed in this nonevaluative filmography on a wide range of traditional and contemporary crafts and their creators.

Schrank, Jeffrey. *Guide to Short Films*. Rochelle Park, N.J.: Hayden, 1979. 197 pp. Creative, entertaining short films (228 entries) are described, with illustrations. A distributors list with addresses and a subject index are provided.

Sternburg, Janet. "Non-Sexist Films for Children." *Sightlines* 8, no. 1 (Fall 1974): 8–18. Fifty-one films that depict nonstereotyped behavior are highlighted.

Trojan, Judith. *American Family Life Films*. Metuchen, N.J.: Scarecrow, 1981. 508 pp. Two thousand short and feature-length films on subjects relating to family concerns are listed alphabetically, with brief annotations and distributor information. Subject and title indexes are included.

Wynar, Lubomyr R., and Buttlar, Lois. *Ethnic Film and Filmstrip Guide for Libraries and Media Centers: A Selective Filmography*. Littleton, Colo.: Libraries Unlimited, 1980. 277 pp. An annotated guide to 1,400 films and filmstrips on the culture and the experience of 46 American ethnic groups.

Locating and Using Film and Video

Audiovisual Marketplace 1982: A Multimedia Guide. 12th ed. New York: R. R. Bowker, 1982. 471 pp. This annual reference work provides listings of audiovisual software, audiovisual hardware, and reference sources. Names, addresses, and telephone numbers are supplied for producers, distributors, equipment manufacturers, associations, and many other services, and the reference section includes a calendar of events along with other lists.

Berger, James L., comp. and ed. *Educators' Guide to Free Audio and Video Materials*. 28th ed. Randolph, Wis.: Educators Progress Service, 1981. 297 pp. A guide to help teachers select free films, filmstrips, slides, cassettes, and videotapes. The 961 titles (including 415 videotapes) listed and briefly described are organized by broad subject headings. There is also a detailed subject index, a title index, and a source and availability index.

Blackaby, Linda, Georgakas, Dan, and Margolis, Barbara. *In Focus: A Guide to Using Films*. New York: Cine Information, 1980. 206 pp. Provides practical hints for community programmers based on firsthand experiences, with information on selecting films, acquiring them inexpensively, leading discussions, publicizing and evaluating films, purchasing equipment, and setting up programs. A resources chapter lists organizations, programming guides, and periodicals.

Brown, James W., ed. *Educational Media Yearbook 1982*. Littleton, Colo.: Libraries Unlimited, 1982. 450 pp. This is a source of up-to-date information about the field of educational media/instructional technology. A guide to organizations, associations, and doctoral and master's programs and a directory of funding sources are featured as well as a mediagraphy listing print and nonprint resources and a directory of producers, distributors, and publishers.

Diffor, John C., and Diffor, Elaine N., eds. *Educators Guide to Free Films*. Randolph, Wis.: Educators Progress Service, 1981. 790 pp. Some 4,825 items that cover a wide variety of curriculum-related subjects are listed in this reference source for teachers.

Educational Film Locator of the Consortium of University Film Centers and R. R. Bowker. 2nd ed. New York: R. R. Bowker, 1980. 2,611 pp. Over 40,000 films available for rental or sale from the 50 member institutions of the Consortium and from film producers and distributors are listed. A subject and audience-level index, a series listing, an index of foreign film titles, and a directory of publishers and distributors are included.

Emmens, Carol, ed. *Children's Media Market Place*. 2nd ed. New York: Neal-Schuman, 1981. 450 pp. This directory of children's media sources includes lists of publishers, audiovisual producers and distributors, periodicals, children's television program sources, organizations, federal grants, awards, and a bibliography.

Factfile. Los Angeles: The American Film Institute. Reference information on various topics in film and television is offered in this series of periodically updated documents: *Film and Television Periodicals in English; Careers in Film and Television; Film/Video Festivals and Awards; Guide to Classroom Use of Film/Video; Women and Film/Television; Independent Film and Video; Movie and TV Nostalgia; Film Music; Animation; Third World Cinema; Film/Television: A Research Guide; Film/Television: Grants, Scholarships, Special Programs; Films about Motion Pictures and Television*.

Index to Educational Video Tapes. 5th ed. Los Angeles: National Information Center for Educational Media (NICEM), University of Southern California, 1980. Approximately 16,000 commercially produced educational videotapes are listed, with technical information and a brief description provided for each one.

Index to 16mm Educational Films. 7th ed. 4 vols. Los Angeles: National Information Center for Educational Media (NICEM), University of Southern California, 1980. Approximately 100,000 commercially produced films are listed, with technical information and a brief description provided for each one.

Kazdin, Genevieve. "Tapes for Kids: 10 Things to Look for. . . ." *Video Review* 2, no. 6 (June 1981): 46–69. Guidelines for parents concerned about the suitability of the content of a videotape or disc. Some of the author's "things to look for" include color, length, sound track, language level, violence, audio and video quality, and potential for stimulating interest.

Laybourne, Kit, and Ciancolo, Pauline, eds. *Doing the Media: A Portfolio of*

Activities, Ideas and Resources. Rev. ed. New York: McGraw-Hill, 1979. 212 pp. An illustrated collection of writings on media philosophy, activities, goals, and resources. The essays cover such subjects as the importance of media programs, photography, film-making, video, sound, and other media formats, and there is an annotated resource section.

Limbacher, James L., comp. and ed. *Feature Films on 8mm, 16mm and Videotape.* 6th ed. New York: R. R. Bowker, 1979. 447 pp. A directory of feature films, videotapes, and serials available for rental, sale, and lease in nontheatrical situations. Updates appear regularly in *Sightlines* magazine.

Miller, Hannah Elsas. *Films in the Classroom: A Practical Guide.* Metuchen, N.J.: Scarecrow, 1979. 313 pp. Offers ideas on selecting, showing, and using 16mm films with students; with filmographies and appendixes, including lists of organizations, sources of free and inexpensive motion pictures, and a list of relevant journals.

Rehrauer, George. *Film User's Handbook: A Basic Manual for Managing Library Film Services.* New York: R. R. Bowker, 1975. 301 pp. A guide for film librarians that covers programming, cataloguing and organizing collections, selecting and maintaining equipment, and film library administration.

Sive, Mary Robinson. *Selecting Instructional Media: A Guide to Audiovisual and Other Instructional Media Lists.* 3rd ed. Littleton, Colo.: Libraries Unlimited, 1982. 300 pp. An annotated guide to approximately 400 selected media lists for K–12, organized into comprehensive lists, lists by subjects, and lists by media.

Thomas, James L., ed. *Nonprint in the Elementary Curriculum: Readings for Reference.* Littleton, Colo.: Libraries Unlimited, 1982. 155 pp. Twenty-three articles by practitioners discuss the variety of ways in which nonprint materials can be used in the classroom.

Thomas, James L., ed. *Nonprint in the Secondary Curriculum: Readings for Reference.* Littleton, Colo.: Libraries Unlimited, 1982. 215 pp. Twenty-seven articles by teachers and librarians discuss the use of nonprint materials in the classroom.

The Video Source Book. 3rd ed. Syosset, N.Y.: National Video Clearinghouse, 1982. 1,568 pp. Some 34,311 videotape and disc program titles are listed, bringing together the catalogs of 653 distributors. Brief descriptions, technical information, audience, and acquisition-availability (rent, loan, purchase, or license) information are provided. There is a subject index and a list of distributors, with addresses.

The Videotape/Disc Guide: Children's Programs. Syosset, N.Y.: National Video Clearinghouse, 1980. 134 pp. Some 2,000 prerecorded children's program title listings are supplied, with brief descriptions, formats, running times, casts, directors, producers, and information on where to buy or rent. Includes illustrations and articles on video, as well as a subject index.

Weaver, Kathleen, ed. *Film Programmer's Guide to 16mm Rentals.* 3rd ed. Albany, Calif.: Reel Research, 1980. 320 pp. A listing of 14,000 films, both features and shorts, available from 105 distributors. Entries include country of origin, date of release, running time, distributor, and rental costs.

Appendix 1
Filmmakers/
Producers/Directors

Aaron, Jane
Kuumba: Simon's New Sound

ACI Films
At Your Fingertips (Series)

Adato, Perry Miller
Anonymous Was a Woman
Georgia O'Keeffe
Nevelson in Process

Ahnemann, Michael
Siu Mei Wong: Who Shall I Be?

Amitai, Ami
Taleb and His Lamb

Anderson, Amelia
Scott Joplin: King of Ragtime Composers

Anderson, Yvonne
Masterpiece

Anthony, Joseph
Walter Kerr on Theater

Asselin, Paul and Asselin, Diane
Dinky Hocker

Associated Council of the Arts
Art Is

Avildsen, John
Dance on a May Day

Bachrach, Doro
The Electric Grandmother
The Gold Bug
Rodeo Red and the Runaway

The Seven Wishes of Joanna Peabody
Sunshine's on the Way

Baker, Diane
Portrait of Grandpa Doc

Balla, Nicholas
The Bear and the Mouse

Ballard, Carroll
The Black Stallion

Bank, Mira
Anonymous Was a Woman

Barbera, Joseph
Charlotte's Web

Barnes, John
The Art of Silence: Pantomimes with Marcel
  Marceau (Series)

Barron, Arthur
The Jolly Corner
My Hands Are the Tools of My Soul
Parker Adderson, Philosopher

Barron, Evelyn
The Tap Dance Kid

Bass, Saul
Notes on the Popular Arts
Why Man Creates

Bauman, Suzanne
The Artist Was a Woman

Beaudry-Cowling, Diane
Maud Lewis: A World Without Shadows

Bell, Mary
The Artist Was a Woman

Bennett, Richard
Very Good Friends

Bernal, William
The Foolish Frog

Besen, Ellen
Sea Dream

Bessie, Dan
Peter and the Wolf
The Notorious Jumping Frog of Calaveras
County

BFA
Dragon Stew

Biggs, Julian
Paddle to the Sea

Bill, Tony
The Ransom of Red Chief

Black Music Association
Black Music in America: From Then till Now
Black Music in America: The Seventies

Black, Noel
The Electric Grandmother
The Golden Honeymoon
I'm a Fool

Blackwood, Christian
Tapdancin'

Blank, Les
Del Mero Corazón: Love Songs of the Southwest

Blank, Tom
Dinky Hocker

Bloomberg, Robert
Animation Pie
Kuumba: Simon's New Sound

Bosustow, Nick
The Incredible Book Escape (Series)
The Legend of Sleepy Hollow
Nate the Great Goes Undercover

Bosustow, Stephen
Madeline

Stephen Bosustow Productions
Evan's Corner

The Guitar: From Stone Age through Solid
Rock
The Legend of John Henry
My Mother Is the Most Beautiful Woman in
the World

Bozzetto, Bruno
The Last Meow: Sibelius's "Valse Triste"
Let It Bee: Vivaldi's "Concerto in C-dur"

Brandt, Yanna
Superlative Horse

British Broadcasting Corporation
The Shakespeare Plays (Series)

Buchbinder, Paul
The Hare and the Tortoise (2nd Edition)

Budner, Gerald
A Is for Architecture (Revised Version)

Burke, Terry
Track Stars: The Unseen Heroes of Movie
Sound

Burnford, Paul
Camera Magic: The Art of Special Effects
Frame by Frame

Centron Corporation
Henry Moore: Master Sculptor
Poetry for Fun: Dares and Dreams
Poetry for Fun: Poems about Animals
Poetry for Fun: Troolier Coolier

Chagrin, Claude and Chagrin, Julian
The Concert
The Morning Spider

Chaplin, Charles
City Lights
The Gold Rush
Modern Times

Chase, Doris
Full Circle: The Work of Doris Chase

Chevry, Bernard
Love of Life

**Chuck Olin Associates for the Art Institute of
Chicago**
Museum: Behind the Scenes at the Art Insti-
tute of Chicago

Clark, James B.
And Now Miguel
The Island of the Blue Dolphins

Cleman Film Enterprises
Maria of the Pueblos

Cochran, Alexander
Apt. 3
Hush Little Baby

Collins, Judy
Antonia: Portrait of a Woman

Concepts Unlimited
Norman Rockwell's World . . . An American
    Dream

Cook, Fielder
From the Mixed-Up Files of Mrs. Basil E.
    Frankweiler

Coppola, Francis Ford
The Black Stallion

Crawley Films
The Loon's Necklace

Crocus Productions
Whazzat?

Csicsery, George Paul
Tealia

Daly, Tom
A Is for Architecture (Revised Version)
Beware, Beware My Beauty Fair
Eskimo Artist—Kenojuak
In Praise of Hands
The Living Stone

Darino, Eduardo
The Bird, the Fox and the Full Moon

Davenport, Tom
From the Brothers Grimm: American Versions
    of Fairytale Classics (Series)

Davies, Jon
Silver Blaze

Davis, Bill
The Notorious Jumping Frog of Calaveras
    County

De Nonno, Tony
One Generation Is Not Enough

DEFA Studios
Little Red Riding Hood
The Seven Ravens

Deitch, Gene
The Beast of Monsieur Racine

The Foolish Frog
Harold's Fairy Tale
Moon Man
Patrick
A Picture for Harold's Room
Smile for Auntie
A Story—A Story
Strega Nonna
The Swineherd
Teeny-Tiny and the Witch-Woman
The Three Robbers
The Ugly Duckling
Where the Wild Things Are
Zlateh the Goat

Deneen, William
Silver Blaze
The Ugly Little Boy

DePatie-Freleng Productions
The Cat in the Hat

Depovere, Christian
Puppet Magic

Deubel, Robert
Norman Rockwell's World . . . An American
    Dream

DiMuro, J. V., II
Listen!

Disney, Walt
Casey at the Bat
Four Artists Paint One Tree
History of Animation
Sleeping Beauty
Toot, Whistle, Plunk and Boom
A World Is Born

Dokumenta Productions
The Magic Pipes

Dornhelm, Robert
The Children of Theater Street

Dourmashkin, Barbara
Isabella and the Magic Brush

Drouin, Jacques
Mindscape

Dunning, George
Yellow Submarine

Eames, Ray and Eames, Charles
Degas in the Metropolitan

Educational Broadcasting Corporation
Cherry Tree Carol

**Educational Film Center,
North Springfield, VA**
Images and Things (Series)

Elikann, Larry
The Amazing Cosmic Awareness of Duffy
  Moon
The Horrible Honchos
Rookie of the Year

Engel, Herman J.
The Clay Circus
Documentary

Fanshel, Susan
Nevelson in Process

Feeney, John
Eskimo Artist—Kenojuak
The Living Stone

Ferrero, Pat
Quilts in Women's Lives

Ferris, William
Give My Poor Heart Ease: Mississippi Delta
  Bluesman

Fertik, William
The Bolero

Fichter, Richard
The Story of Good King Huemac

Fierlinger, Paul
It's So Nice to Have a Wolf Around the
  House

Fillinger, Paul
Houses Have History

FilmFair Communications
Paddington Bear (Series)

Filmpolski
Tales of Hiawatha

**Fine Arts Museum of Boston, Department of
Public Education**
Masterpiece

Finley, Ron
New York City Too Far from Tampa Blues

Fiore, Robert
Full of Life A-dancin'

Flicker, Theodore J.
Jacob Two-Two Meets the Hooded Fang

Foreman, Stephen
The Seven Wishes of Joanna Peabody

Fox, Beryl
Images of the Wild

Freitag, Cynthia
The Cow Who Fell in the Canal
Norman the Doorman

Friedman, Sonya
The Bronze Zoo
Documentary

Fuest, Robert
The Gold Bug

Furrer, Urs
Superlative Horse

Gakken Film
Beauty and the Beast
Clever Hiko-Ichi (A Japanese Tale)
Mr. Goshu, the Cellist

Gardiner, Bob
Closed Mondays

Geller, Robert
The American Short Story (Series)

Geromini, Clyde
Sleeping Beauty

Gianini, Giulio
An Italian in Algiers
Pulcinella

Gilford, Joseph
Max

Glover, Guy
Aucassin and Nicolette
The Light Fantastick
The Street

Godmilow, Jill
Antonia: Portrait of a Woman
Nevelson in Process

Goldman, Stuart A.
Sandsong

Gottlieb, Linda
Big Henry and the Polka Dot Kid
The Case of the Elevator Duck

Snowbound
Summer of My German Soldier

Grant, Barbara
The Tap Dance Kid

**Greater Washington Educational
Telecommunications Association, Inc.**
The Best of Cover to Cover (Series)

Gruebel, Jim
Horse Flickers

Guenette and Schnickel
SPFX: The Making of The Empire Strikes Back

Guenette, Robert
The Making of Star Wars
SPFX: The Making of The Empire Strikes Back

Gulkin, Harry
Jacob Two-Two Meets the Hooded Fang

Hahn, David
In a Rehearsal Room

Haines, Randa
The Jilting of Granny Weatherall

Halberstadt, Hans
Stained Glass—Painting with Light

Hammerich, Paul
The Swineherd
The Ugly Duckling

Hanna, William
Charlotte's Web

Harris, Tom
A Boy Creates

Healy, Deborah
Little Birds
The Owl and the Pussycat

Hershey, Anne
Never Give Up: Imogen Cunningham

Herz, Michael
Dance on a May Day

Hirsch, Michael
The Devil and Daniel Mouse
How We Made "The Devil and Daniel
    Mouse"

Hood, Kit
Ida Makes a Movie and Learns to Tell the
    Truth

Hopkins, Don
Images of the Wild

Hubley, Faith
The Big Bang and Other Creation Myths

Institut für Film und Bild
Bremen Town Musicians
The Shoemaker and the Elves

Internews Productions
Puppet Magic

Izen, Marshall
The Isle of Joy

Jackson, Lamont
Paul's Case

Jacobs, Lewis
The Raven

Jittlov, Mike
The Wizard of Speed and Time

Jodoin, René
Monsieur Pointu

Jones, Chuck
Mowgli's Brothers
Rikki-Tikki-Tavi

Jones, Dewitt
Robert Frost's New England

Jordan, Glenn
The Displaced Person

Joseph, John
Gravity Is My Enemy

Kadar, Jan
The Blue Hotel

Karkowsky, Nancy Faye
The First Moving Picture Show

Kaufman, Lloyd
Dance on a May Day

Kentucky Authority for ETV, Lexington
Images and Things (Series)

KETC-TV, St. Louis
Images and Things (Series)

King Features-Subafilms
Yellow Submarine

Kleiser, Randal
Portrait of Grandpa Doc

Koenig, Wolf
Aucassin and Nicolette
The Light Fantastick
The Lion and the Mouse
The Street

Korty, John
The Music School

Kraft, Doreen
Black Dawn

Kratky Films
Leonardo's Diary
Moon Man

Krizsan, Les
Medoonak, the Stormmaker

Kroll, Nathan
Pavarotti at Juilliard, Program 1

Kurtz, Gary
The Making of Star Wars

Kutten, Ellen Jane
Tealia

Labrosse, Jean-Michel
Duel-Duo

LaFleur, Jean
Beware, Beware My Beauty Fair

Lamb, Derek
I Know an Old Lady Who Swallowed a Fly
This Is Your Museum Speaking

Lambart, Evelyn
The Lion and the Mouse

Lammers, Paul
The Joy of Bach

Lamorisse, Albert
The Red Balloon

Larkin, Ryan
Street Musique

Lathan, Stan
Almos' a Man
The Sky Is Gray

Lawrence, Carol Munday
Kuumba: Simon's New Sound

Lax, Jennifer
Max

Leaf, Caroline
The Owl Who Married a Goose
The Street

Leduc, André
Monsieur Pointu

le Flaguais, Franck
The Boy Who Heard Music

Lightfoot, Norman
Images of the Wild

Littig, Eileen
The Folk Book (Series)

Lloyd, Robin
Black Dawn

Longpré, Bernard
Monsieur Pointu

Loubert, Patrick
The Devil and Daniel Mouse
How We Made "The Devil and Daniel
  Mouse"

Low, Colin
A Is for Architecture (Revised Version)
I Know an Old Lady Who Swallowed a Fly
In Praise of Hands

Luzzati, Emanuele
An Italian in Algiers
Pulcinella

Mack, Earle
The Children of Theater Street

Magyar, Dexso
Rappaccini's Daughter

Manasse, George
Dance on a May Day

Mandel, Robert
Sunshine's on the Way

Marks, Aleksandar
Cowherd Marko

Marquand, Richard
Big Henry and the Polka Dot Kid
Luke Was There

Mason, Bill
Paddle to the Sea

Mason, John
Museum: Behind the Scenes at the Art
  Institute of Chicago

McDermott, Gerald
Anansi the Spider
Arrow to the Sun
The Magic Tree

McLaren, Ian
Medoonak, the Stormmaker

McLaren, Norman
Ballet Adagio
A Chairy Tale
Hen Hop
Pas de Deux

Messina, Cedric
The Shakespeare Plays (Series)

Meyerhoff, Marianne
A Tale of Till

Miller, Allan
The Bolero
Romeo and Juliet in Kansas City

Miller, Jonathan
The Shakespeare Plays (Series)

Miller, Leah
The Hundred Penny Box

Mills, Michael
The Happy Prince

Mills, Reginald
Peter Rabbit and Tales of Beatrix Potter

Minimal Produckter
The Fisherman and His Wife

Mischer, Don
Twyla Tharp: Making TV Dance

Mitchell Seltzer Productions
Nate the Great Goes Undercover

Moretti, Pierre
The Owl Who Married a Goose

Morrison, Jane
The White Heron

Morse, Barry
The Ugly Little Boy

Moss, Carleton
Two Centuries of Black American Art

Moyer, Larry
Lafcadio, the Lion Who Shot Back

Moynihan, Frank
Keith
Martin the Cobbler

National Film Board of Canada
The Bead Game
A Chairy Tale
Images of the Wild
Medoonak, The Stormmaker
Mindscape
Street Musique

Neary, Brian
Listen!

Nelvana
The Devil and Daniel Mouse

Nevell, Richard
Full of Life A-dancin'

NEWIST
The Folk Book (Series)

Nichols, Charles A.
Charlotte's Web

Nierenberg, George T.
No Maps on My Taps

Noble, Nigel
Close Harmony

Nowytski, Slavko
Pysanka: The Ukrainian Easter Egg

O'Connor, Mike
The Morning Spider

O'Hara, Gerry
Paganini Strikes Again

Pajon Arts
The Gingerbread Man

Palardy, Jean
Ti-Jean Goes Lumbering

Pastic, George
The Violin

Patel, Ishu
The Bead Game

Patenaude, Michel
The Light Fantastick

Patris, S. G.
Love of Life

Paul, Millie
Mirrors: Reflections of a Culture
Under the Covers: American Quilts

Pérez, Severo
The Notorious Jumping Frog of Calaveras
  County

Petričić, Neven
Cowherd Marko

Piel, David
Harold and the Purple Crayon

Pierson, Art
Whazzat?

Pope, Amanda C.
The Incredible San Francisco Artists' Soap
  Box Derby

Powell, Michael
The Red Shoes

Prather, Maurice
Maria of the Pueblos

Pressburger, Emeric
The Red Shoes

Pressman, Michael N.
People Don't Dance to Jazz

Pyramid Films
Two Centuries of Black American Art

Radnitz, Robert B.
And Now Miguel
The Island of the Blue Dolphins

Randell, Cyril
Paganini Strikes Again

Raulston, Rhonda
Horse Flickers

Reed, Sir Carol
Oliver!

Reichenbach, François
Love of Life

Reiniger, Lotte
Aucassin and Nicolette

Riss, Sheldon
Alligators All Around
Chicken Soup with Rice
One Was Johnny
Pierre
Really Rosie

Ritchie, Michael
Film: The Art of the Impossible

Robertsco/Aeicor/Sorcery Films
The Sorcerer's Apprentice

Rocky Mountain Productions, Inc.
Antonia: Portrait of a Woman

Rosellini, Jim
Diro and His Talking Musical Bow

Rosenberg, Marian
The Ransom of Red Chief (Learning Corp. of
  America version)

Rosenblum, Ralph
The Greatest Man in the World
The Man That Corrupted Hadleyburg

Rubbo, Michael
The Bear and the Mouse

Rudolph, Ken
Gallery

Sacher, Otto
Little Red Riding Hood

Salsman, Bert
Rodeo Red and the Runaway

Saltzman, Paul and Saltzman, Deepa
World Cultures and Youth (Series)

Salzman, Glen
Nikkolina

Samuelson, Jerry
Camera Magic: The Art of Special Effects
Frame by Frame

Sandler Films
Melody

Sarault, Gaston
Duel-Duo

Saudek, Robert
Film: The Art of the Impossible
Walter Kerr on Theater

Sauerman, Bernard B.
Apple Dolls

Schindel, Morton
Harold and the Purple Crayon
Harold's Fairy Tale
Hush Little Baby

In a Spring Garden
Norman the Doorman
Patrick
A Picture for Harold's Room
Smile for Auntie
The Snowy Day
A Story—A Story
Strega Nonna
Teeny-Tiny and the Witch-Woman
The Three Robbers
Where the Wild Things Are
Whistle for Willie
Wynken, Blynken and Nod
Zlateh the Goat

Schmidt, Egan
The Ugly Duckling

Schuyler, Linda
Ida Makes a Movie and Learns to Tell the
  Truth

Schwerin, Jules Victor
Mahalia Jackson

Sears, Roebuck
Art Is

Sefranka, Bruno
Puppets of Jiri Trnka

Sendak, Maurice
Alligators All Around
Chicken Soup with Rice
One Was Johnny
Pierre
Really Rosie

Shadburn, Susan
Claymation

Shafman, Arthur
Mime Vignettes/Mummenschanz

Shannon, Kathleen
Maud Lewis: A World Without Shadows
Sea Dream

Shedd, Ben A.
Poetry for People Who Hate Poetry with
  Roger Steffens (Series)

Shostak, Murray
The Happy Prince

Silver, Joan Micklin
Bernice Bobs Her Hair
The Case of the Elevator Duck

Smight, Jack
Roll of Thunder, Hear My Cry

Smith, Brian Trenchard
Movie Stuntmen

Smith, Clive A.
The Devil and Daniel Mouse
How We Made "The Devil and Daniel
  Mouse"

Smith, Daniel G.
Ponies of Miklaengi

Smith, Lynn
This Is Your Museum Speaking

Snowsill, Tony
The Man, the Snake and the Fox

Somersaulter, Lillian and Somersaulter, J. P.
The Gingerbread Man

Sonnenschein, David
Little Red Riding Hood: A Balinese-Oregon
  Adaptation

Soyuzmult Film Studio
The Nutcracker

Stapp, Philip
Homage to François Couperin

Steffens/Shedd Poetry Films
Poetry for People Who Hate Poetry with
  Roger Steffens (Series)

Sterling, William
Alice's Adventures in Wonderland

Stitt, Bill
Horse Flickers

Strachwitz, Chris
Del Mero Corazón: Love Songs of the
  Southwest

Stussy, Jan
Gravity Is My Enemy

Sugarman, Andrew
Mandy's Grandmother

Svatek, Peter
Beware, Beware My Beauty Fair

Swanni Films, Inc.
My Hands Are the Tools of My Soul

Swarthe, Robert
Ink, Paint, Scratch
Kick Me

Tahse, Martin
A Special Gift
Very Good Friends

Takamoto, Iwao
Charlotte's Web

Talbot, Jim
Mime Vignettes/Mummenschanz

Tamini, Sargon
Right On/Be Free

Tangney, Ralph
Lorraine Hansberry: The Black Experience
  in the Creation of Drama

Tasker, Rex
Medoonak, the Stormmaker

Templeton, Gary
The Case of the Cosmic Comic
Ponies of Miklaengi

Thompson, Don
The Ugly Little Boy

Time-Life Films
Life Goes to the Movies (Series)
The Shakespeare Plays (Series)

Trick Films, Dresden
The Seven Ravens

Trnka, Jiri
Puppets of Jiri Trnka

Tuchner, Michael
Summer of My German Soldier

Turell, Saul
Paul Robeson: Tribute to an Artist

20th Century-Fox TV
Life Goes to the Movies (Series)

The Twyla Tharp Dance Foundation
Twyla Tharp: Making TV Dance

Valenta, Vladimir
Teach Me to Dance

Van Deusen, Pieter
The Hundred Penny Box

Verrall, Robert
A Is for Architecture (Revised Version)
This Is Your Museum Speaking

Vinton, Will
Claymation
Closed Mondays
The Creation
The Little Prince
Martin the Cobbler
Mountain Music
Rip Van Winkle

Wadhams, Wayne
What Time Is the Next Swan?

WDCN-TV, Nashville
Music and Me (Series)

Weiss, Sam
The Legend of John Henry
Nate the Great Goes Undercover

Werner, Peter
Barn Burning

WETA-TV, Washington, DC
From Jumpstreet (Series)

WGBH-TV, Boston
Creative Kids Series

Wheeler, Anne
Teach Me to Dance

Wiemer, Christel
The Seven Ravens

Wilcox, Patrick
Puppet Magic

Wilson, Daniel
The Amazing Cosmic Awareness of Duffy
  Moon
The Horrible Honchos
New York City Too Far from Tampa Blues
Rookie of the Year

Winkler, Donald
In Praise of Hands

Wittman, Mal
The Snowy Day
Whistle for Willie

Wolff, Lothar
The Joy of Bach

Wood, Elizabeth
Full Circle: The Work of Doris Chase

WTTW-TV, Chicago
You Call That Art?!

Yates, Rebecca
Nikkolina

Young, Andrew
Snowbound

Young, Robert
Soldier's Home

Zagreb Film
Cowherd Marko

Zeffirelli, Franco
Romeo and Juliet (Films Inc. Version)

Zeman, Karel
The Princess and the Pearls

Appendix 2
Distributors

ABC Wide World of Learning
1330 Ave. of the Americas
New York, NY 10019
(212) 887-5000

The Artist Was a Woman

African Family Films
Box 1109
Venice, CA 90291
(213) 392-1020

Diro and His Talking Musical Bow

Agency for Instructional Television
Box A
Bloomington, IN 47402
(812) 339-2203

The Folk Book (Series)
Images and Things (Series)
Music and Me (Series)

The American Federation of Arts
41 E. 64 St.
New York, NY 10021
(212) 988-7700

Museum: Behind the Scenes at the Art Institute of Chicago

Argus Communications
7440 Natchez Ave.
Niles, IL 60648
(312) 647-7800

Mime Vignettes/Mummenschanz

Arthur Mokin Productions
17 W. 60 St.
New York, NY 10023
(212) 757-4868

The Man, the Snake and the Fox

Barr Films
Box 5667
Pasadena, CA 91107
(213) 793-6153

The Notorious Jumping Frog of Calaveras County
The Nutcracker
Stained Glass—Painting with Light
Taleb and His Lamb

Beacon Films
Box 575
Norwood, MA 02062
(617) 762-0811

The Devil and Daniel Mouse
How We Made "The Devil and Daniel Mouse"
Kuumba: Simon's New Sound

Benchmark Films
145 Scarborough Rd.
Briarcliff Manor, NY 10510
(914) 762-3838´

Images of the Wild
The Lion and the Mouse

BFA Educational Media
468 Park Ave. S.
New York, NY 10016
(800) 221-1274; (212) 684-5910 (NY)

The Cat in the Hat
Dragon Stew
Evan's Corner
My Mother Is the Most Beautiful Woman in
    the World

Billy Budd Films
235 E. 57 St.
New York, NY 10022
(212) 755-3968

Claymation
The Creation
Keith
The Little Prince
Martin the Cobbler
Rip Van Winkle

Blackwood Productions
251 W. 57 St.
New York, NY 10019
(212) 247-4710

Tapdancin'

Brazos Films
10341-F San Pablo Ave.
El Cerrito, CA 94530
(415) 525-1495

Del Mero Corazón: Love Songs of the South-
    west

Carousel Films
1501 Broadway
New York, NY 10036
(212) 354-0315

Max

Center for Southern Folklore
Box 40105Z
1216 Peabody
Memphis, TN 38104
(901) 726-4205

Give My Poor Heart Ease: Mississippi Delta
    Bluesman

Centron
Box 687
1621 W. Ninth St.
Lawrence, KS 66044
(913) 843-0400

Henry Moore: Master Sculptor
Poetry for Fun: Dares and Dreams
Poetry for Fun: Poems about Animals
Poetry for Fun: Troolier Coolier
Maria of the Pueblos

Children's Television International
3 Skyline Place, Suite 1100
5201 Leesburg Pike
Falls Church, VA 22041
(703) 379-2707

The Best of Cover to Cover (Series)

Churchill Films
662 N. Robertson Blvd.
Los Angeles, CA 90069
(213) 537-5110

Gravity Is My Enemy
Houses Have History
The Hundred Penny Box
The Incredible Book Escape (Series)
Mirrors: Reflections of a Culture
Nate the Great Goes Undercover
Poetry for People Who Hate Poetry with
    Roger Steffens (Series)
Robert Frost's New England

**Cinema Shares International Distribution
    Corporation**
450 Park Ave.
New York, NY 10022
(212) 421-3371

Jacob Two-Two Meets the Hooded Fang

Coe Film Associates
65 E. 96 St.
New York, NY 10028
(212) 831-5355

Anansi the Spider
Arrow to the Sun
At Your Fingertips (Series)
The Bead Game
The Bear and the Mouse
The Boy Who Heard Music
Bremen Town Musicians
The Clay Circus
Duel-Duo
The Guitar: From Stone Age through Solid
    Rock
Hailstones and Halibut Bones (Parts I & II)
Hen Hop
Homage to François Couperin
Horse Flickers
In a Rehearsal Room

Ink, Paint, Scratch
Isabella and the Magic Brush
Keith
Kick Me
Kuumba: Simon's New Sound
The Legend of Sleepy Hollow
The Lion and the Mouse
Listen!
The Magic Tree
The Man, the Snake and the Fox
Maud Lewis: A World without Shadows
Max
Medoonak, the Stormmaker
Mr. Goshu, the Cellist
The Owl Who Married a Goose
Paddington Bear (Series)
The Practical Princess
Sandsong
Sea Dream
Shoemaker and the Elves
The Street
This Is Your Museum Speaking
Ti-Jean Goes Lumbering

Corinth Films
410 E. 62 St.
New York, NY 10021
(212) 421-4770

The Children of Theater Street

Coronet Films & Video
65 E. South Water St.
Chicago, IL 60601
(800) 621-2131; (312) 977-4000 (IL)

Beauty and the Beast
Clever Hiko-Ichi: A Japanese Tale
The Gingerbread Man
World Cultures and Youth (Series)

De Nonno Pix
7119 Shore Rd.
Brooklyn, NY 11209
(212) 582-4240

One Generation Is Not Enough

Direct Cinema Limited
Box 69589
Los Angeles, CA 90069
(213) 656-4700

No Maps on My Taps

Distribution Sixteen
32 W. 40 St., Suite 2-L
New York, NY 10018
(212) 730-0280

An Italian in Algiers
Pulcinella

Encyclopaedia Britannica Educational Corporation
425 N. Michigan Ave.
Chicago, IL 60611
(312) 321-7105

The Art of Silence: Pantomimes with Marcel
    Marceau (Series)
A Boy Creates
The Hare and the Tortoise (2nd Edition)
The Loon's Necklace
Whazzat?

Film Wright
4530 18 St.
San Francisco, CA 94114
(415) 863-6100

Animation Pie

FilmFair Communications
Box 1728, 10900 Ventura Blvd.
Studio City, CA 91604
(213) 985-0244

Isabella and the Magic Brush
Listen!
Paddington Bear (Series)
Right On/Be Free
A Tale of Till

Films for the Humanities
Box 2053
Princeton, NJ 08540
(609) 452-1128

Lorraine Hansberry: The Black Experience in
    the Creation of Drama

Films Incorporated
733 Green Bay Rd.
Wilmette, IL 60091
(800) 323-4222; (312) 256-3200 (IL)

Alice's Adventures in Wonderland
Anonymous Was a Woman
Bremen Town Musicians
Charlotte's Web
City Lights
Creative Kids Series

From the Mixed-Up Files of Mrs. Basil E.
   Frankweiler
Georgia O'Keeffe
The Gold Rush
In a Rehearsal Room
The Last Meow: Sibelius's "Valse Triste"
Let It Bee: Vivaldi's "Concerto in C-dur"
The Making of Star Wars
Modern Times
Nevelson in Process
Norman Rockwell's World . . . An American
   Dream
Paul Robeson: Tribute to an Artist
Peter Rabbit and Tales of Beatrix Potter
Romeo and Juliet
The Shoemaker and the Elves
Silver Blaze
Sleeping Beauty
SPFX: The Making of The Empire Strikes Back
The Story of Good King Huemac
Teach Me to Dance

Great Plains National
Box 80669
Lincoln, NE 68501
(402) 472-2007

From Jumpstreet (Series)

**ICAP (Independent Cinema Artists &
   Producers)**
625 Broadway
New York, NY 10012
(212) 533-9180

People Don't Dance to Jazz
Pysanka: The Ukrainian Easter Egg

Icarus Films
200 Park Ave. S., Room 1319
New York, NY 10003
(212) 674-3375

Black Dawn

International Film Bureau
332 S. Michigan Ave.
Chicago, IL 60604
(312) 427-4545

A Is for Architecture (Revised Edition)
A Chairy Tale
Cowherd Marko
Hen Hop
I Know an Old Lady Who Swallowed a Fly
Medoonak, the Stormmaker
Mr. Goshu, the Cellist

Puppet Magic
Ti-Jean Goes Lumbering

International Film Foundation
200 W. 72 St.
New York, NY 10023
(212) 580-1111

Homage to François Couperin

Janus Films
45 Fifth Ave.
New York, NY 10022
(212) 753-7100

Paganini Strikes Again

Learning Corporation of America
1350 Ave. of the Americas
New York, NY 10019
(212) 397-9360

Big Henry and the Polka Dot Kid
Black Music in America: From Then till Now
Black Music in America: The Seventies
The Case of the Elevator Duck
Close Harmony
Dance on a May Day
Dinky Hocker
The Electric Grandmother
Film: The Art of the Impossible
The Gold Bug
Ida Makes a Movie and Learns to Tell the
   Truth
It's So Nice to Have a Wolf Around the
   House
Lafcadio, the Lion Who Shot Back
Little Red Riding Hood
Luke Was There
Madeline
Movie Stuntmen
Nikkolina
Pas de Deux
The Princess and the Pearls
The Ransom of Red Chief
The Red Shoes
Rodeo Red and the Runaway
Roll of Thunder, Hear My Cry
The Seven Ravens
The Seven Wishes of Joanna Peabody
Silver Blaze
Siu Mei Wong: Who Shall I Be?
Snowbound
Street Musique
Summer of My German Soldier
Sunshine's on the Way

The Tap Dance Kid
Track Stars: The Unseen Heroes of Movie
  Sound
The Ugly Little Boy
Very Good Friends
The Violin
Walter Kerr on Theater
The White Heron

The Little Red Filmhouse
666 N. Robertson Blvd.
Los Angeles, CA 90069
(213) 855-0241
Ink, Paint, Scratch
Kick Me

Lutheran Film Associates Library
One Main Place
Dallas, TX 75250
(214) 747-8048
The Joy of Bach

Macmillan Films
34 MacQuesten Pkwy. S.
Mount Vernon, NY 10550
(914) 664-4277; (914) 664-5051
The Gold Rush
The Red Balloon

Modern Talking Picture Service
5000 Park St. N.
St. Petersburg, FL 33709
(813) 541-7571
Art Is

National Film Board of Canada
1251 Ave. of the Americas, 16th fl.
New York, NY 10020
(212) 586-5131
Aucassin and Nicolette
The Bear and the Mouse
Duel-Duo
Eskimo Artist—Kenojuak
In Praise of Hands
The Light Fantastick
The Living Stone
The Owl Who Married a Goose
Paddle to the Sea
The Street
This Is Your Museum Speaking

New Day Films
Box 315
Franklin Lakes, NJ 07417
(201) 891-8240

Quilts in Women's Lives

New Yorker Films
16 W. 61 St.
New York, NY 10023
(212) 247-6110
Love of Life

PBS Video
475 L'Enfant Plaza S.W.
Washington, DC 20024
(800) 424-7963; (202) 488-5220 (DC)
You Call That Art?!

PCI
626 Justin Ave.
Glendale, CA 91201
(213) 240-9300
At Your Fingertips (Series)
Cherry Tree Carol
Melody

Perspective Films & Video
65 E. South Water St.
Chicago, IL 60601
(800) 621-2131; (312) 977-4000 (IL)
The American Short Story (Series)
Full Circle: The Work of Doris Chase
The Isle of Joy
Leonardo's Diary

Phoenix Films and Video
470 Park Ave. S.
New York, NY 10016
(212) 684-5910
Antonia: Portrait of a Woman
Beware, Beware My Beauty Fair
The First Moving Picture Show
Full of Life A-dancin'
The Incredible San Francisco Artists' Soap
  Box Derby
Mahalia Jackson
Mandy's Grandmother
Maud Lewis: A World without Shadows
Never Give Up: Imogen Cunningham
Pavarotti at Juilliard, Program 1
Ponies of Miklaengi
Portrait of Grandpa Doc
Puppets of Jiri Trnka
Sea Dream
Superlative Horse
Tealia
Twyla Tharp: Making TV Dance
What Time Is the Next Swan?

Pyramid Film & Video

Box 1048
Santa Monica, CA 90406
(800) 421-2304; (213) 828-7577 (CA)

Ballet Adagio
The Bead Game
The Big Bang and Other Creation Myths
The Bolero
Camera Magic: The Art of Special Effects
Closed Mondays
The Concert
Degas in the Metropolitan
Frame by Frame
Gallery
The Happy Prince
The Legend of John Henry
The Legend of Sleepy Hollow
Mindscape
Monsieur Pointu
The Morning Spider
Mountain Music
Notes on the Popular Arts
Peter and the Wolf
Romeo and Juliet in Kansas City
Scott Joplin: King of Ragtime Composers
The Sorcerer's Apprentice
Two Centuries of Black American Art
Under the Covers: American Quilts
Why Man Creates
The Wizard of Speed and Time

Sterling Educational Films

241 E. 34 St.
New York, NY 10016
(212) 683-6300

Hailstones and Halibut Bones (Parts I & II)
The Magic Pipes
Tales of Hiawatha

Texture Films

1600 Broadway
New York, NY 10019
(212) 586-6960

Anansi the Spider
Arrow to the Sun
The Bird, the Fox and the Full Moon
The Boy Who Heard Music
The Bronze Zoo
The Clay Circus
Documentary
Horse Flickers
Little Birds

Little Red Riding Hood: A Balinese-Oregon
  Adaptation
The Magic Tree
My Hands Are the Tools of My Soul
The Owl and the Pussycat
The Raven

Time-Life Video

1271 Ave. of the Americas
New York, NY 10022
(212) 841-4554

The Amazing Cosmic Awareness of Duffy
  Moon
The Horrible Honchos
Life Goes to the Movies (Series)
New York City Too Far from Tampa Blues
Rookie of the Year
The Shakespeare Plays (Series)
A Special Gift

Tom Davenport Films

Route 1, Box 124
Delaplane, VA 22025
(703) 592-3701

From the Brothers Grimm: American Versions
  of Fairytale Classics (Series)

Twyman Films

Box 605
4700 Wadsworth Rd.
Dayton, OH 45401
(800) 543-9594; (513) 276-5941 (OH)

And Now Miguel
The Island of the Blue Dolphins
Oliver!
The Red Balloon
Yellow Submarine

United Artists

729 Seventh Ave.
New York, NY 10019
(212) 245-6000

The Black Stallion

Walt Disney Educational Media

500 S. Buena Vista St.
Burbank, CA 91521
(800) 423-2555; (213) 841-2000 (CA)

Casey at the Bat
Four Artists Paint One Tree
History of Animation
Sleeping Beauty
Toot, Whistle, Plunk and Boom
A World Is Born

Weston Woods
Weston, CT 06883
(800) 243-5020; (203) 226-3355 (CT)

Alligators All Around
Apt. 3
The Beast of Monsieur Racine
The Case of the Cosmic Comic
Chicken Soup with Rice
The Cow Who Fell in the Canal
The Fisherman and His Wife
The Foolish Frog
Harold and the Purple Crayon
Harold's Fairy Tale
Hush Little Baby
In a Spring Garden
Moon Man
Norman the Doorman
One Was Johnny
Patrick
A Picture for Harold's Room
Pierre
Really Rosie
Smile for Auntie
The Snowy Day
A Story—A Story
Strega Nonna
The Swineherd
Teeny-Tiny and the Witch-Woman
The Three Robbers
The Ugly Duckling
Where the Wild Things Are
Whistle for Willie
Wynken, Blynken and Nod
Zlateh the Goat

Wombat Productions
Box 70
Little Lake, Glendale Rd.
Ossining, NY 10562
(914) 762-0011

Apple Dolls
Sandsong

Xerox Films
Communications Park Video & Film
Box 4000
Mount Kisco, NY 10549
(914) 666-4100

The Guitar: From Stone Age through Solid
    Rock
Mowgli's Brothers
Rikki-Tikki-Tavi

Yellow Ball Workshop
62 Tarbell Ave.
Lexington, MA 02173
(617) 862-4283

Masterpiece

Subject Index

Title Index